T0319976

Designing International Environmental Agreements

NEW HORIZONS IN ENVIRONMENTAL ECONOMICS

General Editors: Wallace E. Oates, *Professor of Economics, University of Maryland, USA* and Henk Folmer, *Professor of General Economics, Wageningen University and Professor of Environmental Economics, Tilburg University, The Netherlands*

This important series is designed to make a significant contribution to the development of the principles and practices of environmental economics. It includes both theoretical and empirical work. International in scope, it addresses issues of current and future concern in both East and West and in developed and developing countries.

The main purpose of the series is to create a forum for the publication of high quality work and to show how economic analysis can make a contribution to understanding and resolving the environmental problems confronting the world in the twenty-first century.

Recent titles in the series include:

Designing International Environmental Agreements

Incentive Compatible Strategies
for Cost-effective Cooperation

Carsten Schmidt

University of Konstanz, Germany

NEW HORIZONS IN ENVIRONMENTAL ECONOMICS

Edward Elgar
Cheltenham, UK • Northampton, MA, USA

Published by
Edward Elgar Publishing Limited
Glensanda House
Montpellier Parade
Cheltenham
Glos GL50 1UA
UK

Edward Elgar Publishing, Inc.
136 West Street
Suite 202
Northampton
Massachusetts 01060
USA

A catalogue record for this book
is available from the British Library

Library of Congress Cataloguing in Publication Data

Schmidt, Carsten, 1966–
        Designing international environmental agreements : incentive compatible
strategies for cost-effective cooperation / Carsten Schmidt.
        (New horizons in environmental economics)
        Includes bibliographical references and index.
        1. Environmental economics. 2. Environmental policy—International
cooperation. 3. Environmental policy—Cost effectiveness. I. Title. II. Series.

HC79.E5 S2843 2000
333.7—dc21

                                                                                                        00–029412

ISBN 1 84064 352 8

Printed and bound in Great Britain by Biddles Ltd, *www.biddles.co.uk*

Für Ute und Amanda

Contents

List of Figures

List of Tables

List of Abbreviations

CBA	Cost–benefit Analysis
CDM	Clean Development Mechanism
CFC	Chlorofluorocarbon
COP	Conference of the Parties to the Rio Convention
ET	Emissions Trading
EU	European Union
FCCC	Framework Convention on Climate Change
GDP	Gross Domestic Product
GEF	Global Environment Facility
GHGs	Greenhouse Gases
GWP	Greenhouse Warming Potential
HCFCs	Halogenated Chlorofluorocarbons
IEA	International Environmental Agreement
IPCC	Intergovernmental Panel on Climate Change
JI	Joint Implementation
KP	Kyoto Protocol
MP	Montreal Protocol
MPMF	Montreal Protocol Multilateral Fund
OECD	Organization for Economic Cooperation and Development
UNCED	United Nations Conference on Environment and Development
UNCTAD	United Nations Conference on Trade and Development
UNDP	United Nations Development Program
UNEP	United Nations Environment Program
UNIDO	United Nations Industrial Development Organization
VOC	Volatile Hydrocarbon
WMO	World Meteorological Organization

Preface

This book is about international environmental economics. Its aim is to investigate the interrelations between cost-effective and incentive compatible approaches of nations cooperating on common environmental resources. International environmental policy is a rapidly growing field of research not only in economic science. Therefore, the present volume cannot provide final answers; rather it contributes to the ongoing discussion by focussing on selected but crucial aspects.

The book is based on a PhD dissertation accepted by the Department of Economics at the University of Konstanz, Germany. It was supervised by Prof. Bernd Genser and Prof. Ernst Mohr (University of St. Gallen). The oral examens took place on 19 May 2000. The study was written while I was a member of the long-term research program *Internationalization of the Economy* (Sonderforschungsbereich 178) at the University of Konstanz, Germany. I gratefully acknowledge financial support by the 'Deutsche Forschungsgemeinschaft' and the 'Landesgraduiertenförderung Baden-Württemberg'.

During the course of my studies in Konstanz I have profited from the help of many people. I am above all indebted to my supervisor Bernd Genser, who supported me continuously and who gave me the opportunity to work within a stimulating and cooperative environment. I am grateful to the members of his research unit, Wolfgang Eggert, Frank Hettich, Christoph John, Sebastian Killinger, Margarita Steinhart and especially Andreas Haufler, for their valuable advice and company.

I am indebted to Ernst Mohr and Josef Janssen, both at the University of St. Gallen, whose cooperation and assistance during common projects I greatly appreciated. I am further grateful to Suzi Kerr, Wallace Oates, Ingmar Prucha and Robert Schwab for their hospitality and instructive advice during my research visit to the University of Maryland, College Park, USA. To the former speaker of the Sonderforschungsbereich 178, Hans-Jürgen Vosgerau, I owe thanks for supporting this research visit and for making it possible for so many interesting economists to come to

Konstanz. Among others, I greatly benefitted from discussions with Rolf Bommer, Lucas Bretschger, Michael Finus, Martin Kolmar, Engelbert Plassmann and Günther Schulze.

The book would not have been possible in this form without the assistance of my brother, who spent a considerable amount of his spare time carefully reading the manuscript and correcting my English. I am indebted to my parents for their confidence. The greatest thanks of all I owe to my wife Regina. She not only tolerated the project, but encouraged and supported me in the most wonderful way.

Bad Vilbel, June 2000

Chapter 1

Introduction

The detrimental impacts of human behavior on the natural environment are manifold and range from the individual to the global level. The man-made degradation of the environment, though, does not occur as an act of deliberate destruction. It is caused by economic activities — production and consumption — whose purpose is to satisfy human needs. Nevertheless it is true that the degree and the complex consequences of human interference with the ecosystem have become a considerable threat to the welfare of future generations. Today the most pressing environmental problems have an international or even global character. Among the most prominent examples are the depletion of the stratospheric ozone layer, the anthropogenic greenhouse effect, loss of biodiversity and pollution of international waters. Common sense demands intensified protection of the earth's environmental resources — in some cases urgently.[1] What contribution can economic science make to explain and to help remedy the destruction of our common basis of existence?

Economic theory explains the excessive use of environmental resources by the phenomenon of technological external effects. Environmental externalities represent one important form of market failure which calls for correction by the public sector. For the policy-maker the regulation of environmental externalities comprises two interdependent aspects: one is the choice of the optimal level of environmental protection, the other is the choice of the policy instrument that best accomplishes this standard. The latter aspect concerns in particular the question of how to reach a given environmental standard at minimum social costs. For a long time it has been recognized that cost-effectiveness of environmental policy is an important issue not only on the national, but also on the international

---

[1] Sandler (1997) presents an impressive array of topical global challenges including non-environmental problems such as population growth, international terrorism, disease eradication and peace making.

level. Olson and Zeckhauser, for example, demanded that 'the theory of externalities and collective goods has to be combined with the theory of comparative advantage' (1967, p. 45) and stated that 'the relatively most efficient producer of a given external economy should "specialize" in that externality, and receive different spillovers or ordinary goods in return' (1970, p. 516).

Theoretic as well as applied research in environmental economics have both addressed the above aspects extensively. The theory of environmental policy that shows the superiority of market-based instruments for the regulation of environmental externalities is well established and elaborate. The above choices, though, have to be made with deference to the set of available policy instruments. This is where the geography of environmental problems becomes relevant, because often it is not congruent with the reach of national sovereignty. Whereas national governments are competent and vested with sufficient power to internalize local environmental externalities, this is not true for transboundary ones. These problems must be addressed on the international or even global level. However, the existing international institutions have lacked adequate competence. Therefore, it is inappropriate to apply the traditional theory of environmental policy indiscriminately.

An overview of different ways of coping with environmental problems is presented in Figure 1.1. The traditional approach to internalize transboundary environmental externalities would be to assign the competence for environmental policy to the supranational level. Under ideal conditions this would allow for an efficient internalization and is depicted by the branch 'supranational regulation' in Figure 1.1. In the foreseeable future, however, regulation by a supranational authority is not a realistic option — at least on the global level. Any attempts to deal with international environmental problems thus have to be initiated and backed by national governments. Conceivable strategies to respond to transboundary externalities without a supranational institution have to rely on (i) voluntary agreements among the countries concerned and (ii) unilateral measures. These are the two right-hand branches of Figure 1.1.[2]

From the perspective of national policy-makers it is neither possible nor optimal to implement international environmental policies developed in the context of a *first-best* setting. Decentralized approaches to the management of transboundary pollution necessarily remain *second-best* from an international point of view. This is evident for unilateral strategies as single governments do not dispose of sufficient instruments to

---

[2] Killinger and Schmidt (1998) provide a comprehensive survey on decentralized international environmental policies and discuss the interrelations between unilateral and partial cooperative strategies.

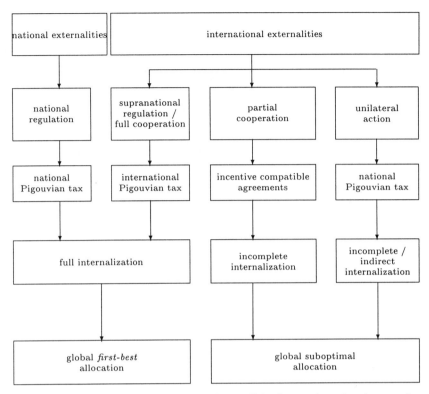

Note: The figure does not indicate second-best policies for purely national externalities. Pigouvian taxes stand for all market-based internalization instruments.

Figure 1.1: First-best and second-best environmental policies

control foreign pollution. It also holds for cooperative solutions. Due to the lack of a supranational authority, sovereign countries cannot be forced to sign environmental treaties nor can their governments credibly commit themselves to the obligations stipulated therein. However, both are indispensable given the strong incentives to free ride on the efforts of other countries in the protection of international environmental resources. Hence, the very reason that rules out a centralized regulation makes it almost impossible for single countries to coordinate their environmental policies efficiently. Negotiations usually last a very long time and are highly likely to fail or lead merely to partial solutions. This pessimistic outlook corresponds to the famous 'tragedy of the commons' described by Hardin (1968).[3]

---

[3] See Barrett (1990) for an introduction to the incentive problems of international

Nevertheless, international environmental cooperation *does* take place and has led to a remarkable number of formal agreements — some of which have been signed by virtually the entire community of countries. Although many environmental conventions have been criticized for not being substantial in an economic sense and merely codifying the status quo, their widespread use suggests that institutions and instruments are available to create incentives for effective and sustainable cooperative solutions. This provokes a number of questions that economic analysis can help to answer:

- Which of the existing international environmental agreements do in fact improve environmental quality substantially compared to the uncoordinated situation?
- Which instruments are employed and should be employed to make countries voluntarily sign and comply with environmental treaties?
- What are the optimal strategies for (sub)coalitions of cooperating countries to maximize their welfare gains from environmental cooperation?

Thus it becomes clear that the design of international environmental policy comprises two dimensions of instrument choice: one is the traditional search for cost-efficient instruments, which policy-makers also face in the context of national environmental externalities; the other concerns instruments which create incentives for cooperation. Both aspects — cost-effectiveness and incentive compatibility — have been analysed extensively in environmental economics. Today there are a great number of contributions on international carbon taxes or globally tradable emission permits as well as on the incentives to cooperate on international environmental resources. However, these two fields of research are still somewhat isolated and in most cases focus on only one aspect at a time. Studies on international cost-effectiveness, for example, usually begin with the premise of perfect enforcement, thereby neglecting implementation and monitoring problems. Similarly, models of international environmental agreements focussing on time consistency generally abstract from the dimension of cost-effectiveness when assuming homogeneous players. This is no coincidence. For 'the design and implementation of workable and cost-effective measures on a global scale are formidable problems, to put it mildly' (Cropper and Oates 1992, p. 731).

The objective of this study is to integrate the aspects of cost-effectiveness and incentive compatibility of international environmental policy. For this purpose, we analyse how economic instruments such as side payments and existing institutions are able to contribute to the

---

environmental cooperation.

success of international environmental agreements. We focus on reciprocal externalities with the properties of a (pure) international public
good and apply the theoretical analysis to two prominent examples: the
anthropogenic greenhouse effect and the depletion of the stratospheric
ozone layer. The analysis is based on a static, partial equilibrium framework. It thus abstracts from important features of international and especially global environmental problems.[4] These simplifications, though,
have been unavoidable when examining cost-effectiveness and strategic
aspects simultaneously. We take three major steps in our analysis. First,
we conceptualize the notions of cost-effectiveness and incentive compatibility and discuss their relevance for international environmental agreements (Chapters 3 and 4). Then in a theoretical analysis we scruti-
nize specific contractual provisions which are relevant for both aspects
(Chapters 5 and 6). Finally, we examine the institutional level. On the
basis of the theoretical analysis, we evaluate whether the existing international institutions achieve cost-effectiveness in global environmental
policy (Chapter 7).

According to this blueprint, the structure of the study is as follows.
Chapter 2 provides relevant background information. First, it introduces
the natural science of the anthropogenic greenhouse effect and the destruction of the stratospheric ozone layer. Subsequently, we review the
international political attempts undertaken so far to tackle these problems. Section 2.3 outlines the theoretical concepts that constitute the
methodological framework of this study: the theory of externalities and
international public goods, cost–benefit analysis and game theory.

In Chapter 3 we qualify the notion of cost-effectiveness and point out
its empirical relevance. Section 3.2 evaluates in a static two-countries,
two-goods model the relative importance of cost-effectiveness when countries differ in size. The non-cooperative Nash and Stackelberg equilibria
are compared with respect to their inefficiency properties. Section 3.3
undertakes a similar analysis for carbon emissions on the basis of an
extended model considering multiple countries and using current data.
Moreover, we show the importance of cost-effectiveness by a survey of
quantitative studies on carbon abatement costs. The chapter concludes

---

[4]We abstract from the fact that greenhouse gas emissions constitute a stock pollutant and do not analyse dynamic aspects in detail. Consequently, issues of optimal
growth and sustainable development are ignored. See, for example, Hettich (2000)
for an analysis of environmental policy within models of endogenous growth. Distortions in other markets which have repercussions with international environmental
policy are discussed only briefly in Section 4.5. See Killinger (2000) for unilateral
environmental policy in the presence of additional distortions and a systematic approach to the 'double-dividend' debate. Finally, national governments are assumed
to be benevolent. See, for example, Schulze and Ursprung (2000) for a survey of the
political-economic aspects of international environmental policy.

by comparing the cost-effectiveness properties of different policy instruments to internalize transboundary environmental externalities.

Chapter 4 surveys recent contributions to the rapidly growing theoretical literature on international environmental cooperation and proposes a taxonomy of instruments to ensure incentive compatibility in international environmental policy. Conceivable strategies to promote a successful coordination of environmental policies despite a merely rudimentary institutional structure on the international level are (i) the choice and detailed form of the internalization instrument itself; (ii) carrot–stick strategies that make cooperative abatement efforts dependent on the past behavior of other countries (internal stabilization); (iii) transfers and sanctions of various forms (external stabilization); (iv) unilateral and accompanying measures taken by single countries or subcoalitions; and (v) long-term provisions to increase the flexibility of agreements and to improve the framework conditions of international negotiations.

Chapter 5 analyses how self-financing transfers can help to overcome the time-consistency problem of international environmental agreements. Within the framework of specific abatement cost and benefit functions we look at a model using conditional transfers and sequential moves of the contracting parties to implement an international environmental agreement. Self-financing transfers prove to be powerful instruments for generating substantial gains from environmental cooperation, even if transfers are limited to compensations for cost-effectiveness of abatement efforts and if more than two countries are involved. The analysis also shows that the prospects for environmental cooperation may rise with greater asymmetry between countries.

Chapter 6 addresses the problem of asymmetric information in international environmental agreements which make use of transfers. We compare the financing of net versus gross incremental abatement costs with respect to the induced incentives for a strategic misrepresentation of environmental preferences. It is shown that it may no longer be optimal for the donor countries to compensate recipient countries only for their net incremental costs of emission abatements. This holds even if the donors are in a position to submit an offer which is optimal for themselves and when the terms of the agreement are differentiated for each possible recipients' type (that is, in the case of a separating equilibrium). In addition, in cases where international transfers have to be based on simple, uniform rules (that is, a pooling equilibrium), realistic scenarios exist where donor as well as recipient countries favor the application of the gross over the net incremental cost concept.

Chapter 7 discusses existing international institutions created to support cost-effectiveness in global environmental policy. We describe the origins and mandate of the Montreal Protocol Multilateral Fund, the Global Environment Facility and the concept of 'joint implementation' within the Framework Convention on Climate Change. We evaluate the operational guidelines of these institutions and concepts against the background of the preceding analysis.

Chapter 8 summarizes the main results of the study and gives an outlook on possible future developments in international environmental policy.

Chapter 2

International Environmental Problems

This chapter provides background information relevant for the study of international environmental externalities. First, we outline the natural science of two environmental problems with a high priority on the international political agenda: the anthropogenic greenhouse effect and the depletion of the stratospheric ozone layer. Both problems possess not only an international dimension but even a global one. Subsequently, we review the political attempts undertaken so far to tackle these problems. The third part of the chapter describes the theoretical concepts that constitute the methodological framework of this study: the theory of externalities and international public goods, cost–benefit analysis and game theory.

2.1 Natural Scientific Background

2.1.1 The Anthropogenic Greenhouse Effect

Currently most scientific experts agree that anthropogenic emission of greenhouse gases (GHGs) will result in global warming. The reports of the Intergovernmental Panel on Climate Change forecast an increase in the mean global temperature by about 2 degrees Celsius (with estimations ranging from 1 to 3.5 degrees Celsius) over the next century if no countermeasures are taken (IPCC 1996, p. 5). In contrast, since the last ice age the average temperature has fluctuated within a range of only 1 degree Celsius. One important consequence of global warming will be a general rise of sea levels. The IPCC estimates an average increase in sea levels by about 50 cm (estimations ranging from 15 to 95 cm) until the year 2100 under a 'business-as-usual' scenario. Since the beginning of industrialization at the end of the nineteenth century, average mean temperatures have already risen by 0.3 to 0.6 degrees Celsius and global sea levels have risen by 10 to 25 cm. Global warming is going to have severe worldwide effects in various spheres such as agriculture, forestry, coastal areas and human health. The question of how to deal with this human-induced climate change involves various (social, economic, political, scientific) aspects that interact in a complex manner. First of all, sufficient knowledge about the behavior of the natural system is required in order to address the problem of global warming in a rational way. In the following we therefore briefly outline the natural science of climate change.

The greenhouse effect[1] is a natural phenomenon that enables life to exist on earth: without it the average temperature would be about 33 degrees Celsius lower. The radiation of the sun is the essential factor for the global climate. Certain gases in the earth's atmosphere permit shortwave, high-energy radiation from the sun to reach the earth's surface, but hold back part of the radiation which the earth in turn reflects towards the atmosphere. This phenomenon leads to a rise in average surface temperatures and is therefore called the 'greenhouse effect'. Besides water vapor (H_2O), the most important greenhouse gases are carbon dioxide (CO_2), methane (CH_4) and nitrous oxide (N_2O).[2]

The possibility of an additional, *anthropogenic* greenhouse effect was discovered by the Swedish scientist Arrhenius in 1896. With the beginning of industrialization, humankind has caused an enormous increase in the emission of various gases which have an impact on the global climate. Carbon dioxide is the most important of them. In the mid-1980s it was responsible for approximately 53 per cent of *instantaneous* greenhouse warming (Table 2.1). The other key gases are chlorofluorocarbons (CFCs, 21 per cent), methane (17 per cent) and nitrous oxides (8 per cent).[3] The relative importance of these gases differs both because

---

[1] See Cline (1991) for an introduction and Houghton et al. (1996) for a comprehensive study on the natural science of the greenhouse effect.

[2] At present, water vapor, clouds and CO_2 together are responsible for about 90 per cent of the total greenhouse effect; the contribution of water vapor alone is about 65 per cent (Enquête-Kommission 1991, p. 215). The bulk of the atmosphere is made up of oxygen and nitrogen which are not GHGs.

[3] The immediate contribution of ozone (O_3) which is also a greenhouse gas is difficult to assess as ozone concentrations vary strongly both geographically and over time. Estimates of its relative contribution range from 3 to 7 per cent. Other emissions connected with industrial production which influence the climate system are volatile hydrocarbons (VOCs) and carbon monoxide (CO). Nitrogen oxides (NO_x) are of importance as they contribute to an increased formation of ozone in the atmosphere. See Enquête-Kommission (1991, Table 11) for a listing of gases that indirectly

Table 2.1: Contributions and warming potentials of greenhouse gases

GHG	Instantaneous[a] Contribution[b]	GWP[c]	Total Contribution[b]	GWP[c]
CO_2	53.2	1	80.3	1
CFCs	21.4	3,970–5,750	8.8	1,500–4,500
CH_4	17.3	58	2.2	9
N_2O	8.1	206	8.7	190

Notes:
a. Immediate effects valid for the mid-1980s.
b. Relative contributions to the anthropogenic greenhouse effect in per cent, defined as the increase in atmospheric concentration of a GHG times its current radiative impact.
c. Global warming potential in relation to the radiative impact of the same mass (in kilogram) of CO_2.

Sources: Nordhaus (1991a, Table 2); Enquête-Kommission (1991, Tables 9, 10).

of the different quantities emitted and because of their different radiative impacts. The latter can be expressed by calculating a 'greenhouse warming potential' (GWP) for each of the GHGs. CFCs, for example, trap about four to six thousand times as much heat as an equivalent amount (that is, mass) of carbon dioxide, while the radiative impact of methane is about sixty times higher than that of CO_2 (Table 2.1).

Determining the relative importance of different greenhouse gases on the basis of their *immediate* impact on the climate system, however, is defective. It ignores the fact that greenhouse gases constitute *stock pollutants* with considerable lifetimes in the atmosphere and are transformed over time into other substances. CO_2, for example, stays in the atmosphere for up to 200 years and therefore has a particularly strong influence on the climate system. A more accurate index, therefore, is one that measures the *total* warming potential of a GHG over the indefinite future (Nordhaus 1991a, p. 38). Comparing the instantaneous and the total relative contributions as well as the respective greenhouse warming potentials of the GHGs in Table 2.1 shows that with regard to long-term climate change, carbon dioxide is even more important: The relative contributions of the various gases to the anthropogenic green-

contribute to global warming.

house effect then are about 80 per cent for CO_2, nearly 9 per cent for CFCs and nitrous oxide, and 2 per cent for methane. Furthermore, CO_2 emissions are also a key factor because no removal (end-of-pipe) technology is currently available. By contrast, backstop technologies for other GHGs have been improved considerably, so that the emissions of these gases could be limited or even reduced.

Bolin (1997) lists the key features of the complex climate system as follows:

- a 0.5 degree increase of the mean surface temperature during the twentieth century;
- a continuous increase of atmospheric GHG concentrations;
- because of their long lifetime in the atmosphere (between 10 and 150 years), GHGs become quite well mixed so that concentrations are about the same all around the world;
- a delay by 40 to 70 per cent in the increase of the global mean temperature caused by anthropogenic emissions of greenhouse gases;
- enhanced concentrations of sulfate aerosols resulting from combustion of fossil fuels and smoke from the burning of organic substances which tend to cool the atmosphere; because of the short atmospheric lifetimes (a couple of weeks) and the uneven distribution of aerosols, this cooling effect is patchy and reacts very fast to a change of emissions;
- limited certainty about the human influence on the global climate because indicators of climate change are still in the range of natural variability;
- insufficient knowledge about the regional impacts of global climate change.

All in all, it is still very difficult to assess how dramatic human-induced climate change is going to be and how quickly it may come about. Most scientists are still reluctant to make predictions about the quantitative dimensions of global warming, particularly about its spatial distribution and timing. The impacts in terms of precipitation, extreme weather situations, agricultural productivity and so on are equally uncertain. Nevertheless, the great majority of climatologists agrees that the anthropogenic greenhouse effect is real and that the global average temperature will rise over the next hundred years (Houghton et al. 1996). Furthermore, there are good reasons to suspect that future predictions on global warming are going to be more and more reliable and detailed, with further increasing complexity of the climate models and processing capacity of the hardware that is used.

What are the main economic activities that cause greenhouse gas emissions? Methane is largely a result of solid wastes, coal mining, oil and

gas production, various agricultural activities (especially wet rice culti-
vation) and livestock. Nitrous oxides are emitted mainly through the
use of fertilizers and through energy production, CFCs in the course
of different industrial production processes.[4] Carbon dioxide is emitted
mainly by burning fossil fuels and by deforestation. Combustion of fossil fuels like carbon, oil and gas is by far the most important source of
human GHG emissions. These emissions stem from energy production
and transformation industries (57 per cent), the residential, commercial
and institutional sectors (16 per cent), industry as an energy user (13
per cent) and transportation (14 per cent). Table 2.2 illustrates the im-

Table 2.2: Primary energy sources in 1990

Energy source	Contribution (%)
Fossil Fuels	75.3
Oil	33.3
Gas	18.4
Coal	23.6
Nuclear	4.9
Hydro	5.5
Biomass	14.3

Source: Houghton et al. (1996).

portance of fossil fuels for present energy production: about 75 per cent
of the total energy supply in the world is produced by burning oil, gas
and coal.

Another way of looking at the sources of GHG emissions is to examine their regional distribution. With regard to CO_2 emissions, national
emission quantities are — at least at present — strongly concentrated:
the three top emitters (the USA, the former USSR, and the EU) account
for about 55 per cent of the world's industrial emissions, the top fifteen
emitting countries account for more than 88 per cent (see Table 3.2).
In 1990, the industrialized world (OECD countries and economies in
transition) was responsible for about two-thirds of global energy-related
CO_2 emissions (Table 3.2). This picture is even more distinct when
we look at historical emissions which have accumulated since the be-

---

[4]While CFCs contribute directly to the greenhouse effect, there is also an indirect
opposite effect via the ozone hole (*Nature*, vol. 372, p. 348, 1994). The latter makes
ultra violet radiation passing the stratosphere trigger a chemical process in the troposphere, which results in an increased number of high clouds reflecting the sunlight
before entering the deeper atmosphere. See also Section 2.1.2 on CFCs.

ginning of industrialization: industrialized countries are responsible for roughly 90 per cent of the stock in CO_2. It is unlikely, however, that this pattern will continue to be valid in the future. In the course of the economic development of highly populated countries like China and India, these countries are going to be more and more important for an effective climate policy (as well as for the protection of other international environmental resources). Furthermore, taking into account the effects of land-use changes (especially tropical deforestation) and other important greenhouse gases like methane, it becomes clear that many other countries also contribute significantly to the anthropogenic greenhouse effect. Hence, an effective climate policy has to include a great number of countries — now and in the future.

In principle, measures against potential damages of climate change can be grouped in two categories: mitigation and adaptation (IPCC 1996).[5] Deciding about global environmental policy is not a matter of choosing between one of these options, but a question of an 'optimal mix', that is, how much of a climate change can be tolerated and adapted to and how much should be mitigated.[6] It is still very difficult to answer this question, not only because the consequences of climate change are uncertain and traditional cost–benefit analyses are of little help given the limited knowledge of future damages, but also because for many people the symptoms of human-induced climate change are still not clear enough for climate change to be considered a serious future threat at all. However, waiting for clear evidence may take a long time and require more costly measures than the precautionary ones which are available now. The inertia of both the natural and the socioeconomic systems also suggests that the countermeasures against harmful climate change have to be taken in a long-term perspective. Despite substantial uncertainty about the precise consequences of global warming, it thus makes sense to implement climate policies now. This renders the analysis of mitigation options a crucial part of the problem of finding optimal ways to deal with climate change. The present study applies the concept of cost-effectiveness merely to mitigation policies and abstains from their comparison with costs of adaptation options. This does not mean that the relevance of adaptation is ignored. Rather, we focus on cost-effective ways to mitigate climate change to a certain extent and do not deal with corresponding levels of adaptation (see Section 3.1).

---

[5]See the contribution of working group II to the second assessment report of the IPCC for a comprehensive overview on adaptation and mitigation options (Watson et al. (eds) 1996).

[6]In line with this, the various CO_2 emission scenarios proposed by the IPCC all imply atmospheric CO_2 concentrations that lie below the one which would result from 'business as usual', but that are above present or even preindustrial concentrations.

The contribution of working group II to the second assessment report of the Intergovernmental Panel on Climate Change summarizes available technologies, policies and measures for mitigating climate change (Watson et al. (eds.) 1996, Part III). It provides a comprehensive overview of ways to limit and reduce GHG emissions and to enhance GHG sinks under the Framework Convention on Climate Change. As an example of the innumerable technological options to reduce GHG emissions, consider the central issue of substituting fossil fuels with other means of energy production. Not only may well-known renewable sources of energy be exploited more efficiently to replace fossil fuels, but also other technologies so far neglected may be further developed and used on a larger scale. One example is the fusion of hydrogen and oxygen to water.

Of course, all human-induced emissions of greenhouse gases have to be evaluated in order to determine the cost-effective mitigation strategy. Global warming is a problem caused by myriads of GHG-emitting activities all over the world. This is exactly the reason why the implementation of marked-based (that is, cost-effective) internalization instruments is a crucial issue in climate policy. Nevertheless, the above considerations illustrate that the use of fossil fuels and the induced changes to the turnover of carbon in the ecosystem play a major role in designing preventive measures. Given the marked dominance of fossil fuels for present energy production (see Table 2.2), curbing climate change obviously requires a reorientation of long-term energy supply and demand. Any such policy is going to have far-reaching consequences on economic activity. It is this circumstance that makes an effective, internationally coordinated climate policy particularly difficult to achieve.

2.1.2   The Stratospheric Ozone Layer

Life on earth is protected against dangerous solar radiation by a layer of air with relatively high concentrations of ozone molecules. The ozone shield stretches from 12 to 25 km overhead and hinders the passage of ultraviolet radiation to the earth's surface. In particular, the powerful short-wave UV-B radiation damages various biological systems. It is a health hazard; it causes or promotes skin cancer, cataracts, allergic reactions and immune insufficiency. It reduces the growth of plants and has adverse affects on crop yields, possibly also on entire food-chain systems. It also damages certain materials, in particular plastic, and increases smog.

Ozone, the three-atom molecule of oxygen (O_3), is generated in a chemical reaction triggered by sunlight above the tropics, from where global air circulation transports some of it to the poles. The delicate ozone equilibrium in the stratosphere is destabilized by the release of anthropogenic trace gases, particularly CFCs and halogens. Characteristic ozone-destroying elements are chlorine in CFCs and bromine in halogens. During their long lifetime, which for some compounds lasts up to 100 years, CFCs and halogens emitted into the troposphere slowly migrate to the stratosphere. There the compounds are broken up by high-energy solar radiation and their chlorine or bromine parts are released. Each of these parts then catalyses the destruction of a myriad of ozone molecules. This chain reaction depletes the ozone layer which in turn allows harmful UV-B radiation to reach the earth's surface.[7] Apart from depleting the ozone layer, CFCs and related compounds are very effective greenhouse gases. Thus, these problems cannot be treated separately from each other.[8]

The main virtue of the CFCs is their chemical stability. They are not toxic since they do not react with other chemicals, and they are not inflammable. Moreover, they are cheap to produce. These properties have made them attractive inputs in industrialized production processes. CFCs have been widely used as coolants in refrigeration (Freon), as foam-blowing agents (Styrofoam), as aerosol propellants in spray cans and as solvents in the electronic industry and in dry-cleaning. Halogens, a similar chemical, are used mainly in fire fighting. Besides CFCs and halogens there are other ozone-depleting substances that have been added to the list of controlled substances by the London and Copenhagen amendments to the Montreal Protocol (see Section 2.2.2). In 1986, world consumption of CFCs and halogens was 1.14 million tons with a total ozone-depletion potential of 1.23 million tons. The main places of production were the USA (29 per cent), Western Europe (37 per cent), Eastern Europe (12 per cent) and Asia, Pacific and Latin America (22 per cent). In 1984/85, per-capita consumption of CFC-11/12 was about 0.85 kg in the USA and in the European Community; in China it was 0.02 kg.

Although every part of the world is affected by ozone depletion, there are some systematic regional differences concerning the impacts as well as the perceived political valuation. Whereas less depletion occurs around the equator, depletion levels are considerably higher towards the poles with a particularly heavy loss of stratospheric ozone after the extremely cold antarctic winter, generating the phenomenon of the 'ozone hole'. This ozone hole has started to widen over the southernmost part of South America, New Zealand and southern Australia. A similar ozone hole has

---

[7]The above interrelations were detected in 1974 by Mario Molina and Sherwood Rowland. See Heister (1993) and Sandler (1997) for the natural science of the 'ozone hole'.

[8]For interdependencies between ozone-layer depletion and global warming see also note 4 in Section 2.1.1.

not yet opened up over the North Pole. However, depressed ozone levels and a serious increase in chlorine concentrations have been registered in the northern hemisphere, too. Apart from this pattern, the valuation of damage caused by UV-B is likely to differ between regions and countries of different political systems and levels of economic development. For example, the political valuation of diseases and lost lives is probably lower in less-developed countries. Taken together, there is a considerable difference in the perceived benefits of ozone layer protection measures in less-developed countries in comparison to highly developed countries. Not only is the distribution of damages biassed against the industrialized countries as the latter are generally located closer to the poles, but also these countries have a higher valuation of such damages. This picture is confirmed by the fact that countries such as Canada, Norway, Finland, Australia and New Zealand were those who fought most vigorously for a strong ozone treaty (Benedick 1991).

2.2 The History of Global Environmental Policy

The need to address environmental problems of international dimension through coordinated action was clearly recognized in the first report to the Club of Rome, 'Limits to Growth', in 1971. It was further elaborated at the conference on Environment and Development in Stockholm in 1972 and in the First Environmental Action Programme of the European Community in 1973. New aspects of the protection of the international environment — especially the notion of sustainable development — were addressed by the 'Brundtland Commission' in its report *Our Common Future* (Brundtland 1987). Since then, international environmental cooperation has been intensified and has led to a remarkable number of environmental conventions. Some of them have been signed by almost the entire community of countries.[9] It has yet to be verified, though, whether these agreements have in fact significantly improved the ecological situation compared to that before environmental policies were internationally coordinated. In some cases (as, for example, in the case of the International Whaling Commission) this seems not to hold; rather, these treaties codify 'business as usual'. In order to be able to evaluate the effectiveness of existing international environmental agreements it is necessary to know how negotiations on certain issues evolved, on what exactly the cooperating parties agreed and how successfully these

---

[9]For an actual and detailed inventory of international environmental agreements, see Bergesen and Parmann (1997).

agreements have been implemented so far. As an example from the great number of issues in international environmental policy, we concentrate on those two environmental problems which have been described in the preceding section: global warming and the depletion of the ozone layer.

2.2.1   The Anthropogenic Greenhouse Effect

With the aim of achieving significant reductions in GHG emissions, more than 170 nations signed the United Nations Framework Convention on Climate Change (FCCC) in June 1992. The ultimate objective of the convention is a

> stabilization of greenhouse gas concentrations in the atmosphere at a level that would prevent dangerous anthropogenic interference with the climate system. Such a level should be achieved within a time-frame sufficient to allow ecosystems to adapt naturally to climate change, to ensure that food production is not threatened, and to enable economic development to proceed in a sustainable manner. (FCCC, Art. 2)[10]

This goal is to be reached in two steps: first, by reducing present global GHG emissions to appropriate levels, and second, by stabilizing atmospheric GHG concentrations in the long run. Unfortunately, the convention remained a mere declaration of intent as it does not specify the policy measures by which the above goals are to be achieved. The only explicit commitment was a declaration of the industrialized countries to reduce their annual GHG emissions until the year 2000 to 1990 levels. Nevertheless, the Framework Convention was an important step in global climate policy in so far as it laid the basis for further negotiations on explicit quantitative emission targets. To this end, the signatories agreed to convene a regular 'Conference of the Parties to the Framework Convention' and to continue negotiating a binding protocol with quantitative reduction obligations. This agreement is intended to replace the FCCC, which expires in the year 2000.

The first conference of the parties (COP-1) in 1995 neither agreed on explicit reduction targets nor discussed the financial aspects of international climate policy such as higher contributions to the Global Environment Facility. Its most important outcome was the 'Berlin Mandate' — an agenda to continue negotiating on binding commitments of industrialized countries after the year 2000. The representatives of the 116 countries present in Berlin also agreed on a pilot phase for the concept of 'joint implementation' (see Section 7.3). Furthermore, for the

---

[10]The text of the Framework Convention on Climate Change ('Rio Convention') is available on the internet under www.unfccc.de.

first time some developing countries — in particular the group of small island countries (AOSIS) — played an active role during negotiations at COP-1.

The second conference of the parties (COP-2) took place in 1996 in Geneva. Its main purpose was to take stock and to give a fresh impetus to the negotiations on a binding protocol. This was achieved by producing the 'Geneva Ministerial Declaration'. The declaration emphasized the need to accelerate the Berlin Mandate talks on strengthening the convention, in particular by making commitments in the post-2000 period legally binding. The second conference of the parties also decided to continue the pilot phase on 'activities implemented jointly'.

In 1997, the negotiations following the Rio Convention finally resulted in a binding protocol which specifies explicit reduction targets for the most important GHG-emitting countries. This protocol was negotiated at the third conference of parties (COP-3) on 1-12 December in Kyoto, Japan and is therefore referred to as the 'Kyoto Protocol' (KP). It contains agreement on three main topics:[11]

- the basket of greenhouse gases is enlarged from three to six gases;[12]
- sinks for GHGs are included, allowing for sequestration induced by reforestation, for example, of tropical rain forests;
- the KP stipulates a reduction and limitation of GHG emissions by Annex I countries (that is, industrialized countries and/or countries in transition to a market economy) which ensures a collective decrease in GHG emissions by at least 5 per cent below 1990 levels within the first period of commitment from 2008 to 2012.

To fulfill the overall emission reduction target, the member states of the European Union (EU) as a group committed themselves to a reduction in their GHG emissions of 8 per cent with respect to 1990 levels,[13] the USA 7 per cent and Japan 6 per cent.[14] Other important GHG-emitting countries such as China and India, however, are not subject to any abatement obligation at all. Originally, the EU advocated a much

---

[11] The text of the Kyoto Protocol is available on the internet under www.unfccc.de.

[12] The three new gases added to the 'first basket' (CO_2, CH_4 and N_2O) are hydrofluorocarbons (HFCs), perfluorocarbons (PFCs) and sulphur hexafluoride (SF_6).

[13] Meanwhile, the EU member states have negotiated the national burden sharing required to reach the EU target of the KP: Germany agreed on a reduction obligation of 21 per cent, Austria 13 per cent, the UK 12.5 per cent and Italy 6.5 per cent. France stabilizes its current emissions, whereas countries such as Spain and Portugal may increase their emissions by 15 and 27 per cent, respectively. Regardless of this agreement at the EU level, the new German government elected in 1998 has confirmed its unilateral and more ambitious 25 per cent target.

[14] See Annex B of the KP for a complete listing of the quantitative reduction obligations of all Annex I countries.

more ambitious reduction proposal: minus 7.5 per cent by the year 2005 and minus 15 per cent by the year 2010 compared with 1990 levels for *all* industrialized countries (Table 2.3). By contrast, the USA proposed

Table 2.3: Declarations on carbon dioxide emission reductions

1988	World Conference on the Changing Atmosphere in Toronto recommends a reduction of current annual CO_2 emissions by 20 per cent until 2005 and by 50 per cent until 2050
1990	German Enquête Commission recommends a reduction of the 1987 level of CO_2 emissions by 40 per cent until 2020 and by 70–80 per cent until 2050
1992	At UNCED in Rio, industrialized countries declare they will reduce their annual CO_2 emissions to the level of 1990 until 2000
April 1995	First conference of the parties to the FCCC (COP-1) in Berlin: Small-island countries propose that industrialized countries reduce their 1990 level of CO_2 emissions by 20 per cent until 2005; German government declares it will reduce the 1990 level of national CO_2 emissions by 25 per cent until 2005
June 1997	EU declares it will reduce its most important GHG emissions in two steps (and proposes the same target for all industrialized countries): by 7.5 per cent until 2005 and by 15 per cent until 2010 compared to 1990 emissions
December 1997	USA proposes stabilizing its national emissions on 1990 levels in the period between 2008 and 2012 and identifying reduction objectives for 2012 to 2017, depending on commitments by developing countries

a mere stabilization of emissions at 1990 levels in the period between 2008 and 2012 and wanted to make the identification of later reduction objectives dependent on a commitment by developing countries.

No agreement has yet been reached on long-term stabilization of emissions. If, for example, the global mean temperature were not to increase by more than 2 degrees Celsius above current levels, CO_2 concentrations should not exceed 450 to 500 parts per million which corresponds to 60–80 per cent of the preindustrial level. Although this goal is compatible with further increasing global CO_2 emissions during the next few decades, emissions will then have to decline drastically and must converge in the long run to approximately half of current annual emission quantities (IPCC 1996, pp. 9–10, Figure 1b). Long-term stabilization of emissions will be a difficult task considering increases in energy consumption in conjunction with a growing world population. According to UN estimates, the world population will rise from 5.8 billion in 1997 to approximately 8.1 billion in 2020. On the basis of current trends, energy consumption will almost have doubled by 2020, more than 50 per cent of energy demand coming from densely populated developing countries.

The Kyoto Protocol provides for several 'flexibility instruments' whose purpose is to increase the international cost-effectiveness of emission reductions. The Protocol differentiates between the following instruments: 'Joint Implementation' (JI), the 'Clean Development Mechanism' (CDM) and 'Emissions Trading' (ET). JI is a project-based emission reduction between Annex I countries (that is, industrialized countries and transformation economies), and the CDM is between Annex I and non-Annex I countries (that is, mainly between industrialized and developing countries). ET is the most general instrument as it allows emission quantities to be traded globally or at the national level and is not necessarily project based. Although these instruments are poorly elaborated at present, their inclusion in the Kyoto Protocol may prove to be a major achievement in the long run. From an economic perspective they are a first step towards a market-oriented and thus cost-effective internalization of global externalities.[15] The general success of the Kyoto Protocol is difficult to evaluate. Reduction targets fall short of what had been hoped for by the public and do not solve the climate problem, especially with regard to the long-run stabilization of GHG concentrations. Moreover, the Kyoto Protocol comes into force only when at least 55 countries have ratified it, which accounts for at least 55 per cent of the CO_2 emissions of Annex I countries. Debates in the US congress demonstrate that ratification by national parliaments may end up in a deadlock, as some countries make their ratification dependent on the ratification of others. Given that for the first time an agreement on precise dates and individual reduction obligations has been negotiated (see Table 2.4), the Kyoto Protocol is nevertheless an important first step towards an environmentally sustainable path of economic development.

---

[15] See Section 7.3 for a critical discussion of the concept of 'joint implementation' as stipulated in the Kyoto Protocol.

Table 2.4: Diplomacy on the global environment

1958	Continuous monitoring of CO_2 concentrations in the atmosphere started at Mauna Loa on Hawaii and at the South Pole
1972	1st Global Environment Conference in Stockholm establishes UNEP
1979	World Climate Conference is held in Geneva; World Climate Program of the WMO
1985	Conference of ICSU, UNEP and WMO in Villach/Austria; Vienna Convention on the protection of the ozone layer
1987	World Commission on Environment and Development develops the concept of *sustainable development* ('Brundtland Report')
1988	World Conference on the Changing Atmosphere and Implications for Global Security in Toronto
November 1988	Convocation of the IPCC by UNEP and WMO
September 1989	International Conference on air pollution and climate change in Nordwijk: Japan, UK, USSR, USA refuse explicit reduction targets
October/ November 1990	World Climate Conference in Geneva; scientific and political discussion of the first report of the IPCC
21 December 1990	UN Resolution 45/212 'Protection of global climate for present and future generations of mankind' by the UN's 45th general assembly
June 1992	UNCED – 'Rio Convention' signed by 176 countries; industrialized countries declare they will reduce their CO_2 emissions to 1990 levels by the year 2000
21 March 1994	FCCC comes into force
28 March – 7 April 1995	1st Conference of the Parties of the Rio Convention in Berlin (COP-1); 'Berlin Mandate' for the negotiation of a protocol on emission reduction commitments of industrialized countries after 2000 (to be adopted at COP-3)
July 1996	2nd Conference of the Parties in Geneva (COP-2); Geneva Ministerial Declaration
June 1997	Extraordinary General Assembly of the UN in New York on 'Environment and Sustainable Development'
1–12 December 1997	3rd Conference of the Parties in Kyoto (COP-3); Kyoto Protocol with explicit GHG emission obligations for Annex I countries
November 1998	4th Conference of the Parties in Buenos Aires (COP-4)

From the beginning, the German government played an active role in the international debate on global climate policy (see Table 2.5). In 1990,

Table 2.5: German initiatives on climate policy

December 1987	German Parliament installs the Enquête Commission (*Vorsorge zum Schutz der Erdatmosphäre*)
1990	German government launches climate protection program (*Klimaschutzprogramm*)
1994	German government presents a list of items (*Elementepapier*) to be included in a future protocol to the climate convention: stabilization of GHG concentrations, technical measures, protection of forests, JI; German government declares it will reduce the 1987 level of national CO_2 emissions by 25–30 % until 2005
April 1995	German government declares it will reduce the 1990 level of national CO_2 emissions by 25 % until 2005 during first meeting of contracting parties of the Rio Convention in Berlin; self-commitment of the German automobile industry to decrease the 1990 level of CO_2 emissions caused by German car traffic by at least 25 % until 2005 through lower petrol consumption
March 1996	19 federations of the industrial and energy sector declare they will reduce their 1990 specific CO_2 emissions by 20 % until the year 2005
June 1997	Together with Brazil, Singapore and South Africa, Germany presents a 'Joint Global Initiative' during extraordinary general assembly of the UN
End 1998	New German government confirms national 25 % reduction target
1999	First stage of ecological tax reform comes into force

it launched a 'climate protection program' which consists of more than 130 individual measures, ranging from regulative legislation on technical standards over subsidization of environmentally friendly investments to environmental taxation. Nevertheless, these measures have so far been insufficient to meet the German reduction targets (Table 2.5).

According to the second report on climate protection (*Kli-maschutzbericht*) issued by the German government in April 1997, CO_2 emissions in Germany have decreased by only 12 per cent between 1990 and 1995. According to the current trend (that is, without additional measures), CO_2 emissions will have decreased by only 15 per cent by 2005 in contrast to the official 25 per cent target declared by the German government in 1995 in Berlin.[16] In 1996, annual CO_2 emissions increased again for the first time since 1990 and were 1.7 per cent higher than in 1995, making it even more difficult to meet the ambitious German reduction target.

Hence, despite the great number of existing regulations for climate protection in Germany, in their essence they do not suffice and are sometimes even contradictory. For example, new regulations in the construction sector are intended to increase the use of insulation materials. Those materials, however, at present are still produced with the help of HCFCs as a foaming agent. The latter substances are still permitted by the Montreal Protocol, but possess a global warming potential that is about five thousand times higher than that of carbon dioxide. Another example of counterproductive German legislation is the abolition of the 'Kohlepfennig' which subsidized coal-mining for energy production. Instead of replacing this coal duty with a carbon or energy tax it was abolished altogether, resulting in lower electricity prices.

There have also been several initiatives by the private sector in Germany. Important branches of the industrial sector tried to obviate imminent environmental legislation by declarations of self-commitment (see Table 2.5). The most important one is the declaration by 19 federations of the industrial and energy sectors from March 1996 which contains a self-commitment to reduce the 1990 level of specific CO_2 emissions by 20 per cent until the year 2005.[17] Another example of a voluntary abatement effort is the German aluminum industry which has committed itself to reducing its 1990 emissions of longlasting greenhouse gases (methanes) by 50 per cent until 2005. It remains to be shown, though, whether these voluntary measures will contribute effectively to the national GHG emission target. The German environmental protection agency (*Umweltbundesamt*), for example, estimates that CO_2 emissions induced by German car traffic will rise in the next ten years by 20 per cent even if average fuel consumption can be reduced to 5 liters per 100 km. This conflicts with the 1995 declaration of the association

---

[16] *Frankfurter Allgemeine Zeitung*, 17 April 1997.

[17] This self-commitment covers 71 per cent of industrial energy consumption and almost 100 per cent of public energy supply, as well as some of the emissions from households.

of the German automobile industry that the 1990 level of CO_2 emissions caused by German car traffic should be reduced by at least 25 per cent until 2005 through lower petrol consumption.[18]

It is broadly recognized by economists that a comprehensive approach to internalize externalities generated by anthropogenic CO_2 emissions could consist of some kind of carbon or energy tax. This policy instrument is able to reach all types of pollution-generating activities and to account for cost-effectiveness of abatement activities (see Section 3.4). Until recently, though, an ecological tax reform has not seriously been on the political agenda in Germany and many other countries.[19] In Germany, the political situation has changed with the elections for the national parliament in autumn 1998. The new German government — a coalition of the social-democratic party (SPD) and the ecologist party (*Bündnis 90/ Die Grünen*) — introduced a national ecological tax reform (*Ökosteuer*) in April 1999. The reform provides that specific taxes on the use of electricity and fossil fuels are to be increased in several steps. The additional tax revenue is mainly used to reduce the social security contributions that have to be paid in connection with labor income. The latter policy measure is thought to have positive effects on the labor market, as it reduces the effective tax rate on labor income and the price of labor in production. The idea is to improve environmental quality and at the same time to reap a 'second dividend' which consists in less unemployment. Besides contentious details of the German ecological tax reform,[20] a unilateral approach to address a global environmental problem such as climate change is in general inefficient — both from an economic and from an ecological perspective.[21] If a unilateral approach is nevertheless thought to be necessary, it should be undertaken jointly by the industrialized countries. The EU may play a predominant role in this context as the political integration of its member states is advanced and agreement on a joint strategy may be relatively easy. Therefore, not only the German government but also the European Commission should revise their current tax policy agenda and shift the focus on to a European environmental tax reform (Genser et al. 1999).

---

[18] *Süddeutsche Zeitung*, 13 April 1995, p. 36.

[19] See *Frankfurter Rundschau*, 27 August 1997, p. 21, on political pressures against the ecological tax reform in Germany and *Zeitpunkte*, ed. 6/1995, p. 27 for the collapse of the European CO_2/energy tax proposal in 1995.

[20] Objections have been raised, for example, that energy-intensive sectors are being exempted from the new energy tax and that implicit tax rates on CO_2 emissions vary substantially, depending on the source of energy used. See Sachverständigenrat (1998, pp. 271–5) for a discussion of the German ecological tax reform and Killinger (2000) for a comprehensive analysis of the possibility of a 'double dividend'.

[21] See Section 4.5 for a detailed discussion of unilateral environmental policies.

2.2.2   The Stratospheric Ozone Layer

About a decade after the discovery of the destructive potential of CFCs for the stratospheric ozone layer in 1974, the first international agreement was reached to tackle this global environmental problem. In September 1987, 24 countries and the European Community signed the Montreal Protocol (MP) on the control of substances that deplete the ozone layer (see Table 2.6). It was clear from the beginning that an effective agreement had to ensure the participation of developing countries. Otherwise, sooner or later a 'leakage problem' would have emerged from developing countries that produce the controlled substances for export and/or for growing domestic markets. However, developing countries were initially barely interested in the protection of the ozone layer.[22] On the one hand, these countries showed no awareness of the potential damages that the destruction of the ozone layer would cause, particularly as the 'ozone holes' constituted a direct threat only to industrialized countries in the southern and northern hemispheres. On the other hand, developing countries did not want to renounce the benefits of a class of cheap industrial chemicals that had also contributed to the economic development of industrialized countries. For the developing countries, paying a higher price for substitutes of these substances amounted to a payment for the environmental damage that the industrialized world had caused in the course of their economic development. In their perspective, the industrialized countries' attempts to ban the global use of CFCs amounted to 'environmental imperialism'.

Therefore, in the negotiations leading to the Montreal Protocol the major challenge for the group of industrialized countries was to convince the developing countries that participation in an ozone treaty would in no way hamper their national economic development. For this purpose three different instruments were devised: first, the MP allowed a grace period of ten years for developing countries before they were to meet its obligations. Second, trade sanctions against countries staying outside the agreement were defined.[23] Third, the agreement provided for side payments to the developing countries in order to guarantee their cooperation in the long run, and subsequently in 1990 the parties to the MP agreed to establish the 'Montreal Protocol Multilateral Fund' (MPMF) to assist developing countries with their costs of phasing out ozone-depleting substances (London amendments, see Table 2.6).

---

[22] See Benedick (1991) or DeSombre and Kauffman (1996) for details of the ozone negotiations.

[23] Article 4 MP specifies banning trade with non-parties, first in controlled substances, then in products containing controlled substances, and finally in goods that are produced with controlled substances.

Table 2.6: International ozone policy

1930	CFCs are discovered by T. Midgley
1974	M. Molina and S. Rowland describe the destructive potential of CFCs for the stratospheric ozone layer
1978	CFCs in aerosols (spray cans) are banned in the USA
March 1985	Vienna Convention (signed by 20 nations and the European Community): no quantitative controls on ozone-depleting substances
September 1987	Montreal Protocol (signed by 24 countries and the EC): control of some substances, 10-year grace period for developing countries to meet obligations, trade sanctions
May 1989	First conference of the parties to the MP in Helsinki: a financial mechanism to support developing countries in controlling ozone depleting substances is proposed
June 1990	London amendments to the MP: MPMF established as an 'interim fund' with a volume of US$160 million for the three following years (1991–93); stricter controls and inclusion of additional substances; 10-year grace period retained; China joins the MPMF
November 1992	Copenhagen amendments to the MP: introduction of a phase-out schedule for HCFCs; controls on consumption and production of methyl bromide; MPMF reauthorized on a permanent basis and funding increased to US$240 million; Brazil, India and most other developing countries join the MPMF
November 1993	Fifth meeting of the parties in Bangkok: MPMF is provided with US$510 million for its second three-year period from 1994–96
1995	Seventh meeting of the parties in Vienna: phase-out schedule for HCFCs is strengthened (industrialized countries phase out consumption but not production by 2030, developing countries by 2040); discussion of data reporting and non-compliance issues
September 1997	Ninth meeting of the parties in Montreal: phase-out schedule for methyl bromide is strengthened; establishment of a licensing system to combat illegal trade in substances; improvement in the data reporting system; review of the non-compliance procedure

Sources: Parson and Greene (1995, p. 20); Oberthür (1997).

Subsequent international negotiations have led to several amendments of the Montreal Protocol. These not only secured financial assistance to developing countries by establishing the MPMF on a permanent basis (Copenhagen amendments in 1992, see Table 2.6), but also intensified the phase-out of ozone-depleting substances by tightening time schedules and by including additional substances. The rapid growth of HCFC production and consumption, for example, which has more than doubled since 1989 and which accounts for about 10 per cent of current consumption made it necessary to reach agreement also on the control of this class of substances. Later meetings of the parties to the Montreal Protocol have been characterized by a switch of the focus from strengthening control targets towards the successful implementation of these targets. Dealing with non-compliance, illegal trade in controlled substances and the functioning of the data reporting system have been major issues both at the Vienna meeting in 1995 and at the 10th anniversary meeting 1997 in Montreal. In sum, it is too early for a definitive evaluation of the Montreal process. Although the main ozone-depleting substances have been almost completely phased out in industrialized countries, production and consumption is rising in important developing countries such as China and India. To date, worldwide consumption of harmful substances still amounts to approximately 25–30 per cent of the level before the introduction of international controls (Oberthür 1997, Table 2). Furthermore, important problems with respect to monitoring and compliance remain to be solved (see Section 7.2).

2.3   Theoretical Framework

Having outlined the natural science and politics of two important international environmental problems, we now turn in the remainder of this chapter to the theoretical framework of this study. The following concepts of economic theory are applied: externalities and public goods, cost–benefit analysis and game theory. We devote a subsection to each of these three concepts, introduce the specific models used in the later chapters and establish their appropriateness for the present analysis.

2.3.1   Transboundary Externalities and International Public Goods

Economic theory explains the excessive use of environmental resources by the phenomenon of technological externalities, that is, negative effects of one economic agent's behavior on the utility or production of other agents who are not compensated by the market mechanism (Baumol and Oates 1988, pp. 15–18). Externalities represent one important form of market failure that calls for correction by the public sector. *International* environmental externalities are characterized by the fact that their spatial reach is greater than the territory of the single political jurisdictions affected by the externality. These problems do not represent an exceptional but rather a typical form of detrimental externalities among individuals sharing common natural resources. The environmental consequences of economic activity do not stop at politically determined national borders, but depend on complex biological and physical causalities. Consequently one fundamental characteristic of transboundary externalities is the number of countries that are involved. Another typical feature is the direction of the external effects which can be unidirectional, reciprocal or a mixture of both.[24]

This study confines itself to reciprocal transboundary externalities that possess a completely symmetric character involving all countries. In other words it is assumed that the pollutant mixes uniformly so that the emissions of all countries contribute in the same way to pollution, and for environmental quality it does not matter where the emissions originate.[25] The externality in this case can be interpreted as the provision of a (pure) global public bad. Inversely, emission reduction activities of single countries feature the aspects of a (pure) international public good: abatements are to the benefit of all countries (non-rivalry) and no country can be excluded from the benefits that a single country's efforts generate (non-excludability). Global environmental problems such as climate change and the destruction of the ozone layer have these properties. It will be pointed out later that problems of cost-effectiveness and incentive compatibility remain basically the same for externalities that are more of a directional or regional type and that generally the analysis also applies for those problems.

Interpreting national policies to protect international environmental resources as the supply of an international public good allows us to focus on the following two issues: (i) with more than one country suffering from pollution, each government has an incentive to take a free ride on

---

[24]Every environmental problem can be characterized by a transport coefficient matrix that describes how much of one unit of polluting emissions released in a particular location is deposited within that location itself and how much of it is exported towards other locations. See, for example, Mäler (1989) for an application to the 'acid rain' problem in Europe.

[25]We abstract from other important characteristics, such as the temporal dimension or the degree of uncertainty on the causes and consequences of an environmental problem. See, for example, Ploeg and de Zeeuw (1992) for an introduction to the theory of international *stock* externalities. For the role of uncertainty in climate policy, see, for example, Larson and Tobey (1994).

the efforts of other countries; (ii) with more than one polluting country one is faced with the problem of how abatement measures should be allocated among them in a way that minimizes overall abatement costs, that is, that ensures international cost-effectiveness. These aspects become predominant in the case of 'global commons' where all countries contribute to the problem and all countries are also victims of it.[26] Furthermore, the above interpretation allows us to apply the normative and positive theory of public-good provision to international environmental policy. The notion of *international public goods* is in fact not new and a particular strand of literature in public economics is devoted to this subject.[27]

One of the starting-points for the normative theory of public goods in general was the seminal contribution of Samuelson (1954).[28] Analogously to the case of national public goods it is possible to derive conditions under which the provision of an international public good is Pareto optimal. In a first-best framework, global efficiency is reached when each national government considers the beneficial effects of the supply of the international public good not only for its own welfare, but also for the welfare of all other nations. If the public good is provided decentrally by many heterogeneous countries, the traditional Samuelson condition is modified: a globally efficient allocation is reached when the sum of the marginal rates of substitution of all individuals in all countries is equal to the marginal rate of transformation of each national economy. This condition implies that the aggregate provision of the public good reaches an efficient level and simultanously is produced at minimum global costs.

---

[26]The original interpretation of the term 'global commons' is a legal one and covers common access resources such as the deep seas, the Antarctic or the radiation spectrum. From an economic perspective, there is no systematic difference from other global environmental problems such as climate change or the destruction of the ozone layer.

[27]See, for example, Braden and Bromley (1981) or Kindleberger (1986); Terasaki (1992) analyses the optimum supply of international public goods between two small open economies and compares the Nash and Stackelberg equilibria; Ihori (1996) analyses the consequences of productivity differentials for the decentralized provision of international public goods; the empirical test of Murdoch and Sandler (1997) on CFC emission abatements confirms the theory of decentralized supply of international public goods. Markusen (1975a, 1975b) derived optimal tax structures with international externalities and analysed optimality conditions for international environmental cooperation. For earlier work on comparative advantage and trade in the production of international public goods see, for example, Connolly (1970, 1972) and Kiesling (1974). Olson (1965) put forward the theory of collective action and Olson and Zeckhauser (1966) were the first to apply this theory to the international level in the context of defense expenditures.

[28]The discussion on the *Pareto*-optimal supply of public goods has already started with Wicksell (1896). See Cornes and Sandler (1986) or Arnold (1992) for an introduction, and Richter and Wiegard (1993) for a survey of the literature.

The former aspect implies full internalization of the positive external effects on other countries; the latter means that the marginal costs of public-good provision are equalized across all countries. As this model forms the basis for the analysis in the later chapters, we continue by giving a brief analytical and graphical representation of it.

Consider a world of two countries A and B with a world population N living in these two countries ($N = n_A + n_B$). National populations are exogenously given, that is, there is no migration between these countries. In both countries, individuals derive utility from the consumption of a private good x and a pure international public good Q. The strictly concave utility function of individual i living in country k is

$$U_k^i = U_k^i(x_k^i, Q), \quad \text{with} \quad i = 1, ..., n_k \quad \text{and} \quad k = A, B. \quad (2.1)$$

Utility functions are twice differentiable and increasing in their arguments. For the purpose of national and international welfare comparisons we further assume that utility is measurable on an absolute scale and that it is interpersonally comparable. The public good is pure in the sense that it makes no difference where it is provided, implying that national contributions are perfect substitutes. The total amount Q of the international environmental good is a function of national contributions q_A and q_B:

$$Q = f(q_A, q_B). \quad (2.2)$$

National income Y_k of country k is exogenously given and can be spent either on private consumption X or for contributing q units to the international public good Q. Normalizing the price of the private good to unity, national budget constraints are given by

$$Y_k = X_k + T_k(q_k), \quad \text{with} \quad X_k = \sum x_k^i, \quad i = 1, ..., n_k \quad (2.3)$$
$$\partial T_k/\partial q_k > 0, \quad \partial^2 T_k/\partial q_k^2 \geq 0, \quad k = A, B.$$

$T_k(q_k)$ are the opportunity costs of country k for providing q units to the international environmental good Q. The costs of providing cne unit of q_k may vary, whereas the price of the private good is held constant. $T'(q)$ represents the marginal rate of transformation ($dX/dq = -T'(q)$). The second derivative of $T(q)$ determines the curvature of the transformation line, that is, the available technology.

Social welfare is characterized by an individualistic social welfare function W of the Bergson–Samuelson type that is increasing in all arguments, twice differentiable and concave. National welfare U depends directly on the utilities of the individuals belonging to that country and indirectly on their consumption bundles:

$$U_k = U_k(u_k^1, ..., u_k^{n_k}) = U_k[u_k^1(x_k^1, Q), ..., u_k^{n_k}(x_k^{n_k}, Q)], \quad k = A, B. \quad (2.4)$$

Correspondingly, global welfare is a function of the utilities of all individuals in both countries:

$$W = W(U_A, U_B) = W(u_A^1, ..., u_A^{n_A}, u_B^1, ..., u_B^{n_B}). \quad (2.5)$$

Global welfare maximization
Globally optimal provision levels of the international public good Q are derived through maximization of global welfare W by choosing globally optimal contributions q_A and q_B as well as optimal quantities x_k^i simultaneously, subject to the global budget constraint:

$$\max \ W[u_A^1(x_A^1, Q), \ldots, u_B^{n_B}(x_B^{n_B}, Q)] \quad (2.6)$$
$$\text{s.t.} \quad Y = X + T_A(q_A) + T_B(q_B).$$

Combining the first-order conditions for a globally efficient outcome yields

$$\sum_{k=A}^{B} \sum_{i=1}^{n_k} \frac{\partial U_k^i / \partial Q}{\partial U_k^i / \partial x_k^i} = T_k'(q_k), \qquad k = A, B, \quad (2.7)$$

which represents the Samuelson condition for the globally efficient provision of a pure international public good. It requires that the sum over all individual marginal rates of substitution in the world equals the marginal costs of providing q in both countries.

Pareto-optimal bargaining solutions
The existence of international public goods implies that international cooperation on the provision of these goods is required to achieve a Pareto-optimal allocation of public and private goods.[29] The Samuelson condition (2.7) can be illustrated graphically by integrating the production possibility frontiers of the countries to one common frontier and by bringing together the system of indifference curves into one graph. In such a graph we can depict a set of Pareto-optimal allocations as well as situations that are Pareto superior to the uncoordinated situation.

In Figure 2.1 the two strictly concave transformation curves $T_A T_A'$ and $T_B T_B'$ are depicted. Country B is assumed to have a comparative advantage in the production of the international public good, this being

---

[29]The following is based on Arnold (1984) who applies the Samuelson condition in a simple two-countries, two-goods model to international environmental problems.

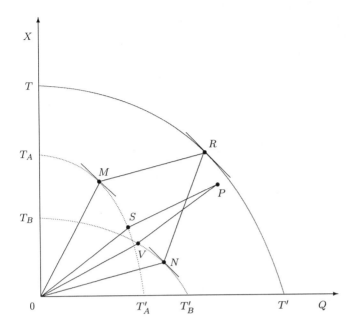

Figure 2.1: Cost-effective contributions to an international public good

reflected in a relatively smaller slope (in absolute values) of the transformation curve. The common production possibility frontier TT' can be derived as the set of linear combinations of those pairs of points that are characterized by equal marginal rates of transformation in both countries. Due to the concavity assumption there is always only one such combination $-dX_A/dq_A = -dX_B/dq_B = -dX/dQ$. The latter condition is fulfilled, for example, for points M and N whose added vectors yield point R. By contrast, when the marginal rates of transformation are not equal (points S and V), the global production possibility frontier is not reached (point P).

Assuming that the preferences of a country's population can be represented by a set of social indifference curves, the set of indifference curves for one country (country A) can be directly inserted into Figure 2.1. The welfare of the other country (country B) can be depicted using the procedure developed by Shibata (1971).[30] The resulting graph is Figure 2.2. The lens enclosed by the social indifference curves W_A^1 and $\tilde{W}_B^1$ represents the set of Pareto superior allocations which improves the welfare of both

---

[30] See Appendix A.1 for a detailed description of the procedure, and Arnold (1984, pp. 121–3) for the case of linear production possibility frontiers.

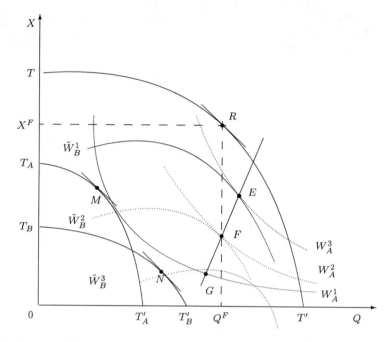

Figure 2.2: Efficient cooperative supply of an international public good

countries compared to the uncoordinated situation. Line EG represents the set of Pareto-optimal allocations. Due to the graphical construction, the Samuelson condition $\sum MRS = MRT_A = MRT_B$ holds in every point on EG. The strategic behavior of national governments and the specific circumstances of the bargaining problem determine whether and on which of these points the countries may agree. If, for example, countries agree on F, amounts Q^F of the public good and X^F of the private good are produced by the corresponding national production vectors N and M. Country A grants to B a transfer in units of the private good and enjoys in exchange a higher supply of the public good by B in which the latter has a comparative advantage.

National welfare maximization

The opposite benchmark is a situation without any cooperation. This is the case when the countries involved know the potential gains from cooperating on the supply of the international public good, but do not succeed in negotiating and implementing an agreement. Each government then maximizes national welfare subject to its exogenous income by choosing the nationally optimal contribution q_k to the international environmental good. We assume Nash behavior of each government, that is, the contribution level of the other country $\bar{q}$ is taken as given.[31] The optimization problem for each country k is:

$$\max_{q_k, x_k} U_k[u_k^1(x_k^1, Q), ..., u_k^{n_k}(x_k^{n_k}, Q)] \qquad (2.8)$$

$$\text{s.t.} \quad Y_k = X_k + T_k(q_k),$$

$$Q = f(q_A, q_B),$$

$$X_k = \sum_{i=1}^{n_k} x_k^i, \quad k = A, B.$$

Differentiating the Lagrangian of the maximization problem with respect to control variables x_k^i and q_k and rearranging yields the necessary condition that implicitly determines the *national* optimal provision level q_k for each country k:

$$\sum_{i=1}^{n_k} \frac{\partial U_k^i / \partial Q}{\partial U_k^i / \partial x_k^i} = T_k'(q_k), \qquad k = A, B. \qquad (2.9)$$

Condition (2.9) would represent the Samuelson condition if the public good was purely national. However, as Q is an *international* public good, efficiency condition (2.9) ensures national optimal provision levels, but does not characterize internationally efficient allocations.

Olson (1965) has already pointed out that the number of agents involved in the decentralized provision of a public good is essential for individual behavior and thus for the overall outcome. This is an important aspect of international environmental policy, too. It is established that the smaller the group of countries involved in a transboundary pollution problem, the easier it is in general for the governments to coordinate their actions, to suppress opportunistic behavior and to achieve mutual gains from environmental cooperation. One reason for the influence of group size on the uncoordinated provision of public goods is that free-riding incentives vary with group size. This is illustrated in Figure 2.3.[32] Let $C'(Q)$ be the constant marginal costs of public good provision Q and let N be the inverse compensated demand functions for the public good.

[31] It may be inappropriate to assume Nash behavior when only a few countries are involved in the pollution problem because each government may realize the impact of its own behavior on the other governments' decisions. Taking into account 'non-zero conjectures', however, does not change the results fundamentally and will not be examined here. Cornes and Sandler (1986, ch. 9.3) demonstrate how non-zero conjectures can be taken into account without changing the general framework.

[32] The graph is taken from Arnold (1992, p. 100); see McMillan (1979) for a survey on different aspects of the free-rider problem.

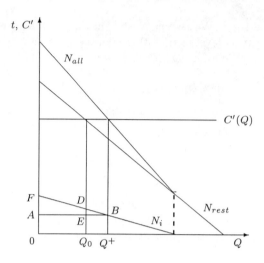

Figure 2.3: Preferences for a public good and free-riding incentives

Given aggregate demand N_{rest} of the other individual(s), individual i has no incentive to reveal its true marginal willingness to pay N_i. If it did so, it could consume the higher amount Q^+, but would have to bear a financial burden $0ABQ^+$. By contrast, if the individual could make the regulator believe that it has no preference for the public good, it would not have to contribute anything to finance the provision of Q but could nevertheless consume amount Q_0 by free-riding on the contributions of the other individuals. This is a rational strategy as the increase in consumer surplus EDB when revealing the true preference is smaller than the loss in terms of the financial burden $0AEQ_0$. If individuals are identical, all behave in this way and no positive amounts of the public good will be supplied in equilibrium. By contrast, if the inverse (pseudo) demand function N_{rest} does not represent the aggregate demand of a great number of individuals but rather of one single agent, this individual voluntarily finances the amount Q_0 of the public good. Hence, free-riding is not as severe as in the case where aggregate demand N_{all} is composed of many individual demand components. The incentive structure underlying this socially inefficient free-riding behavior corresponds to the type of situation described by the game-theoretic 'prisoner's dilemma' (see Section 2.3.3).

Comparing conditions (2.9) and (2.7) we can summarize as follows (Arnold 1984, p. 118): as long as more than one country is involved there will be underprovision with the international public good because single countries do not choose abatement levels that take into account the positive effects on welfare in the rest of the world. Moreover, even if national governments considered to some extent the positive international spillovers of their own decisions, uncoordinated policies generate additional welfare losses when the marginal costs of providing the international environmental good are not equalized. Only if all countries totally internalize the spillovers or if they are completely homogeneous, is cost-effectiveness ensured automatically. Hence, the comparison of optimality conditions (2.9) and (2.7) shows two interdependent sources of inefficiency: the first one is given through the possibility of taking a *free ride* on the contributions of other countries; the second one results from *comparative advantages* in the provision of the international public good not being exploited. Which of these inefficiencies is quantitatively more important depends on the characteristics of the countries and of the international environmental problem. Therefore in the following we shall consider different scenarios of asymmetry between the countries and specify the general model in terms of costs and benefits of emission abatements.

2.3.2 Cost–benefit Analysis

The purpose of this section is to introduce the basic concept of cost–benefit analysis (CBA) and to hint at its limitations within the context of international environmental policy.[33] In any political decision-making the perceived benefits of policy measures are compared either explicitly or implicitly to their costs. Economic cost–benefit analysis provides an analytical tool which helps to compare on a systematic, quantitative basis the social consequences of alternative policy actions. CBA thus allows us to assess the relative attractiveness of given policy projects. In the context of environmental policy-making, cost–benefit analysis is used to answer the following questions (Munasinghe et al. 1996, p. 150):

- How much should environmentally harmful emissions be reduced?
- When should emissions be reduced?
- How should emissions be reduced?
- Who should reduce emissions?

A rational policy to reduce environmentally harmful pollution maximizes the net social benefits of abatement measures, that is, the benefits of reduced pollution minus the associated costs. Such a policy requires

---

[33]It is beyond the scope of this study to discuss the theory and applications of CBA in detail. See, for example, Drèze and Stern (1987) for the welfare theoretic foundation of CBA. Cropper and Oates (1992) survey valuation techniques to assess the non-market values of environmental protection projects. Munasinghe et al. (1996) discuss the applicability of CBA techniques to climate change.

that the environmental benefits of an additional unit of pollution abatement (the marginal abatement benefits) are equal to the costs of an additional unit of emission reduction (the marginal abatement costs). Abatement costs and benefits often reflect the phenomenon of diminishing returns. A standard assumption in environmental economics which is empirically justified from a macro perspective is that the higher the marginal costs of abating emissions, the lower the level of emissions. Furthermore, marginal abatement costs are (close to) zero at the emission level implicitly chosen by a country which does not undertake *any* measures to control its emissions (Nordhaus 1991a). The empirical assessment of abatement benefits is generally more difficult: in most cases, either decreasing or constant marginal abatement benefits are assumed. In either case the net benefit function under these assumptions has a unique maximum at the point where the slopes of the abatement cost curve and the damage cost curve are equal.

The real situation is complicated by manifold biological and economic factors: emissions often generate a stream of environmental damages over a period of time that must be appropriately discounted to their present value; the environmental damage curve may be discontinuous and non-convex; technological progress requires estimation of future abatement costs; abatement measures may exhibit economies of scale which lead to non-monotonies of the abatement cost curve. Furthermore, some projects may generate costs and benefits in other fields ('joint products'). Finally, traditional cost–benefit studies rely on a partial equilibrium analysis and assume that prices and quantities outside the relevant subsystem are ignored, that is, exogenously fixed. For global environmental problems such as climate change, though, considerable effects on prices and terms of trade are to be expected from effective abatement measures. This is the reason for the widespread use of computable general equilibrium models in analysing climate policies (see Section 3.3). The present study nevertheless resorts to a partial equilibrium approach in order to be able to investigate the cost-effectiveness and incentive compatibility of international environmental agreements in a coherent framework. In general, a comprehensive CBA has to take into account all relevant aspects of the environmental problem under scrutiny (for example, uncertainties or irreversibilities) as well as additional constraints on the choice of actions (for example, capital shortages in developing countries).

In traditional cost–benefit analysis all costs and benefits are expressed in monetary units to enable a valuation of the different effects of a project on the basis of a common standard of value. Hence, effects which do not have a market price are also valued in monetary terms. This is regularly the case when the environmental and social benefits of pollution reduction projects have to be quantified. Modern CBA tries to cope with the difficulties that arise from the monetary valuation of such effects by using techniques such as multicriteria and cost-effectiveness analysis. For complex environmental problems such as global warming, though, even with these techniques it proves to be very difficult to make trade-offs between social costs and benefits which do not have straightforward monetized values (Munasinghe et al. 1996). Many environmental cost–benefit studies even look exclusively at the (positive and negative) effects of national environmental policy projects on gross domestic product (GDP). It is generally acknowledged that GDP is not a welfare measure *per se*; rather it is used as a proxy for different components contributing to welfare (Brekke 1994). Using GDP as a welfare measure is particularly problematic in cases where it does not appropriately take into account the depletion of natural resources. There is a growing body of literature which argues that conventional national accounting concepts systematically overestimate GDP growth and therefore should be replaced by 'green accounting'. Even a 'green GDP', though, will not be a perfect welfare measure (Aronsson et al. 1997).

The ideal approach would be to measure utility directly. If a cardinal utility concept that considers all sources of utility were operational, the costs and benefits of emission abatements could be derived directly from individual preferences and measured in welfare terms. We can illustrate this by using the framework introduced above. A government's decision about how much national emissions should be abated ensues from balancing national benefits against costs of unilateral environmental policy. From the public good character of emission abatements, it follows that country k's benefits B_k depend on aggregated abatement efforts in the whole world, while national costs C_k depend only on its own contribution to global abatements. Net abatement benefits π of country k are

$$\pi_k = B_k(Q) - C_k(q_k), \quad k = A, B \qquad (2.10)$$

and national abatements q_k add up to

$$Q = q_A + q_B. \qquad (2.11)$$

The next step is to investigate how net abatement benefits (2.10) are related to the general welfare analysis of the preceding section and what additional assumptions are needed. For the sake of simplicity, assume that all individuals in the world are identical with respect to both their preferences and their exogenous income. Furthermore, countries differ only with respect to population size n_k which enters exogenous national income (2.3) in a trivial way:

$$Y_k = \sum_{i=1}^{n_k} y_k^i = n_k \, \overline{y} = n_k \, x_k + T(q_k), \; y_k^i = \overline{y} \; \forall \, i, \; k = A, B$$
$$\Leftrightarrow x_k = \overline{y} - T(q_k)/n_k. \tag{2.12}$$

Term $T(q_k)$ represents the continuous, increasing and convex abatement technology which is the same for both countries ($T' > 0$, $T'' \geq 0$).

Assuming an additively separable utility function of the form

$$u(x, Q) = \beta(Q) + \gamma(x), \tag{2.13}$$
$$\beta' > 0, \quad \beta'' < 0, \quad \gamma' > 0, \quad \gamma'' < 0,$$

leads to individual net benefits of abatements. A discrete change in the abatement level starting from $Q^0 = 0$ to Q is to be valued by calculating utility with and without abatements. Its difference indicates the absolute change in utility, that is, individual net benefits from abatements:

$$\Delta u(q) = u(x, Q) - u(x^0, Q^0) = \beta(Q) + \gamma(x) - \gamma(\overline{y}). \tag{2.14}$$

Under a utilitarian welfare function, *national* net benefits π_k from abatements are

$$\pi_k(q_k) = n_k \, \Delta u = \underbrace{n_k \, \beta(Q)}_{B_k(Q)} - \underbrace{n_k \left[\gamma(\overline{y}) - \gamma(x_k) \right]}_{C_k(q_k)}. \tag{2.15}$$

Expression (2.15) illustrates how differences in population size (represented by different parameter values n_k) influence national net benefits of emission reductions. We shall come back to this type of asymmetry in Section 3.2.

Policy measures to protect international environmental resources are ultimately decided and implemented by national governments. The benefits and costs of national emission abatements nevertheless depend on the behavior of other countries. Analysing international environmental policy therefore requires a framework which accounts for strategic decision-making and the incentives of single governments (not) to coordinate their actions. This framework is provided by game theory.

2.3.3 Game Theory

Whenever the actions of single agents have an impact on economic variables which in turn affect the decisions of other actors, game theory offers the appropriate theoretical framework to study individual behavior.

In contrast to the scenario of perfectly competitive markets, in game-theoretic models agents are 'large' in the sense that their actions directly influence the economic situation and welfare position of other agents. Individual decisions are made taking into consideration the strategic interdependence between players. The strategic aspect is obvious when agents consider coordinating their actions in order to achieve mutual utility gains. In international environmental policy the most important agents are national governments which are 'large' in the above sense. The analysis of cooperative solutions in international pollution control therefore has to be accomplished within the framework of game theory (Cornes and Sandler 1986, p. 132).[34]

The classical approach to a decentralized internalization of externalities is Coasian bargaining. According to Coase (1960), utility-maximizing individuals (or profit-maximizing firms) agree on a Pareto-optimal allocation of resources through decentralized bargaining, given that the following assumptions hold:[35]

- well-defined property rights;
- perfect information;
- absence of enforcement, monitoring and other transaction costs.

This efficiency result is valid irrespective of the initial allocation of property rights (Coase 1960).[36] It is no longer guaranteed, though, that negotiations lead to an efficient outcome once these conditions are not fulfilled. In fact, stylized facts of international environmental cooperation entail that neither enforceability, nor perfect information can be presumed without neglecting important aspects of the problem. Concerning the property rights on international environmental resources, the initial distribution of rights is in general not legally determined by binding international law, but is based on the traditional use which gives the polluter the right to pollute. Taking the idea of Coasian bargaining as a starting-point for the analysis of international environmental policy, obvious directions of research are to study the prospects for cooperative solutions when either of the above assumptions is relaxed (Mäler 1990, p. 85). Accordingly, in the theoretical analysis of Chapter 5 we relax

---

[34]See, for example, Sandler (1996) or Althammer and Buchholz (1993) for introductions to game-theoretic models of international environmental policy.

[35]See, for example, Mäler (1990, p. 84) who additionally mentions the absence of income effects and the possibility of treating the bargaining problem at stake separately from other issues as preconditions for efficient Coasian bargaining.

[36]Of course, the initial allocation of property rights as well as the bargaining positions of the agents determine the *distribution* of the gains from cooperation, that is, which Pareto optimum emerges.

the assumption of full enforcement, whereas Chapter 6 departs from the scenario of perfect information.

Enforcement is a particularly relevant problem for agreements between sovereign states. Although governments are the principal actors in determining the rules of the game, there is evidence that these rules can be modified and renegotiated at any time. This gives rise to time-inconsistency problems. Asymmetric information is of particular importance in the context of environmental externalities. Preferences for environmental quality are private information and are subject to strategic manipulation in the process of negotiations. In order to implement the social optimum, though, the revelation of true preferences is necessary. Although economic literature has designed mechanisms to create incentives for a true revelation, these are imperfect in the sense that a revelation mechanism may be either not budget neutral[37] or one in which not all players voluntarily participate (Myerson and Satterthwaite 1983). Consequently, aspects of enforcement and asymmetric information cannot be neglected in modeling international environmental agreements. This translates into the requirement to apply models of non-cooperative game theory and bargaining under asymmetric information. In contrast to cooperative game theory, non-cooperative games do not presume that the players are able to engage in binding commitments. The latter is an assumption that does not correspond to the lack of enforcement on the international level. Cooperative solutions may nevertheless come about, but they must be *self-enforcing*.[38]

Without the necessary preconditions for efficient Coasian bargaining, the implementation of globally efficient allocations is hindered by the fact that national governments behave strategically. Although cooperation is also possible in these cases, the public-good character of national abatement efforts generates strong free-riding incentives. One way of describing the strategic interaction of countries involved in transboundary pollution is through the famous 'prisoner's dilemma' game. Table 2.7 illustrates the pay-off matrix of the symmetric two-player, one-shot prisoner's dilemma using a numerical example.[39] The first term in brackets indicates the pay-off of country A, the second that of country B. C denotes 'cooperate', N denotes 'not cooperate'. In this game, free-riding incentives inevitably lead to a 'tragedy of the commons' because non-

---

[37]The Clark–Groves mechanism, for example, allows for a revelation of true preferences as an equilibrium in dominant strategies, but is not budget neutral.

[38]See Chapter 4 for a comprehensive discussion of the enforcement problem in international environmental policy.

[39]See also Figure 3.1, where the pay-off structure of the prisoner's dilemma is derived from a graph on national abatement quantities.

Table 2.7: Symmetric prisoner's dilemma

| | | country *B* | |
		C	N
country *A*	C	(3,3)	(-2,4)
	N	(4,-2)	(0,0)

cooperation is the dominant strategy for each government. Agreeing on joint pollution reduction efforts makes every country better off compared to mutual non-cooperation, but the individual gain is even greater under one-sided non-cooperation. Hence, as long as governments cannot engage in binding commitments, cooperation is not an equilibrium outcome of this game. Instead (N,N) is the unique Nash equilibrium in dominant strategies.

This pessimistic result has to be qualified in a dynamic framework. In a *repeated* prisoner's dilemma game, global efficiency can be sustained by credible sanction strategies as a cooperative equilibrium as long as future pay-offs are not discounted too strongly. This holds for the infinitely repeated prisoner's dilemma (Folk theorem), but under certain conditions also for the finite repetitions (see Section 4.3). Furthermore, an additional dynamic dimension emerges when depositions accumulate over time. In contrast to repeated identical decisions, the presence of *stock externalities* implies that the outcome of previous rounds has an impact on the strategy space and pay-offs in present and future periods. Thus, with stock pollutants, differential game theory is principally the appropriate framework for the analysis of environmental cooperation.[40] Although greenhouse gases as well as ozone-depleting substances both belong to this class of externalities (see Section 2.1) we restrict the analysis to *flow pollutants*. This simplification is permissible in one-shot games on emission abatements because the stock of pollutants is directly determined by the once-and-for-all decision on emission abatements. The static framework of the theoretic analysis in the subsequent chapters in turn is justified because the decision problem of a national government with regard to international environmental cooperation remains basically the same. In particular, the cooperation-enhancing instruments that are proposed and discussed in the later chapters can be applied

---

[40]See Section 4.3 for a brief overview of models of differential game theory with stock pollutants.

both in a static as well as in a dynamic framework. The basic difference is that with repeated interactions the agents have additional instruments at hand to sustain stable cooperation.

When more than two players are involved, free-rider incentives often lead to coordination problems that can be characterized as a 'chicken game' (Lipnowski and Maital 1983). In this case cooperation emerges, but it is only partial (or incomplete). In contrast to the prisoner's dilemma, cooperation in this game is rational even if one or several other players do not cooperate. Each player prefers to be in the position of the outsider who does not cooperate and free rides on the cooperative efforts of others. Yet given that the entire cooperation hinges upon one's own behavior, some (in certain cases all) players prefer to cooperate. Each agent *ex ante* has an incentive to signal not to cooperate, thereby inducing other players' cooperation. Thus, the coordination problem is characterized by multiple equilibria where it is not clear *ex ante* which players are going to cooperate and which not. The pay-off structure of the chicken game is illustrated for two players (countries) in the numerical example of Table 2.8. As in the prisoner's dilemma, mutual

Table 2.8: Chicken game

		country *B*	
		C	N
country *A*	C	(3,3)	(2,4)
	N	(4,2)	(0,0)

cooperation (C,C) is not an equilibrium outcome of the game. However, given that one country does not cooperate, the other prefers to go ahead and does cooperate.[41] In the symmetric chicken game of Table 2.8 there are thus two Nash equilibria: (C,N) and (N,C).

The possibility of multiple equilibria is reduced if the negotiating parties are sufficiently asymmetric with respect to their pay-offs from environmental cooperation and/or their bargaining power (see Section 5.4). In many cases both countries are simultaneously polluters and victims of pollution, but national costs and benefits of abatement efforts are distributed asymmetrically across countries. Depending on the precise pay-off structure, the strategic situation can be characterized either as

---

[41] One-sided 'cooperation' can be interpreted as joint pollution reduction efforts by a subcoalition of countries which cooperate given the non-cooperation of other countries.

an 'asymmetric' prisoner's dilemma or as a 'suasion game'. In the asymmetric prisoner's dilemma the incentive structure is the same as in the symmetric case (that is, non-cooperation is a dominant strategy for both players, see Table 2.7), but the players differ with respect to their individual pay-offs (Table 2.9). In the suasion game, players are so asymmetric

Table 2.9: Asymmetric prisoner's dilemma

		country B	
		C	N
country A	C	(5,2)	(−3,3)
	N	(6,−2)	(2,1)

that only one player is interested in cooperation. In the numerical example of Table 2.10, the dominant strategy for country A is to cooperate, for country B not to cooperate.[42] Country A has to persuade country B to participate in international environmental cooperation. Like the chicken

Table 2.10: Suasion game

		country B	
		C	N
country A	C	(5,2)	(2,3)
	N	(4,−2)	(1,0)

game, the suasion game thus involves a coordination problem. In the asymmetric prisoner's dilemma as well as in the suasion game, cooperation can be sustained if the games are repeated infinitely and discount rates are sufficiently small. However, without side payments the cooperative outcome will not support global efficiency as an equilibrium (Cesar and de Zeeuw 1996).

---

[42] One-sided 'cooperation' can be interpreted here as a subcoalition (for example, the industrialized countries) that engages in joint pollution reduction efforts and tries to make other (developing) countries join.

2.3.4   Conclusions

This chapter has provided necessary background information for the study of international environmental policy. We have outlined the natural science of the two international environmental problems 'global warming' and the 'ozone hole', reported on the political attempts undertaken so far to tackle these problems and described the appropriate theoretical concepts for the economic analysis of international environmental policy. The next two chapters establish the importance of cost-effectiveness and incentive compatibility for international environmental policy in a theoretic analysis and by surveying recent research on these issues. After working out critical points which deserve further investigation, Chapters 5 and 6 proceed to a theoretic analysis in which the role of enforcement and of asymmetric information for both aspects are examined. The results are then used to evaluate existing international institutions to promote cooperation on the global climate and on the protection of the ozone layer.

Chapter 3

Cost-effectiveness

In this chapter we discuss the theoretical concept and empirical relevance of cost-effectiveness in international environmental policy. Based on the theoretical framework introduced in Section 2.3, the notion of cost-effectiveness is qualified and its limitations are addressed in Section 3.1. Subsequently, Section 3.2 evaluates in a static two-countries, two-goods model the relative importance of cost-effectiveness when countries differ in size. In addition, the non-cooperative Nash and Stackelberg equilibria are compared with respect to their inefficiency properties. In Section 3.3 we present numerical simulations of an extended model with multiple countries and additional asymmetries using current data. We also survey quantitative studies on country-specific carbon abatement costs. The chapter concludes with a brief discussion of policy instruments for internalizing transboundary environmental externalities and their cost-effectiveness properties (Section 3.4).

3.1 The Concept of Cost-effectiveness

The basic idea of the concept of cost-effectiveness is to distinguish different aspects of economic efficiency. For detrimental environmental externalities a distinction can be made between the optimal degree to which externality-generating activities are to be reduced and the pattern of activities that allows for this internalization at minimum social costs. In terms of public-good provision it is possible to distinguish between the optimal aggregate supply of a pure public good and how to provide this efficient level. In the simple model of public-good provision outlined in Section 2.3.1, this distinction cannot be made because the underlying theoretical framework is one of a *centralized* provision of the public good. Cost-effectiveness in this context reduces to the requirement that the economy has to be on its production possibility frontier. In the case of reciprocal environmental externalities, however, we are dealing with a public good that is independently supplied and consumed.

The distinction between optimality and cost-efficiency[1] becomes relevant when the classical Samuelson framework is extended to a decentralized and/or intertemporal provision of a pure public good. Then the normative questions arise: what quantities are to be supplied by which economic entities at what point in time? As illustrated in Section 2.3.1 within a static setting, the Samuelson condition for the optimal *decentralized* supply of a pure international public good postulates that the sum over all individuals' marginal rates of substitution has to be equal to the marginal rate of transformation in each national economy. Under adequate convexity/concavity assumptions, this condition uniquely determines the optimal aggregate supply of the international public good. The total supply depends on the marginal benefits of pollution reduction of all individuals involved, both at home and abroad. In addition, due to equal marginal rates of transformation across countries, the Samuelson condition implicitly determines the efficient individual contribution of each country. It guarantees that the international public good is supplied at minimum aggregate costs. However, although a distinction between optimality and cost-effectiveness is possible in principle, it is not meaningful in this framework because both aspects of efficiency are taken into account simultaneously. By contrast, in the presence of additional distortions there may be a reason to compare the gains from reduced underprovision with those of a cost-effective allocation of individual contributions.

A limitation of cost-effectiveness as defined by the traditional Samuelson condition is that the latter is derived in a *first-best* framework. Hence, implementation problems and additional distortions are disregarded. In particular it is assumed that lump-sum taxes and transfers are feasible without restrictions (Samuelson 1954; Atkinson and Stiglitz 1980, Lecture 16). By contrast, when this policy instrument is not (or only in a constrained manner) available, optimality conditions change and the notion of cost-effectiveness has to be qualified.[2] This is an important aspect in the provision of international environmental goods. For various reasons side payments between countries may not be feasible to the extent that is required to implement a first-best solution. If so, the international distribution of income affects the optimal allocation of public-good contributions across countries. Efficiency aspects

---

[1] Cost-efficiency and cost-effectiveness both refer to the same concept and are used interchangeably.

[2] See Bohm (1993b), Chichilnisky and Heal (1994) and Eyckmans et al. (1993) on which the following discussion builds.

can then no longer be separated from equity aspects, corresponding to the traditional distinction between first-best and second-best analysis.

To illustrate how the conditions for the optimal supply of an international public good change when lump-sum transfers are not available, consider the maximization of an international social welfare function W

$$\max_{q_1,\ldots,q_N} \quad W\left[U_1(y_1,Q),\ldots,U_N(y_N,Q)\right] \tag{3.1}$$

where U_k $(k=1,\ldots,N)$ denotes the strictly concave utility of country k that depends on the consumption of an international (environmental) public good Q (with $Q = \sum q_k$) and of a composite private good y_k, called income. As in Section 2.3, the public good is produced by transformation of the initial endowment of income $\bar{y}_k$ in each country. The production technology is given by $y_k = \bar{y}_k - C_k(q_k)$, $C' > 0$, $C'' > 0$. Assume that the set of instruments in the maximization problem (3.1) consists of national abatement levels q_k $(k=1,\ldots,N)$, and that international side payments are *not* available. The first-order conditions for the *second-best* solution are then

$$\sum_{i=1}^{N} \frac{\partial W}{\partial U_i}\frac{\partial U_i}{\partial Q} = \lambda_k \, C_k', \quad \lambda_k \equiv \frac{\partial W}{\partial U_k}\frac{\partial U_k}{\partial y_k}, \quad \forall k \in N, \tag{3.2}$$

with λ_k indicating the weight or marginal social value attached to one additional unit of income in country k. The vector of all λ_k determines the curvature of the social welfare indifference curve, the degree of concavity of W reflecting judgments on the international distribution of wealth.[3] In the case of a utilitarian social welfare function ($\tilde{W} \equiv \sum_k U_k$), the marginal social value coincides with the marginal utility of income.

By contrast, in the first-best scenario where lump-sum transfers are available, the maximization problem can be written as

$$\max_{q_1,\ldots,q_N,T_1,\ldots,T_N} \quad W\left[U_1(y_1,Q),\ldots,U_N(y_N,Q)\right] \tag{3.3}$$

$$\text{s.t.} \quad \sum_{i=1}^{N} T_i = 0, \quad \text{with} \quad y_k = \bar{y}_k - C_k(q_k) + T_k \quad \forall k \in N. \tag{3.4}$$

The first-order conditions with respect to individual contributions are the same as in (3.2). However, we have an additional condition with respect to transfers T_k:

$$\lambda_k = \gamma, \tag{3.5}$$

---

[3] Alternatively, in a game-theoretic context, maximization problem (3.1) also has a positive interpretation. Partial derivatives $\partial W/\partial U_k$ then represent differing bargaining positions or power weights in a bargaining problem between countries (Eyckmans et al. 1993, p. 370).

where γ is the Lagrange multiplier of constraint (3.4). Hence, the lump-sum transfers are used to equalize the marginal social welfare of income (or of the representative private good) across countries. Differing welfare weights λ_k reflect a certain inequality aversion and imply positive lump-sum transfers to countries with higher weights such that the marginal utility of income is lower for these countries. Inserting (3.5) in (3.2) and rewriting yields the familiar first-best Samuelson condition

$$\sum_{i=1}^{N} \frac{\partial U_i/\partial Q}{\partial U_i/\partial y_i} = C_k', \quad \forall\, k \in N. \tag{3.6}$$

Comparing conditions (3.6) and (3.2) illustrates the implications of the availability of international side payments for the optimality conditions. First, the first-best solution is cost-effective, but the second-best is generally not. What is equalized across countries in (3.2) is the term $(\lambda_k\, C_k')$. Hence, with increasing marginal abatement costs, countries with a high marginal social value of income (that is, poor countries) will have to provide less of the international environmental good. The intuitive reason is that in the absence of other instruments for redistribution, differences in abatement costs are used as a second-best instrument to influence the international distribution of wealth. Even though the allocation implied by (3.2) is not cost-effective in the traditional meaning, it is a Pareto-efficient solution. Second, comparing the right-hand sides of (3.2) and (3.6) illustrates that without side payments, the countries' marginal utilities from the public good are weighted by their importance for international welfare. Both results are well known from second-best welfare theory.

Despite the fact that side payments are available only to a limited extent as an instrument in international environmental negotiations, this does not render the concept of cost-effectiveness meaningless. First, for certain specifications of the international social welfare function (that is, when distributional aspects do not matter) it is true that marginal abatement costs are equalized across countries even in the absence of side payments. Second, it can be argued that the optimality of differing marginal abatement costs in the no-transfer scenario stems from a misspecification of marginal abatement costs (Bohm 1993b). When marginal abatement costs are not specified in terms of real output forgone, but in terms of valued opportunity costs,[4] they *are* equalized in the optimum. Third, and most important, by ruling out side payments in the decentralized provision of international public goods it is implicitly

---

[4]'Valued opportunity costs' are defined as the real marginal output forgone times the marginal valuation of this output (Bohm 1993b, p. 7).

assumed that countries rest in autarky and that international trade in the public good is not possible. However, if trade in private goods is an everyday occurrence, accompanied by payments across countries, why should one suspect that countries do not make use of their comparative advantages in the supply of public goods? As long as marginal abatement costs are not equalized there always exist potential gains from trade that wait to be realized. Finally, side payments in fact *are* increasingly employed on the international level, for example in recent environmental treaties. The fact that the amounts we currently observe are still not substantial does not mean that transfers are not granted in other ways. Concessions in other fields of international policy are probably much more important than the amount of dollars that international agencies such as the 'Global Environment Facility' have at their disposal.[5]

Another limitation of the cost-effectiveness concept consists in the potential existence of non-convexities in the production set. The general relevance of such non-convexities in the context of (international) environmental policy stems from the fact that externalities themselves are an important source of non-convexities.[6] The latter imply that uniqueness of the globally efficient allocation is no longer guaranteed, but instead that multiple local maxima exist among which, in practice, it is virtually impossible to identify the global optimum. In the context of the present study, non-uniqueness of (locally) efficient abatements has two main implications: first, there exist several vectors of public-good contributions (or abatement quantities) that all minimize aggregate production costs and thus deserve to be called cost-effective; second, a straightforward measurement of the welfare losses due to non-cooperation is not possible, as this requires a comparison between welfare in the unregulated status quo and in the local maximum which dominates all others.

Nevertheless, cost-effectiveness of international environmental policy *is* an important issue, regardless of whether a unique efficient allocation of abatement measures exists or not. In either scenario, implementing a policy that does not ensure cost-effectiveness of international abatement efforts means that potential efficiency gains are not realized. Moreover, the complications connected with non-convexities are present for all sorts of attempts to reduce pollution to socially optimal levels, irrespective of whether they are market based or not (Baumol and Oates 1988, p. 159). The difficulties of designing optimal environmental policies in the presence of non-convexities can be seen as one major reason to opt for an

---

[5]It was not by accident that the Rio conference in 1992 was called the 'Conference on Environment *and* Development'.

[6]See Baumol and Oates (1988, ch. 8) for an introduction and note 2, p. 111 therein for further references.

environmental standard that is more or less arbitrarily chosen. To reach this standard at minimum costs remains the only aspect of efficiency in environmental decision-making. Therefore, cost-effectiveness is the central idea behind the 'charges and standards' or 'permits and standards' approach.[7]

To circumvent the complications arising with non-uniqueness of the efficient allocation and to allow for a direct comparison between welfare in a non-cooperative status quo and in various cooperative solutions, we confine ourselves to scenarios where uniqueness is ensured. This is the case under the following assumptions:

- quasi-linear preferences over consumption and environmental quality;
- concave, differentiable and increasing utility from pollution abatement; and
- a strictly concave production technology.

These assumptions imply that in all Pareto-optimal states, the vector of individual abatement quantities and thereby also the level of aggregate abatements is unique.[8]

There are manifold facets of the problem to determine a cost-effective international environmental policy. We have already seen that by restricting the analysis to national productivity differentials in the provision of international environmental goods, we conceptualize cost-effectiveness only in a very narrow, static sense. It can be argued that it is quantitatively much more important to ensure cost-effectiveness of international environmental policy over time than across different sources of pollution at a given point of time. The bulk of potential cost-savings that is achievable through the implementation of cost-effective policy instruments may be related to the dynamic efficiency gains that are induced through investments in cleaner production technologies (Palmer et al. 1995, p. 121). We have seen that the intertemporal dimension of cost-effectiveness is especially important for problems such as global warming or the depletion of the ozone layer. Unfortunately, measuring the potential gains of equalizing marginal abatement costs across countries is an extremely difficult task even for current emissions. Empirically estimating the potential cost-savings in a dynamic sense requires even more information. The latter type of information amounts to perfect foresight in areas such as future (abatement) technologies, economic

---

[7]See Baumol and Oates (1988, chs. 11–12) for an introduction. There is, however, one important qualification with respect to cost-effectiveness in this approach: the cost-minimum implemented by a certain permit/charges solution may be a local and not a global minimum (see pp. 172–3).

[8]See Chander and Tulkens (1997, p. 382) for a formal proof.

development, the future status of the biosystem and so on. Even if estimates for this type of information were available, it would require a tremendous processing capacity to derive the efficient vector of individual contributions. Hence, it is basically impossible to make more than very crude statements about how to allocate abatement activities cost-effectively over time, especially for long time spans. In fact, this is precisely why the assessment of potential cost-savings and the search of technologies enabling them should be left to the market mechanism.

In this study we restrict the analysis to the static dimension of cost-effectiveness despite the severe limitations this implies. Most importantly, the intertemporal trade-off between abatement and adaptation policies is not addressed.[9] Moreover, it is differentiated only between countries as sources of environmentally harmful emissions but not between the single economic entities that are the true emitters (companies, households) in these countries. We thus consider cost-effectiveness only at the international level and abstract from the implementation of cost-effective internalization policies in the individual countries. In addition, cost-effectiveness across multiple pollutants which are responsible for the same environmental damage is ignored here as well.[10] Given that strategic interactions in international environmental policy take place mainly between countries (or rather the governments they represent), the restriction to cost-effectiveness in the above sense allows for a consistent framework in the analysis. Furthermore, the static and international concept of cost-effectiveness used here corresponds to the analysis of comparative advantage in international trade theory.

The above limitations and simplifications have to be borne in mind in the subsequent analysis. Besides the informational restrictions described above, they are motivated by the aim to combine the aspects of cost-effectiveness and of incentive compatibility in international pollution control. Before turning to incentive problems it is instructive to justify this integrative approach also from an empirical perspective. If marginal abatement costs barely differed in the unregulated status quo, there would be no point in emphasizing the importance of cost-effectiveness in international environmental agreements. The purpose of Sections 3.2 and 3.3 is to demonstrate that the opposite is true and that cost-effectiveness is indeed of empirical relevance.

---

[9]See the contribution of working group II to the second assessment report of the IPCC for a comprehensive overview on possible impacts of climate change and adaptation options (Watson et al. (eds) 1996, Part II).

[10]Michaelis (1997) analyses a cost-effective climate policy with multiple pollutants. See Victor (1991) for an argument against the inclusion of non-CO_2 gases in a global tradable permit system.

3.2 Cost-effectiveness when Countries Differ in Size

In this section we analyse in a simple model how asymmetries between countries influence the welfare losses due to non-cooperation in international environmental policy. We focus on population size and abstract from other types of heterogeneity such as economic income, abatement technologies, or the information available to governments. Nevertheless, different kinds of heterogeneity may influence the structure of the decision problem in a similar way and therefore may be summarized under just one variable. For the sake of simplicity and in order to be able to present a graphical illustration, we consider only two countries. The set-up is a static, partial equilibrium model of the provision of a pure international public good that is formulated in terms of costs and benefits of emission abatements. The model thus builds on the general framework described in Section 2.3.1 and makes the assumptions necessary for uniqueness of the efficient allocation (see p. 52). By decomposing the aggregate inefficiencies into those that are caused by underprovision of abatement measures and those that are caused by an inefficient distribution of abatements across countries, we show that cost-effectiveness may be relatively important, both under Nash as well as under Stackelberg behavior. The numerical simulations for different scenarios also show that cost-inefficiencies are generally smaller, but aggregate inefficiencies are always greater in the Stackelberg equilibrium.

The present analysis is connected with three strands of literature. The fundamental one is the theory of the private provision of public goods (see Section 2.3.1). The second branch of literature is theoretical and empirical work on cost-effectiveness in international environmental policy which is discussed later in this chapter. The third field of related literature consists of contributions in international environmental economics that analyse the role of different kinds of asymmetries for non-cooperative as well as for cooperative equilibria (see Chapter 4 for a survey).

The section is organized as follows. In Subsection 3.2.1 we describe the model and specify the costs and benefits of emission abatements. Subsections 3.2.2 and 3.2.3 derive the properties of the Nash and the Stackelberg equilibria, respectively. By means of numerical simulations, the welfare losses from underprovision are compared to those from cost-inefficiency for different scenarios of asymmetry between countries. In addition, we compare the efficiency properties of the Nash equilibrium with those of the Stackelberg equilibrium. A discussion of the results and of possible extensions of the model concludes the section.

3.2.1 Costs and Benefits of Emission Abatements

Consider a world of two countries A and B with a world population N ($N = n_A + n_B$). National populations are exogenously given, that is, there is no migration between countries, and all individuals are identical with respect to their preferences and their exogenous income. The national governments of both countries are assumed to maximize the utility of their populations. A government's decision on how much of its national emissions should be abated ensues from balancing national benefits against costs of unilateral environmental policy. Emission abatements represent a pure international public good in the sense that it makes no difference for the environment who abates (that is, national contributions are perfect substitutes) and national abatements q_k add up to

$$Q = q_A + q_B. \tag{3.7}$$

The public-good character of pollution reduction implies that national benefits of emission abatements depend on aggregate abatement Q, whereas national abatement costs depend only on the individual contribution q_k of a country to global abatements. Assuming a one-shot game of complete information and abstracting from general equilibrium effects (for example, changes in the terms of trade through environmental policy), the decision problem reduces to balancing national benefits against costs of abatement efforts, and net abatement benefits π of country k are given by[11]

$$\pi_k = B_k(Q) - C_k(q_k), \quad k = A, B. \tag{3.8}$$

The next step in exploring the properties of a non-cooperative equilibrium is to specify the costs and benefits of abatements. We follow the approach of Barrett (1992a), which allows us to incorporate the population size of a country explicitly. Starting with abatement costs we assume *linearly increasing marginal costs* of abatements, that is, it becomes more costly for a country to reduce additional CO_2 emissions the higher its absolute abatement quantities. This functional specification has been justified as a reasonable approximation for CO_2 emissions (Nordhaus 1991c, p. 929).[12] Furthermore, we know that without additional distortions so that prices reflect social opportunity costs, polluters

---

[11] Although restrictive, assuming additive separability of the underlying preferences is the usual approach in the related literature (see, for example, Barrett 1994, p. 880; Carraro and Siniscalco 1993, p. 311; Chander and Tulkens 1997, p. 381; or example 2 in Eyckmans 1997) and is maintained here as well.

[12] Although empirical estimations on the costs of reducing greenhouse gas emissions differ in their quantitative dimensions, the general shape of the estimated cost sched-

are indifferent between emitting or abating the last unit of emissions. Thus, the cost of abating the first unit of emissions is equal to zero.

Concerning differences in abatement costs between countries, marginal abatement costs may vary for several reasons. For example, there may be different substitution possibilities for energy production or different national abatement technologies available. Another reason is different national base-year emission levels. A larger country, that is, one with a higher base-year emission level, incurs lower marginal abatement costs for any given *absolute* level of abatement (Barrett 1992a, pp. 18–19). Everything else being equal, marginal abatement costs are thus the same in different countries for the same *percentage* of abatement. Writing the base-year emission level as the product of average per-capita emissions and the size of a country's population ($E_k = \bar{e}\, n_k$), marginal abatement costs of country k are

$$C'_k = c_k \frac{q_k}{E_k}, \quad E_k = \bar{e}\, n_k, \tag{3.9}$$

where c_k is an exogenous parameter that determines the slope of the marginal cost function. It reflects, for example, the type of abatement technology that is available. A less expensive abatement technology implies, *ceteris paribus*, a lower value of c. Integrating marginal abatement costs and using the fact that the cost of abating the first unit of emissions is close to zero yields the total abatement cost function. For simplicity we assume here national cost parameters c_k to be the same for all countries:[13]

$$C_k(q_k) = \frac{c}{2} \frac{q_k^2}{n_k}, \quad c \equiv c_k/e > 0. \tag{3.10}$$

The specification of national abatement benefits is more difficult. First of all, despite extensive empirical work with respect to the benefits of curbing climate change,[14] there is still a substantial lack of knowledge on the consequences of global warming for the earth's bio-system and especially its different regional and long-term impacts. Moreover, the individual judgments that people in different countries put on these consequences are private information. Therefore, the adoption of a monotonic, well-behaved benefit function is somewhat arbitrary. If we take into

---

ule is uncontroversial (see Section 3.3.2). Assuming that marginal abatement costs increase at an even steeper rate, as some of the empirical literature suggests, does not change the qualitative results.

[13] By assuming identical values of c_k for all countries, we abstract from heterogeneities other than country size.

[14] See, for example, Cline (1992b, ch. 4), Fankhauser (1995) or OECD (1991, ch. 1).

account long-term effects and assess a significant risk aversion against catastrophic events (Cline 1992a, ch. 6), it is reasonable to presume that marginal damages will increase with the level of greenhouse gas emissions, implying positive but decreasing marginal benefits of reducing carbon emissions. In line with this, we assume here *linearly decreasing marginal benefits* of abatements.[15] Looking again at national differences, marginal abatement benefits are generally higher the greater a country's economic income. The latter can be written as the product of (exogenous) per-capita income and the economy's population size ($Y_k = \bar{y} n_k$). A small and poor country like the Maldives may be relatively more vulnerable to climate change than Germany, but the total damage for Germany would be much greater (Barrett 1992a, p. 21). Correspondingly, the benefits of additional abatements would be much greater for the richer and bigger country. Thus marginal benefits can be written as

$$B'_k = b_k Y_k (a - Q), \quad Y_k = \bar{y} n_k, \tag{3.11}$$

where b_k is an exogenous parameter that determines the slope of the marginal benefit function, and a is the abatement level where marginal benefits would become zero ($a > Q$).[16] As in the case of marginal abatement costs, we abstract from differences in benefit parameter b_k and per-capita income $\bar{y}$. Integrating marginal benefits gives gross abatement benefits of a country:

$$B_k(Q) = n_k \, b \, (aQ - 1/2 \, Q^2), \quad b \equiv b_k \, \bar{y} > 0. \tag{3.12}$$

Having specified the cost and benefit functions of abatements, net benefit function (3.8) becomes[17]

$$\pi_k = n_k \, b \, (aQ - \frac{1}{2} Q^2) - \frac{c}{2} \frac{q_k^2}{n_k}, \quad a > Q, \, b > 0, \, c > 0. \tag{3.13}$$

Balancing marginal benefits against costs determines optimal abatement quantities q_k of country k ($k = A, B$). The way in which a government

---

[15]It can be argued that for CO_2 emissions it is appropriate to assume *constant* marginal abatement benefits (Nordhaus 1991b, p. 148). Assuming constant marginal benefits does not change the qualitative results concerning the relationship between asymmetry in size and the two sources of inefficiency reported below. See Chapters 5 and 6 for models where constant marginal abatement benefits are assumed.

[16]Assuming $a > Q$ ensures that marginal benefits are decreasing and positive over the relevant range of global abatements Q.

[17]Parameters a, b and c are taken to be the same for both countries in order to isolate the effect of asymmetry in population size on the non-cooperative equilibrium. Choosing different parameter values for each country would allow additional asymmetries to be incorporated.

takes into account the abatement activities of another country (that is, its assumptions on the other government's behavior) determines what kind of non-cooperative equilibrium emerges.

3.2.2   Nash Behavior

Let us first look at the properties of the non-cooperative equilibrium when national governments exhibit Nash behavior. In this case each national government independently maximizes net benefit function (3.13) by choosing nationally optimal abatement levels, given the abatement decision of the other country.[18] In the national optimum, marginal abatement benefits $B'(Q)$ are equal to marginal costs $C'(q)$:

$$\frac{\partial \pi_k}{\partial q_k} = n_k \, b \, (a - Q) - \frac{c}{n_k} \, q_k \overset{!}{=} 0 \qquad (3.14)$$

$$\Leftrightarrow \quad n_k \, b \, (a - Q) = \frac{c}{n_k} \, q_k.$$

Solving (3.14) for q_k gives the best reply of country k to given abatement levels $\overline{q}_j$ in the other country:

$$q_A(\overline{q}_B) = \frac{a - \overline{q}_B}{1 + \frac{c}{n_A^2 \, b}}, \qquad (3.15a)$$

$$q_B(\overline{q}_A) = \frac{a - \overline{q}_A}{1 + \frac{c}{n_B^2 \, b}}. \qquad (3.15b)$$

The above reaction functions illustrate that under the present specification, non-cooperative abatement quantities are interdependent. The optimal response of a country to an increase in abatements in the other country is, *ceteris paribus*, to reduce its own abatement efforts, the magnitude of this reaction depending on the slope of a country's best-reply function.[19] If marginal benefits are decreasing and marginal costs are increasing with abatement quantities, an increase (decrease) in abatements in the rest of the world will lower (raise) marginal benefits from national abatements in the home country and this country will decrease

---

[18]This corresponds to the decision problem of a profit-maximizing firm choosing optimal supply quantities in a *Cournot* duopoly. The analogy of externality and public-good issues to oligopoly theory and industrial organization has already been emphasized (among others) by Shibata (1971).

[19]The reaction is increasing with a country's population size and decreasing with c/b.

(increase) its abatement quantities to equalize marginal benefits and costs in the new national optimum. By contrast, when marginal benefits are constant there is no such interdependency.[20] The intersection of the reaction curves determines the *Cournot–Nash* equilibrium denoted by CN. This equilibrium is unique because the reaction curves are linear, and stable since the slopes of the curves are less than 1 in absolute value. Equilibrium abatement quantities q_k^{CN} in countries A and B are

$$q_A^{CN} = \frac{a\, n_A^2}{n_A^2 + n_B^2 + c/b} = \frac{a\, \alpha^2}{\alpha^2 + (1-\alpha)^2 + c/bN^2}, \quad (3.16a)$$

$$q_B^{CN} = \frac{a\, n_B^2}{n_A^2 + n_B^2 + c/b} = \frac{a\,(1-\alpha)^2}{\alpha^2 + (1-\alpha)^2 + c/bN^2}, \quad (3.16b)$$

and the aggregate abatement level is

$$Q^{CN} = \frac{a(n_A^2 + n_B^2)}{n_A^2 + n_B^2 + c/b} = \frac{a\,\left[\alpha^2 + (1-\alpha)^2\right]}{\alpha^2 + (1-\alpha)^2 + c/bN^2}, \quad (3.17)$$

where $\alpha \equiv n_A/N$, $1/2 \le \alpha < 1$.

Parameter α defines the size of country A relative to world population N and indicates the degree of asymmetry between countries.[21] Substituting equilibrium quantities (3.16a and 3.16b) into the global net benefit function

$$\Pi = \pi_A + \pi_B = N\, b \left(aQ - \frac{1}{2}\, Q^2 \right) - \frac{c}{2} \left(\frac{q_A^2}{n_A} + \frac{q_B^2}{n_B} \right) \quad (3.18)$$

gives the global net benefit level Π^{CN} in the Nash equilibrium. We calculate below the respective levels for different scenarios of asymmetry using numerical simulations.

National abatement levels that are *globally* optimal are derived by maximizing the sum of net benefits (3.18) with respect to q_A and q_B. The first-order conditions yield

$$q_k^* = \frac{a\, n_k}{N + c/bN}, \quad k = A, B. \quad (3.19)$$

Aggregate efficient abatements are

$$Q^* = \frac{a}{1 + c/bN^2} \quad (3.20)$$

---

[20] See Chapters 5 and 6 for this specification.

[21] Country A is taken to be the larger country ($0.5 \le \alpha < 1$).

and the level of global net benefits Π^* in the global optimum is

$$\Pi^* = \frac{a^2\, b\, N}{2(1 + c/bN^2)}. \tag{3.21}$$

Aggregate abatement quantities (3.20) and (3.17) differ with respect to the term $[\alpha^2 + (1 - \alpha)^2]$ in the numerator and in the denominator of the right-hand side of equation (3.17). Hence, only in the hypothetical benchmark of $\alpha = 1$ (that is, the total population is allocated in only one country) are non-cooperative aggregate abatements equal to the globally efficient level $(Q^{CN} = Q^*)$. In all other cases non-cooperative abatements only reach a suboptimal level $(Q^{CN} < Q^*)$, reproducing the standard result that decentralization ends in an underprovision of the pure public good.[22] Moreover, aggregate abatement is not only suboptimal, but also its distribution across countries is inefficient. From (3.19) it follows that, in the social optimum, national abatements have to be distributed across countries in the same proportion as the world population: $q_A^*/q_B^* = n_A/n_B = \alpha/(1 - \alpha)$. However, the distribution of abatements in the Nash equilibrium according to (3.16a and 3.16b) is $q_A^{CN}/q_B^{CN} = n_A^2/n_B^2 = \alpha^2/(1 - \alpha)^2$. Thus, the two ratios coincide and cost-effectiveness is reached in the Nash equilibrium only in the symmetric case ($\alpha = 0.5$). If countries differ in size, the bigger country will bear a disproportionately large burden of aggregate abatements. This result reproduces the well-known result of the 'exploitation of the big by the small' (Olson and Zeckhauser 1966).

The globally efficient allocation could be reached through full cooperation of the countries. However, due to the prisoner's dilemma type of decision problem, a full cooperative solution is unlikely to be implemented successfully. The underlying incentive structure is shown in Figure 3.1. It shows the non-cooperative Cournot–Nash equilibrium in abatement quantities for two *symmetric* countries and depicts the payoff matrix of country A. The two linear reaction curves correspond to equations (3.15a and 3.15b). Their intersection CN represents the Cournot–Nash equilibrium. The strategic character of the abatement decision can be illustrated by comparing the iso-net benefit curves $\pi_A(\cdot)$ of country A under alternative hypothetical allocations of abatements. Let C indicate the globally efficient abatement combination (q_A^*, q_B^*).[23]

---

[22]The ratio $\overline{OCN}/\overline{OC}$ in Figure 3.1 reflects the degree of undersupply. This is the 'index of easy riding' of Cornes and Sandler (1986, pp. 80–82).

[23]The incentive structure described below also characterizes abatement vectors which are not Pareto optimal but Pareto superior to CN. In point C, two iso-net benefit curves $\pi_A(C)$ and $\pi_B(C)$ are tangential to each other; the iso-net benefit curve of country B is not drawn in the figure.

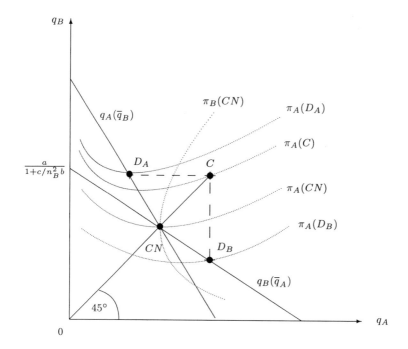

Figure 3.1: Cournot–Nash equilibrium

D_A (D_B) indicates the abatement vector when, starting from the co-operative solution C, country A (B) decides to take a free ride on the cooperative abatement level of the other country and defects uni-laterally. As we see from the iso-net benefit curves drawn for coun-try A in Figure 3.1, the ranking of net benefits under the different allocations $\pi_A(D_A) > \pi_A(C) > \pi_A(CN) > \pi_A(D_B)$ corresponds to the payoff-structure of the 2×2 normal form prisoner's dilemma game $(D, C) \succ (C, C) \succ (D, D) \succ (C, D)$ where defection (D) is the dominant strategy for both players.[24]

We now come back to the questions raised at the beginning of this section. Given the above incentive structure, (i) how are the inefficien-cies through non-cooperation related to the extent of asymmetry in size and (ii) how important are welfare losses through an inefficient alloca-tion of abatements across countries relative to the welfare losses from free-riding and underprovision? As stated already, the basic idea behind the concept of cost-effectiveness is to differentiate different aspects of

---

[24]See Table 2.7 for a numerical example of the symmetric two-player, one-shot prisoner's dilemma in its normal form.

economic efficiency. We can illustrate this differentiation graphically by adapting Figure 3.1 to the case of asymmetric countries (see Figure 3.2). Let country A be the larger country. In the non-cooperative equilibrium

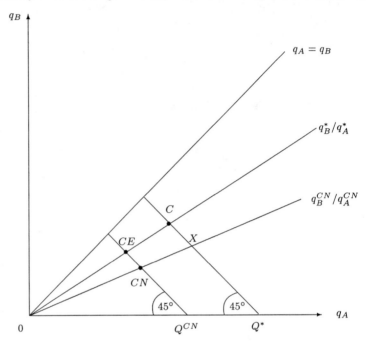

Figure 3.2: Cost-effectiveness versus underprovision

of abatement quantities CN, country A contributes a disproportionally large proportion to the aggregate abatement level. In the globally efficient abatement allocation C, both the aggregate abatement level and country B's share of global abatements are higher and marginal abatement costs are equalized across countries. The abatement vector CE is cost-effective as well (CE lying on the line through the origin and point C), but the aggregate abatement quantity is the same as in the inefficient Nash equilibrium (CE lying on the line with a slope of -1 that goes through CN to the horizontal axis). Hence, in CE global (gross) abatement benefits are the same as in CN, but aggregate abatement costs are lower due to equalization of marginal abatement costs. The potential increase in global welfare from implementing the social optimum C can be separated by comparing the overall cost-savings of implementing allocation CE instead of CN with the increase in global net benefits when implementing C instead of CE. This approach corresponds to a hypothetical policy scenario where, starting from uncoordinated national environmental policies, at first cost-effectiveness is implemented by introducing international trade in abatement quantities and technologies, and then underprovision is eliminated by a first-best international environmental agreement or a supranational regulation.[25] The relative size of these two components depends on the countries' asymmetries and the values of the cost/benefit parameters. To see this we now construct indices to measure the inefficiencies from non-cooperation and calculate their values for different parameter combinations.

The global welfare losses from Nash behavior can be measured by comparing Π^{CN} with Π^*. For this purpose we define the welfare loss ratio

$$\Delta^{CN} \equiv \frac{\Pi^* - \Pi^{CN}}{\Pi^*} \tag{3.22}$$

which measures losses under non-cooperative Nash abatements in per cent of net benefits attainable when abatements are globally efficient. Cost-inefficiencies are measured by comparing Π^{CN} with net benefits Π^{CE} of the hypothetical allocation where aggregate abatements amount to Q^{CN} as in the Nash equilibrium, but are allocated cost-effectively:

$$\Psi^{CN} \equiv \frac{\Pi^{CE} - \Pi^{CN}}{\Pi^*}. \tag{3.23}$$

As Ψ^{CN} goes up, welfare losses through an inefficient international distribution of abatement efforts across countries increase in per cent of net benefits of the social optimum. Analogously, we measure the welfare loss resulting from underprovision by comparing Π^* with Π^{CE}:

$$\Phi^{CN} \equiv \frac{\Pi^* - \Pi^{CE}}{\Pi^*}, \quad \Pi^{CE} \equiv \Pi(Q^{CN}, q_A/q_B = q_A^*/q_B^*). \tag{3.24}$$

By means of these indices the welfare losses from underprovision and from cost-inefficiency can be directly compared with each other and they sum up to $\Delta = \Phi + \Psi$.

In the following, the values of the indices are calculated for different parameter combinations, using numerical simulations.[26] The results are

---

[25] Note that there is an alternative separation involving point X in Figure 3.2. In X, abatements are allocated across countries as in the non-cooperative Nash equilibrium, but reach the same aggregate level as under global efficiency. This approach, however, is inappropriate because in that case globally optimal aggregate abatements would be lower than in C, given the additional constraint that the single countries contribute the same proportions as in the inefficient Nash equilibrium.

[26] Numerical simulations are taken out with the solver algorithm 'Conopt' of the sofware package GAMS.

summarized graphically in Figures 3.3 and 3.4, which indicate the welfare losses from underprovision and from cost-inefficiency when country sizes vary. Besides differences in population size denoted by α, the welfare losses depend on parameters b, c and N. As equations (3.17) and (3.21) show, the outcome is determined by the ratio c/bN^2. Therefore, simulation results are shown in Figure 3.3 for a high value and in Figure 3.4 for a low value of c/bN^2.

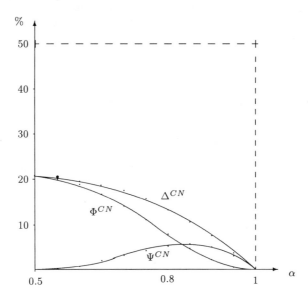

Figure 3.3: Inefficiencies in the Nash equilibrium for high c/bN^2

Comparing the values of welfare loss ratios Φ^{CN} and Ψ^{CN}, Figure 3.3 illustrates that cost-inefficiency is becoming relatively important when countries differ strongly in size and may even exceed the welfare losses resulting from underprovision of abatement efforts. Then, however, aggregate inefficiencies are not as severe as in the case of only moderate asymmetry. The welfare losses generated by 'easy riding' Φ^{CN} are decreasing with the asymmetry in country size. The intuition for this relationship is as follows. Consider for a moment the hypothetical case where the world population is allocated in just one single country ($n_A = N \Leftrightarrow \alpha = 1$). Then, by definition, there are no transnational spillovers, and the decision problem of the government is identical to the problem of a world's central planner. By contrast, when countries are less asymmetric, free-riding on foreign abatement efforts generates inefficiencies, predominantly by the behavior of the smaller country. The latter implies that, in addition to the welfare losses from underprovision, national abatement efforts are not allocated cost-effectively. Cost-effectiveness is reached only in the other benchmark of completely symmetric countries ($\alpha = 0.5$), since countries abate identical quantities at equal marginal costs. In that case, though, international spillovers and induced welfare losses through underprovision are greatest. The non-monotonic relationship between the countries' asymmetry and cost-inefficiency is explained as follows: when countries are very different in size (that is, beyond $\alpha \approx 0.85$ in Figure 3.3), both countries exhibit high (and relatively similar) marginal abatement costs. Marginal costs are high for the big country as it undertakes the bulk of aggregate abatements; they are high for the small country due to the effect of a small population on its marginal abatement costs.

A similar picture results from the scenario of Figure 3.4, where marginal abatement costs increase at a considerably lower rate than related marginal benefits decrease. Here, cost-inefficiencies are relatively

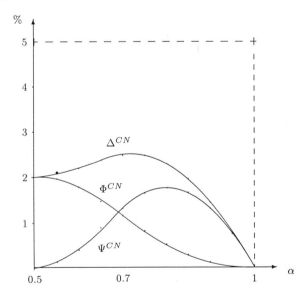

Figure 3.4: Inefficiencies in the Nash equilibrium for low c/bN^2

more important and already exceed the losses from underprovision for less extreme scenarios of asymmetry. If c is small relative to b, however, aggregate welfare losses from non-cooperative abatements as a whole are less severe.[27] In general, cost-inefficiencies are quantitatively more severe, (i) the more asymmetric the countries (up to a critical level) and (ii) the steeper the slope of the marginal abatement cost curve in relation to the slope of the marginal abatement benefit curve.

3.2.3   Stackelberg Behavior

When countries are asymmetric, the nature of the strategic interaction between national governments may change with regard to their strategic behavior. A usual assumption is that the larger country (in our model country A) behaves as a Stackelberg leader. A country that is much larger than its counterpart may be able to commit itself credibly to a certain abatement level or to act first in a non-cooperative game of emission abatements. It may also dispose of a threat potential in other fields of international policy if the small country is vulnerable to actions of the large country. For two reasons one might suspect that the overall welfare losses under Stackelberg behavior are smaller than under Nash behavior. First, the larger country in its leader position is able to make the smaller country abate more and thus reduce the smaller country's underprovision. Second, increasing the share of the smaller country's abatements on the aggregate level reduces the cost-inefficiency in comparison to the Nash equilibrium. In order to investigate whether this intuition is true, we shall analyse the Stackelberg case and compare the two types of equilibria with respect to their (in)efficiency properties.

As only the strategic behavior but not the decision problem changes, the Stackelberg equilibrium is derived on the basis of net-benefit function (3.13). The relatively small country B still takes the abatement efforts of A as given and decides on the basis of its reaction function (3.15b). By contrast, country A as Stackelberg leader chooses an abatement level which induces a decision of country B such as to maximize A's net benefits. In other words, country A maximizes national net benefits not subject to a given abatement level $\bar{q}_B$, but subject to the abatement quantities along country B's reaction function. Deriving the first-order condition for this problem and simplifying yields for leader A

$$q_A^S = \frac{a\,n_A^2}{n_A^2 + b/c\,(n_B^2 + c/b)^2}.$$ (3.25a)

Inserting (3.25a) into B's best reply, the equilibrium abatement level of

---

[27]Notice that the scaling in Figures 3.3 and 3.4 is different.

follower B is

$$q_B^S = \frac{a\left(n_B^2 + c/b\right)^2}{x}, \tag{3.25b}$$

$$x = \left(n_B^2 + c/b\right)^2 + bc\left(n_A^2 + n_B^2 + 2c/b + c/b\, n_A^2/n_B^2 + c^2/b^2\, 1/n_B^2\right).$$

The resulting Stackelberg equilibrium S is illustrated in Figure 3.5.[28] It indicates the gain for country A relative to the Nash equilibrium as

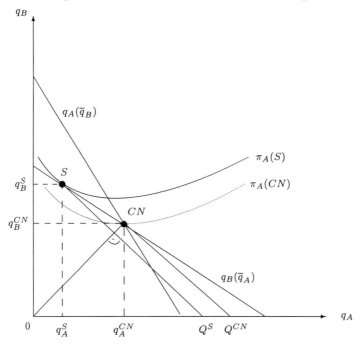

Figure 3.5: Stackelberg equilibrium

well as the consequences for underprovision and cost-effectiveness. By choosing an abatement level q_A^S that is lower than the Nash level, country A causes country B to abate more than in the Nash equilibrium and exploits its position as a leader to improve national welfare at the expense of country B. From a global perspective, though, inefficiencies are even greater in the Stackelberg equilibrium than in the Nash equilib-

---

[28]For comparability with Figure 3.1 the *symmetric* case is shown again, although we motivated Stackelberg behavior for countries of unequal size.

rium. Not only is underprovision more severe $(Q^S < Q^{CN})$,[29] but also cost-effectiveness is not attained: cost-effectiveness in the symmetric case would require that countries abate identical quantities $(q_A^*/q_B^* = n_A/n_B)$ which is not the case (in Figure 3.5, $q_A^S < q_B^S$). The relevant case with Stackelberg behavior, however, is when countries are not symmetric but heterogeneous. As before, we calculate the inefficiency properties of the Stackelberg equilibrium by means of numerical simulations for different values of α and summarize the results in Figure 3.6 for a high and in Figure 3.7 for a low value of (c/bN^2).[30]

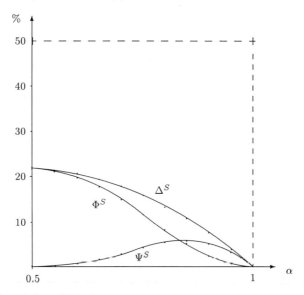

Figure 3.6: Inefficiencies in the Stackelberg equilibrium for high c/bN²

Comparing Figures 3.6 and 3.3 shows that aggregate efficiency losses in the Stackelberg and the Nash equilibria are similar when cost-parameter c is large relative to benefit-parameter b. Although follower B's abatement level is higher than in the Nash equilibrium, leader A's abatements are lower and aggregate underprovision is slightly higher. By contrast, cost-inefficiency is less important under Stackelberg behavior than under Nash behavior because 'leader' A induces 'fol-

---

[29]This is indicated in Figure 3.5 by the lines with slope of -1 that are drawn from the two equilibria to the horizontal axis.

[30]In the simulations shown in Figures 3.6 and 3.7, the same respective values as in Figures 3.3 and 3.4 have been used for c/bN^2.

lower' B to abate more. The latter effect is quantitatively the more important, the lower the value of c/bN^2, that is, the smaller the increase of abatement costs is in comparison to the decrease of abatement benefits.

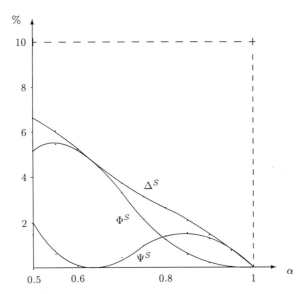

Figure 3.7: Inefficiencies in the Stackelberg equilibrium for low c/bN^2

Figure 3.7 shows that for low values of c/bN^2 and a moderate degree of asymmetry ($\alpha \approx 0.6$) the above effect (that is, that A as a leader induces B to abate relatively more) even induces full cost-effectiveness. By contrast, the welfare losses from 'easy-riding' are always greater under Stackelberg behavior than under Nash behavior, regardless of the countries' heterogeneity. Hence, in the Stackelberg case cost-inefficiencies are generally less important (except for almost symmetric countries), but underprovision is more severe than under Nash behavior. The question therefore arises whether there exist scenarios in which overall inefficiencies in the Stackelberg case are smaller than in the Nash case. Numerical simulations, however, do not confirm this for any parameter combination.

To summarize, separating the two sources of welfare losses from noncooperative behavior shows that, with regard to cost-effectiveness, in many cases the Stackelberg equilibrium is indeed less inefficient than the Nash equilibrium and even full cost-effectiveness may be reached. However, underprovision is always so much more severe in the Stackelberg equilibrium compared to the Nash equilibrium that the overall welfare losses are always greater under Stackelberg behavior (see Table 3.1).

Table 3.1: Inefficiencies of Nash and Stackelberg equilibria

	Symmetry	Moderate asymmetry	Strong asymmetry
Underprovision	$\Phi^S > \Phi^{CN}$	$\Phi^S > \Phi^{CN}$	$\Phi^S \approx \Phi^{CN}$
Cost-inefficiency	$\Psi^S > \Psi^{CN} = 0$	$\Psi^S < \Psi^{CN}$	$\Psi^S \approx \Psi^{CN}$
Aggregate inefficiency	$\Delta^S > \Delta^{CN}$	$\Delta^S > \Delta^{CN}$	$\Delta^S > \Delta^{CN}$

3.2.4   Discussion

The preceding model analysed the two sources of inefficiency from a decentralized, non-cooperative provision of an international environmental good by heterogeneous countries. Inefficiencies arise from free-riding on the abatement efforts of other countries as well as from not exploiting comparative cost advantages in the supply of international environmental goods. For both types of strategic behavior considered, the welfare losses from underprovision become relatively less important in relation to cost-inefficiency the more the countries differ. In those cases, however, aggregate inefficiencies are not as severe as in scenarios of only moderate heterogeneity.

In the light of the potential welfare gains attainable through an effective management of common environmental resources, the attractiveness of coordinating international environmental policies is obvious. The results suggest that the potential welfare gains from a cost-effective distribution of pollution reduction efforts across countries may be substantial. Negotiations on cooperative solutions therefore should try not only to *intensify* national abatement efforts, but also to *redistribute* them in a cost-minimizing way. This can be achieved by using market-based internalization instruments such as tradable emission permits or a pollution tax.

Of course, because the model is highly stylized, the results have to be treated with caution and cannot be applied directly to international environmental policy. The analysis is presented in a static, partial equilibrium framework where prices are not affected; income and emissions are exogenously determined, there is no trade in private goods, and national governments are treated as unit benevolent actors. Beside the above simplifications, the model considers only asymmetries in population size and abstracts from other heterogeneities. The purpose of the analysis, however, is to illustrate the general impact that heterogeneities between countries may have on the welfare losses due to non-cooperative strategic behavior.

To apply the above analysis to global environmental problems it would be necessary to consider more than just two countries. Of course, in a multiple-countries model the two sources of inefficiency described above would also prevail. Their relative importance, however, may change considerably. Intuitively, one would expect that the inefficiencies from underprovision would become more important as the number of countries involved increases. In the extreme case where each country is very small in proportion to the rest of the world, the environmental impact of unilateral abatement efforts will tend towards zero. From a national point of view it is then rational not to undertake any abatements because they only produce costs. As a consequence, cost-inefficiencies become relatively unimportant in a highly disintegrated world. To draw a realistic picture of the relative importance of cost-effectiveness (for example, in the context of global warming) it would be necessary to consider a model that incorporates an empirically plausible number of countries (for example, the 15 countries that account for about 90 per cent of global CO_2 emissions). Moreover, one would also have to take into account other factors that make abatement costs and benefits differ between countries.

One relevant heterogeneity that has not been considered is differences in (per-capita) national income. This aspect, however, can easily be incorporated in the above framework and allows us to capture the fact that national abatement benefits are, *ceteris paribus*, higher for richer countries (that is, there is more to lose from global warming in absolute terms). Countries may also differ with respect to available abatement technologies because of different possibilities for replacing 'dirty' by 'clean' energy production (see, for example, Barbier et al. 1991). This kind of asymmetry could be incorporated by using different parameter values c_k for each country, that is, different slopes of the (marginal) abatement cost function. Another element of an empirically based analysis would be to incorporate explicitly the emission levels in the non-cooperative status quo.

The overall effects of these different asymmetries on the importance of cost-inefficiency are ambiguous. They may either reinforce or counteract each other. For example, if a large country disposes of a cheap abatement technology, the two asymmetries work in the same direction and the above results are strengthened. Which scenario is realistic, for example, for GHG emissions, is an empirical question. In the following section, we address this question for the case of carbon emissions by taking two steps. First, we present results of numerical simulations with current data. Subsequently, Section 3.3.2 reviews recent empirical studies that estimate national costs of reducing carbon emissions.

3.3 Empirical Relevance for Carbon Emissions

3.3.1 A Numerical Simulation Approach

This section presents a methodology to quantify the importance of cost-effective policy approaches in reducing global CO_2 emissions. To this end the model of the previous section is extended to many countries and to additional asymmetries. We choose 1990 as a benchmark year and use data on CO_2 emissions, GDP and population size to calibrate the costs and benefits of emission abatements. The approach incorporates crucial determinants of differences in marginal abatement costs as well as an empirically relevant number of countries in a simple numerical simulation model. Nevertheless, the simulations merely serve illustrative purposes. Calibrating the model on the basis of empirical estimates of abatement costs and benefits would require a dynamic framework in order to take into account the aspects discussed in Section 3.1.[31]

Following Mäler (1989) for the case of 'acid rain' in Europe, we assume that national CO_2 emissions in 1990 represent a non-cooperative Nash equilibrium.[32]   Then we analyse the economic costs of national abatement efforts under different scenarios and compute the respective potential cost-savings in numerical simulation runs. The scenarios being considered are

---

[31] For simulation studies on climate agreements see, for example, Barrett (1992a), Falkinger et al. (1997), Kverndokk (1993), Welsch (1992) or Xepapadeas and Yiannaka (1997).

[32] Alternatively, one could interpret the uncoordinated status quo as behavior which emerges in the absence of *any* environmental concern (see, for example, Fankhauser and Kverndokk 1996). In one of the very few empirical tests of theoretic models on the voluntary provision of international public goods, Murdoch and Sandler (1997) confirm that CFC emission cutbacks are consistent with Nash behavior.

1. a cost-effective reallocation of 1990 global CO_2 emissions (the 'cost-effective 1990 emissions' scenario);
2. proportional emission cuts by Annex B countries to reach the global Kyoto target[33] (the 'proportional Kyoto reductions' scenario);
3. differentiated emission reductions as negotiated in Kyoto[34] (the 'negotiated Kyoto reductions' scenario); and
4. cost-effective emission reductions to reach the global Kyoto target (the 'cost-effective Kyoto reductions' scenario).

By comparing (i) the benchmark scenario (non-cooperative emissions in 1990) with the 'cost-effective 1990 emissions' scenario, (ii) the 'proportional Kyoto reductions' with the 'cost-effective Kyoto reductions' scenario, and (iii) the 'negotiated Kyoto reductions' with the 'cost-effective Kyoto reductions' scenario, it is possible to determine the excess costs of (i) non-cooperative abatements, (ii) proportional abatements to reach the global Kyoto target, and (iii) the differentiated abatement obligations negotiated in Kyoto, respectively.

Statistical data refer to emissions and not to abatements of CO_2. Therefore, we do not run simulations on the basis of abatement net benefits (3.8), but use the inverse formulation where net benefits are a function of emissions. National net benefits from CO_2 emissions are defined as the economic return R minus the environmental damage D from emitting CO_2:

$$\tilde{\pi}_k = R_k(e_k) - D_k(E), \qquad (3.26)$$

where e_k denotes the annual emission quantity of country k and E global emissions ($E = \sum_k e_k$). The specification of abatement costs and benefits is the same as in Section 3.2, that is, we assume linearly decreasing marginal emission benefits (linearly increasing abatement costs) and linearly increasing marginal damage costs (linearly decreasing abatement benefits). With respect to differences in marginal emission costs and damages we assume that a country's marginal emission benefits are *ceteris paribus* higher, the greater its population (as the same absolute abatement quantity implies a smaller individual burden for a country with a higher population), and that the damage costs are *ceteris paribus* higher, the higher a country's economic income (the absolute damage

---

[33] A reduction of GHG emissions by at least 5 per cent below 1990 levels until 2008 to 2012 (Art. 3 Para. 1 KP).

[34] The emission reduction obligations according to Annex B of the KP are: -8 per cent (EU, former Czechoslovakia), -7 per cent (USA), -6 per cent (Japan, Canada, Poland), 0 per cent (former USSR) and +8 per cent (Australia).

being larger for a relatively wealthy country).[35] A specification that
satisfies the above assumptions is

$$\tilde{\pi}_k = 2\,c_k\,n_k\,e_k^{1/2} - 1/2\,d_k\,y_k\,E^2, \qquad (3.27)$$

with $c_k > 0$, $d_k > 0$, $n_k > 0$ and $e_k > 0$, where c_k and d_k are country-
specific emission benefit (that is, abatement cost) and damage parameters, n_k describes a country's population size, and y_k is GDP of country
k.[36]

In the non-cooperative Nash equilibrium, each government expands
its emissions to the level where marginal emission benefits are equal to
marginal damage costs:

$$c_k\,n_k\,e_k^{-1/2} \stackrel{!}{=} d_k\,y_k\,E. \qquad (3.28)$$

For the simulations we need data on the variables and parameters given
in (3.28). National and global emissions, population and GDP figures
are available from annual statistics. Data on cost and damage parameters have to be estimated. To simplify matters, we assume that the
damage parameter d_k is the same for all countries ($d_k = d\,\forall\,k$), that is,
identical environmental preferences for countries with the same economic
income.[37] Given the above information, emission cost parameters c_k can
be calibrated such that (3.28) holds.

The data used in the simulations are summarized in Table 3.2. We
consider the 15 largest emitters which account for almost 90 per cent of
global energy-related CO_2 emissions and neglect emissions from the rest
of the world. Table 3.2 illustrates that emission quantities, population
size and GDP are distributed unevenly across countries not only in absolute terms, but also with respect to per-capita and per-GDP emissions.

---

[35] See, for example, Barrett (1992a, pp. 16–21). The empirical test of Murdoch and
Sandler (1997) confirms a linear relationship between the demand for CFC emission
abatements and national income.

[36] Although this functional specification differs from the one of the previous section
it has the same general properties. The exact inverse formulation to (3.13) would
be $\tilde{\pi}_k = c_k\left(a\,n_k\,e_k - 1/2\,e_k^2\right) - 1/2\,d_k\,y_k\,E^2$, parameter a representing the level of
per-capita emissions where marginal emission benefits become zero. National emis-
sions can then be written as the difference between emissions in the absence of any
environmental concern and abatement quantities: $e_k = a\,n_k - q_k$.

[37] The value of parameter d does not influence the simulation results and is used as
a scaling device.

Table 3.2: Energy-related CO_2 emissions, population and GDP in 1990

	Jurisdiction	CO_2 emissions[a] Absol.	%	Population[b] Absol.	%	GDP[c] Absol.
1	United States	1 347.6	22.89	249.9	4.73	5 489.6
2	Former USSR	1 012.9	17.54	281.5	5.33	1 506.7
3	European Union[d]	847.3	14.67	366.0	6.93	6 676.3
4	China	660.7	11.44	1 155.3	21.86	387.4
5	Japan	289.1	5.00	123.5	2.34	2 932.1
6	India	186.2	3.22	834.7	15.79	305.9
7	Korea (united)	133.1	2.30	64.6	1.22	265.8
8	Canada	111.6	1.93	26.6	0.50	568.1
9	Poland	95.2	1.65	38.1	0.72	58.9
10	Mexico	85.6	1.48	86.1	1.63	244.1
11	South Africa	79.3	1.37	37.1	0.70	102.1
12	Australia	72.6	1.26	17.1	0.32	296.0
13	Iran	57.8	1.00	54.5	1.03	538.1
14	Czechoslovakia	57.6	0.99	15.7	0.29	45.2
15	Brazil	55.4	0.96	144.7	2.74	477.9
Total		5 091.9	88.15	3 495.4	66.13	19 894.2
Rest of world		684.3	11.85	1 789.6	33.87	–
Global		5 776.2	100	5 285.0	100	–

Notes:
a. Estimated energy-related emissions from fossil fuel combustion, cement production and gas flared, in million metric tons of carbon.
b. Mid-year estimates, in millions.
c. At current prices, in billions of US dollars.
d. For compatibility with the European Union's commitment in the Kyoto Protocol, the figures do not represent the member states of the European Community (EC 12) in 1990, but those of the European Union (EU 15) in 1997.

Source: United Nations (1996, Tables 2, 8, 20, 70). Own calculations.

Table 3.3 presents the results of numerical simulations taken out with the above data and model specification. The second column of Table 3.3 indicates which countries have committed themselves to an individual emission cut according to Annex B of the Kyoto Protocol. The third column reports the calibrated values of national emission benefit (that is, abatement cost) parameters c_k. The values in the fourth to the sixth columns show the individual excess costs, expressed in per cent of emission benefits forgone when marginal emission benefits are not equalized. Negative values indicate that under international cost-effectiveness these countries should reduce their emissions and corresponding emission benefits due to their relatively low marginal abatement costs. The bottom row presents the aggregated cost-savings that are possible when marginal emission benefits (abatement costs) are equalized under the alternative scenarios.

The simulation results indicate the existence of substantial welfare losses from cost-inefficiency. Under all three scenarios aggregate emission benefits could be increased by more than 20 per cent through a cost-effective reallocation of emission quantities. However, only the USA and the EU would be designated for an increase of emissions. All other political entities would have to reduce their emissions considerably. A uniform reduction in 1990 emissions of Annex B countries by 5 per cent implies higher cost-inefficiencies than a mere reallocation of the 1990 levels. This result reflects the fact that only Annex B countries with relatively high marginal abatement costs (due to high values of c_k) would reduce their emissions. The difference, however, is small (22.55 vs. 22.98 per cent). Interestingly, a comparison of aggregate cost-inefficiencies under equal versus negotiated percentage reductions reveals that excess costs are slightly higher under the differentiated reduction pattern stipulated in Annex B of the Kyoto Protocol than under the hypothetical uniform reduction scenario. This is because those countries which have relatively higher marginal abatement costs reduce their emissions more. The difference, however, is quantitatively negligible (22.98 vs. 23.01 per cent).

Table 3.3: Simulation results on cost-inefficiencies

Jurisdiction	Annex B	c_k^b	Annual excess costs[a] of		
			1990 non-cooperative emissions[c]	Equal percentage reductions[d]	Negotiated percentage reductions[e]
USA	X	41.06	26.29	26.77	26.78
Former USSR	X	8.67	−62.76	−62.52	−62.52
European Union	X	27.04	39.39	39.78	39.79
China		0.44	−90.43	−90.61	−90.61
Japan	X	20.55	−27.53	−27.07	−27.06
India		0.26	−92.44	−92.58	−92.58
Korea (united)		2.42	−93.43	−93.56	−93.56
Canada	X	11.49	−85.96	−85.87	−85.87
Poland	X	0.77	−98.54	−98.54	−98.54
Mexico		1.34	−93.97	−94.08	−94.08
South Africa		1.25	−97.48	−97.53	−97.53
Australia	X	7.51	−92.68	−92.64	−92.64
Iran		3.82	−86.70	−86.95	−86.95
Czechoslovakia	X	1.11	−98.88	−98.88	−98.88
Brazil		1.25	−88.19	−88.41	−88.41
Total			22.55	22.98	23.01

Notes:
Simulations taken out with GAMS, using data from Table 3.2. Rounded values.
a. In per cent of forgone economic income R due to cost-inefficient emissions.
b. Calibrated values according to (3.28) and assuming $d_k = d \ \forall \ k$. Parameter d is used as a scaling device and does not influence the simulation results.
c. The benchmark (1990 emissions) versus the 'cost-effective 1990 emissions' scenario.
d. The 'proportional Kyoto reductions' versus the 'cost-effective Kyoto reductions' scenario.
e. The 'negotiated Kyoto reductions' versus the 'cost-effective Kyoto reductions' scenario.

The simulation results shown in Table 3.3 are generally in line with the conjecture that industrialized countries bear considerably higher marginal abatement costs than developing countries and economies in transition. The pattern by which emissions would have to be cost-effectively reallocated, however, suggests that important determinants of national abatement costs are lacking in the underlying theoretic model. Canada's emissions, for example, would also be sharply reduced under cost-effectiveness although the value of its cost parameter is relatively high. It is likely that with a more realistic specification of national abatement benefits and costs, the cost-effective reallocation of national emission quantities would tend to be smaller and/or include more jurisdictions which are apt to increase their emissions. Cost-inefficiencies nevertheless may be important because of other relevant factors such as the intertemporal aspect. In any case, the purpose of the above simulation exercise was not to provide an empirically sound assessment of abatement cost differentials between countries. Rather, it served to illustrate a methodology for addressing this issue. The empirical dimension is discussed briefly in the next section by surveying studies that try to assess the national costs of reducing GHG emissions.

3.3.2   Quantitative Studies on CO_2 Abatement Costs

In the 1970s, attempts were made to estimate the economic costs of reducing GHG emissions. Since then, many contributions have been published in this field.[38] It is beyond the scope of this study to give a comprehensive overview of this literature or to discuss systematically the different results and underlying assumptions of these models. Instead, the aim of this section is to summarize the general picture drawn by this literature for carbon abatement cost differentials between countries.

Studies which assess the costs of GHG reduction policies share two main features: first, the focus of most of the work is still on CO_2 emissions whereas other greenhouse gases are ignored; second, there has been a lively, often controversial debate on the magnitude of the costs of mitigating climate change (Hourcade 1996a, p. 268). The latter controversy is in part due to a modeling dichotomy in this field: quantitative studies on the costs of reducing carbon emissions are divided into so-called 'bottom-up' and 'top-down' models. The former models tend to suggest that aggregate costs of GHG mitigation might be low or even negative,

---

[38] One of the pioneering works was Nordhaus (1979). The bulk of quantitative literature on the economic costs of curbing climate change emanated in the early 1990s in connection with the work done by the 'Energy Modeling Forum' as well as a parallel research program of the OECD and its subsequent '1992 Model Comparison Project'.

whereas the latter models tend to suggest the opposite (Hourcade 1996a, p. 286).[39]

The bottom-up or engineering method uses technological cost data to calculate emission reduction potentials achievable through energy-saving and substitution activities in certain countries or sectors. The advantage of this approach lies in its ability to take into account existing inefficiencies in the use of energy resources and to work out the different abatement opportunities and their related costs. This may serve as a basis for comparing (marginal) abatement costs across countries. On the other hand, the simple addition of costs or cost-savings does not withstand a rigorous theoretic analysis: in particular, it is inappropriate to presume prices to be constant when energy is saved and substituted in considerable amounts.

Top-down, macroeconomic studies on the costs of reducing GHG emissions circumvent the disadvantages of the bottom-up approach as they allow for sectoral and international repercussions. In a general equilibrium framework, most of these studies take a long-term, global perspective and predict economywide impacts on the basis of price elasticities, resource intensities, growth and technology parameters. In doing so, they estimate the costs of reducing certain greenhouse gases (mostly CO_2) within a given time span to certain (not necessarily optimal) levels in terms of gross world product forgone. Although top-down studies are better founded on economic theory and mostly disaggregated to several regions with differing characteristics, often they do not focus on the different cost implications of a certain policy scenario (for example, uniform abatement targets) for different regions or countries. Rather, their primary aim is to derive global cost estimates for a given emissions target. Therefore, these studies do not always give a straightforward answer to the question: how big are the potential cost-savings of cost-effective policy approaches?

The majority of top-down models take a global perspective, whereas the bulk of bottom-up models are country-by-country studies. However, the reverse can also be found as an exception to the rule. Looking first at studies that assess GHG abatement costs for single countries, both top-down as well as bottom-up models demonstrate the quantitative importance of cost-effectiveness. For example, several top-down studies that attempt to quantify the macroeconomic impacts of the European Commission's 1992 proposal on a combined CO_2/energy tax report substantial differences with respect to the tax effects on national economic

---

[39]See Hourcade (1996b) for an up-to-date review of mitigation cost studies under these two alternative approaches, and Hourcade (1996a) for a comparison of the bottom-up and top-down methods as well as for other methodological issues.

variables. The tax effects on national GDP range from a 0.72 per cent increase in GDP in Italy to a 0.72 per cent decrease in the UK (Hourcade 1996b, p. 316, Table 9.11). Similarly, bottom-up studies for Europe that aim directly at intercountry comparisons of reduction costs report marginal CO_2 abatement costs between (close to) zero for Denmark, France or Germany and 143 ECU per ton of CO_2 for Spain — even at a moderate level of 5 per cent emission reductions from 1988 levels until 2010 (Hourcade 1996b, p. 318, Table 9.14). The latter results have to be considered with some reservation, as they are in fact the outcome of several, not perfectly standardized country studies. Nevertheless, other bottom-up models report similar results with respect to differences in national reduction costs (Hourcade 1996b, p. 321, Figure 9.12). The feature of bottom-up studies to allow for economic inefficiencies in the baseline and therefore for energy-saving potentials at low or even negative costs becomes particularly relevant in the case of developing countries (and countries in transition) since markets are in general less well functioning and distortions in the energy sector are greater in these countries. For moderate abatement scenarios, studies on developing countries regularly report *negative* marginal abatement costs. For higher reduction targets, costs also become positive and considerably different within this group of countries (Hourcade 1996b, p. 331, Figure 9.20, and p. 332, Figure 9.21).

An enormous cost-saving potential is seen in cost differentials between industrialized and developing countries, based on the more or less explicit conjecture that marginal abatement costs are considerably lower in third world countries and economies in transition. For example, in a 30–40-year time frame the studies cited above estimate average emission reduction costs in these countries to be less than US$ 14 per tonne of CO_2. This is about one-tenth of the costs estimated for some industrialized countries (see above). The presumption that marginal carbon abatement costs are always lower in less-developed countries is challenged by several authors. In a comparison of bottom-up cost estimates for four different countries,[40] Jackson (1995) finds that GHG emission reductions are relatively cheaper in industrialized economies. Moreover, all of the countries — but most noticeably the UK and Denmark — possess a considerable potential for emission reductions at *negative* costs. One explanation for this result is the fact that per-capita energy demand in industrialized countries is much higher than in developing economies. Given this status quo, replacing less-efficient technologies by cheaper ones in a well-developed energy system results in considerably greater

---

[40]The four countries considered are two highly developed economies (Denmark and the UK), one country in transition (Poland) and one developing country (Zimbabwe).

total cost-savings than in countries where the energy system is poorly developed and the demand for energy lower. However, the author himself emphasizes that the results of his comparison have to be treated with great caution and serve merely for the purpose of illustration, since 'the studies themselves have not been carried out on a uniform, equitable basis' (Jackson 1995, p. 127).

A similar result with respect to relative abatement cost advantages is derived by Kverndokk (1993) in a dynamic partial equilibrium analysis for five world regions.[41] By using numerical simulations for a cost-effective implementation of a given emission target,[42] the author concludes that marginal abatement costs are relatively *high* in developing countries. Reasons for this outcome are large reserves of coal and other fossil fuels, fewer energy substitution possibilities and rapid rates of economic growth in developing countries. By contrast, OECD countries (except the USA) exhibit relatively low marginal abatement costs due to a large nuclear power industry as well as a high proportion of undiscovered oil and gas resources (Kverndokk 1993, p. 99). Moreover, compared to the traditional solution of uniform percentage emission reductions, it is shown that a tradable permit solution which allocates emission rights proportional to current emissions (the grandfathering approach) is the only simple rule that makes all countries better off. The global gains from cost-effectiveness compared to the uniform solution are rather low in this case (Kverndokk 1993, p. 106). This result, however, critically depends on the assumption that the five regions represent homogeneous entities where cost-effectiveness within each region is assured by assumption. Increasing the number of countries modifies this picture because the existence of many heterogeneous countries generally increases the quantitative importance of cost-inefficiency.[43]

Assessing and comparing abatement costs of countries that differ substantially with respect to many characteristics requires a global perspective. Country-by-country partial equilibrium analyses are often very difficult to compare because of different underlying assumptions and methodologies, and they also ignore important linkages (for example, via international trade) that may influence the economic impacts of national reduction policies substantially. Most importantly, a global perspective is necessary in order to identify internationally cost-effective emission

---

[41] The regions considered are the USA, other OECD countries, countries in transition (former USSR and other socialist countries), China and the rest of the world.

[42] The emission scenario considered is a 20 per cent worldwide reduction of 1990 emissions from 2000 onwards that roughly corresponds to the (relatively demanding) Toronto target.

[43] Relatively small gains from cost-effectiveness are also reported by other macroeconomic models (see note 12 in Kverndokk 1993).

reduction strategies as in the model presented above. Due to the complexity that is added by considering several countries (or world regions) and by incorporating trade effects, most global analyses use a top-down approach. In line with the regional studies, they estimate global costs of emission abatements which differ widely.[44] Moreover (and in contrast to the results of Kverndokk 1993), many macroeconomic studies assess both considerable potential gains from implementing a cost-effective international policy as well as relatively high abatement costs in the developed world (Hourcade 1996b, p. 339).

In summary, although the precise pattern as well as the quantitative importance of comparative cost advantages in the reduction of carbon emissions across countries is still controversial and needs further investigation, there is a common view that the potential cost-savings from implementing cost-effective global environmental policies are substantial. If so, international negotiations have to focus not only on the overall level of GHG emissions, but also on the choice of instruments that ensure international cost-effectiveness. In the next section, we briefly review the policy instruments for the internalization of environmental externalities and discuss some of their specific characteristics which are relevant in the international context.

3.4   Cost-effective Policy Instruments

The core elements of any international environmental agreement are the international environmental standard chosen and the necessary measures assigned to the different contracting parties. Appropriate policy instruments for meeting the treaty targets have to take into account not only fundamental institutional restrictions and incentive problems which are present on the international level, but also the specific characteristics of the countries involved and the environmental problem at stake. Instrument choice thus comprises two aspects: (i) the internalization of transboundary environmental externalities; and (ii) the incentive compatibility of the terms of an agreement. In the following, we focus on the first question by briefly reviewing the properties of different internalization instruments that can be used in international environmental agreements.[45]

---

[44]See, for example, Clarke et al. (1996) for a comprehensive survey of this class of models and a conceptual framework for analysing the macroeconomic consequences of GHG emission abatements.

[45]We shall abstract from the question of how an agreement is to be implemented on the national level and discuss the instrument choice on the international level only. The choice of appropriate instruments to guarantee incentive compatibility is

In general, we can make a distinction between policy instruments for the internalization of environmental externalities that are market based and those of a command-and-control type. The former comprise emission taxes or tradable emission permits, the latter emission quotas, technology standards or other forms of direct regulation. It is a central result of the theory of environmental policy that an internalization by market-based instruments is the superior policy option since they support the realization of a given environmental standard at the lowest social cost (Baumol and Oates 1988). By contrast, command-and-control type instruments such as uniform, fixed quotas are usually not cost-effective in a static sense, that is, the same environmental effect could be achieved at a lower social cost through a different allocation of abatement efforts across emitters (see Sections 3.2 and 3.3). Furthermore, they are inefficient in a dynamic sense because they do not provide incentives to reduce emissions further by investing in new and cleaner technologies.[46] From the perspective of global efficiency, this holds for transboundary externalities as well. There is some evidence that the dynamic efficiency aspect of economic internalization instruments is important (Tietenberg 1990). In the case of carbon emissions, for example, it is particularly important to develop new disposal technologies since CO_2 is difficult to dispose of, even if it is removed from stack gases (Pearce 1991).

In Section 3.1, it was noted that the cost-effectiveness property of market-based internalization instruments is also ensured when a desirable environmental standard is more or less arbitrarily chosen in a first step (which may correspond, for example, to 'critical loads' of pollution), but is then implemented either by an emission tax or by tradable emission permits. This is the 'charges and standards' or 'permits and standards' approach which has been put forward most prominently by Baumol and Oates (1971). It implies that the principle of optimality is given up and that environmental policy confines itself to a 'satisficing' solution. This latter route is pursued in many international environmental negotiations. It may be justifiable for those environmental problems (such as 'global warming') where, due to their global and intertemporal character, it is very difficult to carry out an explicit cost–benefit analysis. A qualification of the minimum-cost theorem is that it requires a direct and additive relationship between the emissions of pollutants and their environmental impacts. Otherwise, charges have to

---

discussed in Chapter 4.

[46]The empirical relevance of cost-effectiveness is emphasized, for example, by Tietenberg (1985) who finds that for 17 types of emissions to air and water, a move from command-and-control or uniform regulations to cost-effective ways of reaching the same environmental standard would reduce costs by about 7–95 per cent, with a cost reduction of 50 per cent for 10 of the 17 cases examined.

be differentiated among emitters (Baumol and Oates 1988, pp. 169–72). However, important global environmental problems such as the anthropogenic greenhouse effect and the depletion of the ozone layer do have this property.[47]

Under 'ideal' conditions such as perfect competition and perfect information, emission taxes and tradable emission permits are equivalent instruments and both lead to cost-effectiveness (see, for example, Baumol and Oates 1988). The uniform tax rate of an emission unit and the uniform price of a permit are equal to the marginal abatement cost, where the market mechanism ensures that this marginal cost is equalized across all economic agents. The policy-oriented literature on instrument choice for the internalization of international or global environmental externalities discusses both tradable emission permits and international emission or energy taxes (OECD 1992, UNCTAD 1992). Thus far, the aspect of cost-effectiveness is taken into account. However, the equivalence (in a strict sense) holds only under a number of restrictive assumptions, which do not reflect either important stylized facts or implementation issues which are relevant in international environmental policy. In the presence of uncertainty over abatement cost schedules, for example, the equivalence is lost and either taxes or permits are the superior instrument, depending on the relative slopes of the marginal benefit and cost curves (Weitzman 1974). If, for example, global marginal abatement costs increase at a higher rate than the related marginal abatement benefits decline, then the social loss from an incorrectly chosen emission tax is smaller than the loss from a suboptimally chosen amount of total permits; the tax instrument is preferable. On the other hand, discontinuities or the possibility of catastrophic events make a permit system relatively more attractive because it guarantees a certain environmental standard. Under imperfect competition both instruments open up the possibility that large countries will exploit their monopoly power strategically, but with different consequences.[48]

Another important criterion for the choice of the internalization instrument on the international level is the institutional framework that is required and the degree of national sovereignty that has to be delegated to a supranational institution for implementation, monitoring and administration. In principle, both instruments are equivalent in this respect. For both of them, an international institution is needed which

---

[47] Appendix A.2 derives the minimum-cost theorem for the 'permits and standards' approach; for a derivation with respect to charges and for further references, see Baumol and Oates (1988, pp. 165–9).

[48] See, for example, Hoel (1997) or Misiolek and Elder (1989) for the properties of optimal tax and permit instruments in a second-best framework.

determines the actual tax rate or the amount of permits available on the market and which monitors national compliance with emission obligations and redistributes revenue to the single countries. Generally, the question of how to redistribute the revenue from a global emissions tax is equivalent to the question of how to allocate initial emission permits (and future assignments) to the individual countries. Nevertheless institutional details may exist in which the implementation of either a tax or a tradable permit system differs, and these differences have to be taken into account.[49]

Given that the tax instrument is chosen to fight global warming, an emission tax is generally preferable to an energy tax because of its higher precision. Nevertheless, problems of practical feasibility and other considerations may call for at least a mix of tax bases.[50] Furthermore, a tax would have to take into account not only interactions with other economic variables in the presence of distortions in other markets (giving rise to a positive or negative 'double dividend'), but also substantial discrepancies in national energy prices due to manifold distortions on energy markets. Moreover, taxes would have to be adjusted continuously over time in order to approach the global emission level stipulated in the agreement. The norm according to which the revenue from a global emission tax is redistributed to the single countries would be a very sensitive negotiation issue politically. Under a permit system, transaction costs would have to be small in order to enable sufficient transactions on a global permit market. Moreover, inefficiencies caused by imperfectly competitive markets cannot be ignored, given the presence of large countries with monopoly power on world markets (Hahn and Stavins 1992, Koutstaal 1997, Misiolek and Elder 1989).

National governments have been very reluctant to implement market-based instruments for the internalization of environmental externalities, even if they exhibit a purely national character. International environmental negotiations in most cases lead to inflexible solutions, for example, in the form of equal percentage abatement obligations. If the globally optimal environmental standard were chosen, all that would be needed in addition for an efficient internalization is the tradability of those pollution rights. But when the negotiated standard is suboptimal, it is only one step further to implement a market-based solution by

---

[49]See, for example, Hoel (1997, pp. 122–4) or Zhang and Folmer (1995) for a comparison of tradable carbon permits and an international carbon tax with regard to institutional aspects. Tietenberg (1994) discusses implementation issues of a global tradable permit system for carbon emissions.

[50]Manne and Richels (1993) discuss the proposal for a combined energy/CO_2 tax made by the EU Commission; Jorgenson and Wilcoxen (1993) compare the two tax solutions for the USA.

also allowing for tradability of the national quotas. Therefore, given the inclination of national governments to agree on quotas in international environmental negotiations, there is a strong case for tradable permits over an international emission tax. If tradability of these quotas is not (or only to a limited extent) negotiable and the governments agree, for example, merely on proportional emission reductions, then cost-effectiveness is not reached when the countries in the initial situation have differing marginal abatement costs. Even when marginal abatement costs are initially the same, proportional emission reductions will be cost-efficient only if marginal cost schedules are linear (see, for example, Endres 1993).

The Framework Convention on Climate Change takes into account the above considerations and tries to reduce the inefficiency of inflexible quota solutions by allowing for 'activities implemented jointly'. According to this principle, signatories with relatively high marginal abatement costs can fulfill (part of) their obligations in countries with lower marginal abatement costs. Under ideal circumstances and full deductibility of related emission reductions, the concept of *joint implementation* would lead to the equalization of marginal abatement costs across countries and ensure cost-effectiveness. Given that the stipulated abatement obligations of the host countries remain unchanged by such projects, this concept corresponds to trading emissions rights and can be seen as a preliminary step for the implementation of a future tradable permits system.[51] The manner in which the induced emission reductions are deducted from the treaty obligations determines implicitly a transfer between the two countries that participate in a joint implementation project. For example, when the induced abatements are credited in full to the obligations of the high-cost country, the transfer equals zero and the cost-efficiency gains go in total to the high-cost country — a source of massive protest of developing countries against the concept of joint implementation.

A number of additional constraints are relevant for the choice between the above policy instruments. To a large extent, these are due to the international nature of the problem. Given the lack of a supranational authority with sufficient competencies, a centralized regulation of transboundary or even global environmental externalities is not an option at present. Thus international environmental policy is determined at the national level. As national governments neither are concerned with global welfare, nor do they have appropriate instruments at hand to implement a global environmental policy, all attempts to coordinate environmental policies inevitably possess a second-best character (see Fig-

---

[51] See Section 7.3 for a critical discussion of joint implementation as an instrument for introducing a future global tradable emission permit market.

ure 1.1).[52] This is also reflected in the choice of the policy instrument for the internalization of transboundary externalities through international environmental agreements. In general, there is a close relationship between the choice of the internalization instrument and the incentive compatibility of an international environmental agreement. This puts the incentives for individual countries to cooperate on international environmental problems in the foreground. In the following chapter, we therefore discuss the aspect of incentive compatibility and its implications for cost-effectiveness in international environmental policy.

---

[52]Killinger and Schmidt (1998) survey the possibilities and strategic aspects of national environmental policy in view of additional restrictions and distortions.

Chapter 4

Incentive Compatibility

4.1 Introduction

The 1990s have been imbued with a growing concern for international and especially global environmental problems. At the international level this is reflected by political debates and activities such as the 1992 United Nations Conference on Environment and Development (UNCED) in Rio de Janeiro. At the same time, it has also been discussed intensively in the academic sphere. The economic analysis of environmental problems was the subject of intensive research in the 1960s and 1970s. Nevertheless, the increasing preoccupation with transboundary externalities has led to a recent renaissance of research in environmental economics and to a new body of literature. The basic reason for a reformulation of the research program has been summarized concisely by Carraro and Siniscalco (1992, p. 381):

> Standard solutions for [transboundary] environmental externali-
> ties are therefore not available, and the protection of the interna-
> tional commons is left to voluntary agreements among sovereign
> countries. It is precisely this fact which requires a shift in our
> analyses, from a literature on government intervention to a lit-
> erature on negotiation between nations and international policy
> coordination.

Many environmental problems share the features that a great number of countries are involved and that a substantial heterogeneity of these countries can be observed with respect to economic, environmental and other characteristics. These features make it difficult to coordinate environmental policies effectively. Although cooperating on the use of international environmental resources is by definition improving global welfare and is not a zero-sum game, single countries may nevertheless lose by participation in an international environmental agreement.

First, when countries are very asymmetric with respect to the benefits and costs of emission abatements, some of them may not profit from environmental cooperation at all although they contribute to pollution and, therefore, should be part of a cooperative solution. Obviously this holds for unidirectional externalities. In such cases, compensation payments to upstream countries are required in order to reach some kind of Coasian bargaining solution. In the case of more than one polluting country, the additional problem arises as to how to allocate the measures in a way that minimizes overall abatement costs. Again, the allocation of abatement efforts that is internationally cost-effective may not be profitable for some countries without compensation. Second, even in the extreme case of identical countries, every government has an incentive to abstain from an agreement as long as its own abstention does not lead to the entire breakdown of environmental cooperation. The public-good character of environmental policy implies that outsider countries benefit from the efforts of cooperating countries without incurring any costs. This incentive to free ride on the efforts of other countries is the stronger, the more countries are involved because then the behavior of a single country is of only minor importance for the cooperative outcome. Taken together, in many situations it may be difficult to create the necessary *participation incentives* so that all relevant countries join an environmental treaty.

An additional problem of cooperative approaches in international environmental policy is the lack of a supranational authority which can enforce formal agreements between sovereign states. It implies that national governments cannot credibly commit themselves to the obligations and actions stipulated in an environmental convention. The same free-rider incentives that persuade countries not to participate in a coordination of environmental policies also lead to an intrinsic instability of agreements. The stability problem is especially severe when many countries are involved, but it is still an important issue even when there are only a few countries. Therefore, one also has to provide appropriate *compliance incentives* that render cooperation incentive compatible once an environmental convention has come into force. From a global perspective, the basic economic problem is to maximize aggregate welfare gains from international environmental cooperation subject to the above two types of incentive constraints. This translates into the questions of how an agreement should be designed with respect to the international environmental standard, how the required policy measures should be assigned to the different contracting parties and which additional treaty provisions should be adopted to increase the effectiveness and stability of the treaty.

This chapter addresses the questions raised above (i) by giving an up-to-date survey on economic models which analyse incentives for international environmental cooperation and (ii) by categorizing the different instruments proposed in the literature to support incentive compatibility.[1] The survey does *not* claim to reflect the entire spectrum of the literature on transboundary environmental externalities. For example, important aspects of international pollution control such as imperfect and/or incomplete information are reviewed only briefly. Moreover, all models discussed in this chapter assume countries to be 'unit actors' whose governments maximize national welfare.[2] This survey focusses on the economic instruments that stimulate and sustain cooperation on the internalization of transboundary or even global environmental externalities.[3] It is thus oriented towards contributions that explore the possibilities of compensating for the fundamental lack of institutional structure on the international level.[4]

Instruments for promoting and stabilizing international environmental cooperation generally influence both the incentives for participation and compliance. Some provisions even produce a conflict between cooperation incentives *ex ante* and *ex post*. There is thus no point in grouping conceivable strategies according to the type of incentives they affect. Instead, we classify the instruments according to how narrowly they are related to the environmental policies of national governments. Beginning with the choice and design of the internalization instrument itself, we gradually enlarge the strategy space of the players (the national governments) and increase the complexity of the underlying decision problem to discuss additional possible instruments. The strategy space is enlarged first by adding the time dimension to the decision problem (that is, by assuming repeated decisions on pollution abatement) and then by allowing for various forms of compensation as additional instrument variables. The underlying decision problem is extended to take into account utility interdependencies (that is, additional arguments in utility/welfare functions) and interdependencies with other markets (that

---

[1] This chapter is an extended version of Schmidt (2000).

[2] See Schulze and Ursprung (2000) for a survey of the political economy of international environmental policy.

[3] We do not consider arguments that call for an international coordination of policies even in the case of purely national environmental problems (see, for example, Hoel 1997, Kox and van der Tak 1996).

[4] Mäler (1990) provides a comprehensive taxonomy of international environmental externalities and an excellent introductory survey on important theoretical aspects of their internalization through international cooperation. For a brief overview, see Carraro and Siniscalco (1992); for a policy-oriented survey, see Verbruggen and Jansen (1995).

is, general equilibrium effects). Combinations of these extensions and of
related instruments are certainly possible and realistic, but we discuss
them separately to keep the argumentation clear.

The structure of the survey is as follows.[5] In Section 4.2 we discuss
the influence of the choice and shaping of the internalization instrument
on the incentives to engage in environmental cooperation. Section 4.3
expands the strategy set to multiple periods and considers treaty provisions that make future abatement efforts of observant parties dependent
on the (potentially defecting) behavior of other countries. This way of
warranting incentives for cooperation, which exploits the fact that environmental policy decisions are repeated, is referred to as *internal stabilization*. In Section 4.4 the strategy space is enlarged to compensations
and sanctions of various forms (monetary side payments, issue linkage,
trade sanctions and so on) to induce cooperation. They are labeled
external stabilization instruments as they are not necessarily restricted
to cooperation on environmental externalities. Section 4.5 investigates
how unilateral and accompanying measures of single countries or subcoalitions cohere with the incentives to participate in and comply with
an environmental convention. These may be motivated by special preference structures (altruism, reputation, social norms and so on) or by
general equilibrium effects of abatement activities. Section 4.6 briefly
addresses long-term measures in the form of flexible adjustments of an
agreement to changing circumstances and of improved framework conditions for international negotiations. Section 4.7 concludes and motivates
the two directions of theoretical analysis treated in Chapters 5 and 6.

4.2   The Choice of Internalization Instrument

The first-best instrument for providing sufficient incentives for national governments to sign and comply with international environmental
treaties is lump-sum taxes and transfers that work as a reward (sanction)
for (non-)cooperative behavior. In a second-best world where international lump-sum transfers and taxes are not, or only to a limited extent,
possible, the question arises as to which type of internalization instrument harmonizes best with the incentive compatibility requirement. In
the following, we look first at explanations for the widespread use of
uniform quota solutions in international environmental policy. Subsequently, we introduce the market-oriented instrument of 'joint implemen-

---

[5]See also Heister et al. (1995) who distinguish internal and external stabilization
instruments and flexible adjustments to an agreement.

tation' that is proposed as a supplementary element of a quota agreement in climate policy. The section closes with a discussion of market-based instruments, comparing international emission taxes to tradable emission permits and presenting some suggestions for increasing the incentives to cooperate if these instruments are chosen in an agreement.

National governments have been very reluctant to implement market-based instruments for the internalization of environmental externalities. In most cases, international environmental negotiations lead to uniform or inflexible solutions, for example, in the form of equal percentage abatement obligations. Since quotas are without doubt an inefficient instrument, one has to ask why they are none the less an element of so many negotiations on international pollution control in reality. There are several reasons for this phenomenon.[6] First, uniform solutions are apparently 'fair'.[7] Moreover, negotiating complex and differentiated solutions is associated with high transaction costs and manifold informational problems. Asymmetric information on the valuations of environmental quality and uncertainty about the working of the ecosystem often make it very difficult to determine economically efficient, differentiated strategies to internalize international environmental externalities.[8] In addition, when several agreements are possible (that is, in the presence of multiple equilibria), simple rules such as uniform quotas may serve as a 'focal point' during negotiations.

Whenever countries are heterogeneous and compensation payments are ruled out, there is a close relationship between the choice of the internalization instrument, the agreed international environmental standard and the incentives to cooperate (Barrett 1992b). If asymmetric countries are assumed to negotiate on equal (percentage) reductions and the outcome is determined by the median country of the coalition, some but not all countries involved in the pollution problem will cooperate in equilibrium (Hoel 1992b). The stricter the chosen environmental standard and the higher the requirements on incentive compatibility, the fewer the countries that will find it in their interest to participate in the agreement which *ceteris paribus* decreases the global level of pollution

---

[6] In the context of purely national pollution, it is known from the political–economic analysis of command-and-control policies that quotas may create rents whereas taxes do not. This may also be an important explanation in an international context, but it is disregarded here.

[7] The aspect of equity and the impact of different principles of burden sharing, especially rules of equal sacrifice, on the incentives to sign a global climate treaty are analysed in Welsch (1992).

[8] Due to lack of space, we do not discuss these aspects in detail. See, for example, Larson and Tobey (1994) for the role of uncertainty in global climate policy.

reduction.[9]

A partial cooperative solution emerges not only when the use of a quota instrument is an exogenously given constraint. The same result is derived by Finus and Rundshagen (1998) in an extended framework where the choice of the internalization instrument is endogenously determined, participation as well as compliance incentives are taken into account, and in which the preferences of the marginal signatory (instead of the median country of the coalition) are decisive for the outcome of the agreement. Moreover, in most cases the negotiating governments agree on a uniform quota and not on an emission tax although the latter is (due to its cost-effectiveness property) preferable from a global perspective. However, from the perspective of the country that is the 'bottleneck' in the negotiations and decisive for the terms of the agreement — the country with the lowest environmental preferences — the quota is superior to the tax. In the quota regime, all countries carry the same abatement burden in relation to their perceived abatement benefits, whereas under the tax regime the lower the environmental preferences, the higher the relative burden.[10] This corresponds to an analysis of Kverndokk (1993) suggesting that the poorest countries in the world would have the highest costs of reducing emissions relative to GDP when carbon emissions are allocated cost-effectively. Hence, although uniform quotas restrict the number of participating countries, the use of taxes or emission permits is an even greater disincentive for many countries to sign an international environmental treaty. The quota instrument is likely to be chosen in an environmental treaty, especially when national governments have to compromise on 'the smallest common denominator' and when international side payments are not possible.

Given the multidimensionality of international economic relations, an additional argument exists for not pursuing an environmental policy that would be optimal in a first-best world. This is shown by Mohr (1995) in a general equilibrium framework with overlapping generations where two countries are linked to each other not only by environmental externalities, but also via international debt. Although the countries may agree to implement an international tradable-permit scheme, they will

---

[9]Correspondingly, in the case of only two asymmetric countries, uniform emission reductions have to be set at suboptimal levels for an international environmental agreement to exist at all (Endres 1993).

[10]The relative burden is defined as national abatement benefits compared to their costs. Due to the authors' assumption that countries differ only with respect to abatement benefits but not with respect to costs, under the tax regime all countries will reduce their emissions to identical absolute quantities, irrespective of their abatement benefits. Hence, countries with lower environmental preferences will bear a relatively higher burden in terms of utility.

not necessarily trade emission permits in quantities such that marginal abatement costs are equalized across countries. This is the case if the debt steady state is constrained by country sovereignty, that is, if the loans are not as high as they were with full international enforcement of debt treaties. Yet, if the debtor country is a net exporter of emission permits, selling permits functions as a substitute for the procurement of capital by international debts. Consequently, it may be in the interest of the creditor country to reduce its demand for emission permits below the cost-effective level, thereby ensuring that the supply of capital in the debtor country does not exceed the level where debts are not settled. This is a second-best argument: as another market (the market for debt) is imperfect with respect to the enforcement of contracts on the international level, it is not necessarily optimal to select the first-best instrument for the environmental problem. Market-based internalization instruments not only may be inferior with respect to the incentives they provide for environmental cooperation, but also may increase the imperfections in other markets such as international debt.[11]

In Section 3.4 it was seen that the use of quotas in international environmental agreements may give rise to substantial cost-inefficiencies as countries generally differ with respect to many characteristics and thereby in marginal abatement costs. In order to avoid the cost-inefficiencies of uniform solutions to some extent, certain governments have pushed for at least a limited possibility of trading emission rights internationally. The most prominent example of this is the concept of 'activities implemented jointly' that was put down in the Framework Convention on Climate Change. It stipulates that two (or more) parties to the convention have the right to implement emission abatement measures jointly if they find it in their interest. According to this provision, contracting parties with relatively high marginal abatement costs can fulfill (part of) their abatement obligations by purchasing abatement activities in countries with low marginal abatement costs. The realized abatement quantities in the other country are at least partially credited to the donor country. Purchasing abatements implicitly introduces international transfer payments and is equivalent to trading emission rights: under ideal conditions, the combination of a quota agreement and 'joint implementation' (JI) would lead to international cost-effectiveness. It thus corresponds to the approach of Baumol/Oates of first setting a global environmental standard and then selecting a cost-minimzing instrument to achieve this target. Even if the scope for JI projects is

---

[11] However, Mohr (1995) shows that the introduction of cross-default clauses allows for a full strategic stabilization of the permit scheme. See Section 4.4 for a discussion of this strategy.

restricted and search and monitoring costs are high, some authors (for example, Bohm 1994) regard it as a first step towards a future system of tradable emission permits. Under ideal conditions with perfect foresight and in the absence of transaction costs, there is economically no difference between joint implementation and emission permit trading. Yet the issue of incentive compatibility is crucial in the context of joint implementation as well. It remains unclear why there should be incentives for JI projects while it was not possible to sign a contract including a market-based internalization instrument in the first place. So far, this aspect has not been addressed sufficiently in the discussion on the superiority of joint implementation.

The comparison of emission taxes and tradable emission permits in Section 3.4 has made it clear that both instruments possess similar characteristics with respect to cooperation incentives. The differences between market-based internalization instruments rather lie in institutional aspects. If there are no restrictions on the way tax revenue or initial permits can be allocated to individual countries, the allocation rule may be designed to support the broad and lasting participation of countries which would otherwise abstain from cooperation. This is possible even if the international assignment of emission permits has to be based on simple rules, such as status quo emissions ('grandfathering'), cumulated historic emissions, current GDP or national population size. The same holds for rules that determine the redistribution of tax revenue to the cooperating countries. Each of the two rules distributes the gains from environmental cooperation in favor of specific countries. Uniform percentage reductions, the grandfathering of permits or an assignment according to current GDP generally favor industrialized countries, whereas population size (equal per-capita emission rights) or cumulated historic emissions (that is, giving developing countries the right to 'catch up') as a base would benefit the developing countries, in particular because of the substantial subsequent trade of permits between industrialized and developing countries.[12] One way of increasing the acceptability of a tradable permits solution could be to mix different allocation rules by constructing a weighted average of different criteria, the weights being adjusted over time. A formula for such an allocation rule is

$$Q_k = Q \left(w_H \Gamma_{t_0,H,k} + w_Y \Gamma_{t_0,Y,k} + w_P \Gamma_{t_0,P,k} \right) \tag{4.1}$$

where k represents the country in question, Q_k is the emission quota and Q the global emissions target, subscripts H, Y and P refer to status quo

---

[12] A study by Kverndokk (1993) estimates payments to the developing countries of 6 per cent of GDP from the USA and and 3 per cent of GDP from the other OECD countries in the year 2000.

emissions, GDP and population, respectively; parameters w_i refer to the weight assigned to each rule ($w_H + w_Y + w_P = 1$); Γ represents the country's share in the relevant global aggregate; and subscript t_0 refers to the base year (Zhang and Folmer 1995, p. 139). In order to reconcile the differing interests of industrialized and developing countries, Pearce (1990) proposes starting out with a grandfathering regime and then changing emission entitlements over time in such a way that rising permits of developing countries less than offset declining permits of industrialized countries. Cline (1992a) expects that an agreement which shifts the weights of such a rule over time towards the population rule would have the best chance of broad and lasting support. All of the above proposals redistribute the gains from environmental cooperation by granting compensation to certain countries. In the preceding discussion on internalization instruments, this option had been ruled out since it constitutes an instrument which provides cooperation incentives of its own and is treated separately in Section 4.4 in more detail.

The discussion of the utilization of market-based as well as command-and-control instruments in international environmental agreements has shown that uniform solutions often generate greater incentives for international environmental cooperation. It has also elucidated that the distributional effects of potential internalization instruments in international environmental policy become predominant, once international lump-sum taxes and transfers are not (or only to a limited extent) possible. Without these first-best instruments, globally efficient cooperative solutions will not be accepted by countries which are worse off under cooperation. With distortionary international transfers, the optimal cooperative solution will be second best. In general, suggestions on the choice of internalization instruments have in common that they focus on stimulating the incentives to participate in an environmental agreement and ignore the incentives to comply with the obligations each party has committed to in a treaty.[13] In order to cope with this time-consistency problem, additional instruments are required. One way of enlarging the strategy space of governments is to extend the time horizon of environmental policy, that is, by assuming repeated decisions on pollution abatement. If breaching an environmental treaty can be sanctioned, for example, through lower cooperative abatements in future periods, this 'shadow of the future' is likely to make countries comply with their obligations more carefully. Creating cooperation incentives by sanctioning non-cooperative behavior in future periods is discussed in the subsequent

---

[13]See Laffont and Tirole (1996) for an analysis of the impact of spot and future markets for tradable pollution permits on the potential polluters' compliance and investment decisions.

section.

4.3   Internal Stabilization

Cooperating countries can exploit the fact that environmental policy measures are taken repeatedly. They can agree to sanction unilateral non-compliance with less ambitious internalization efforts in future periods. This behavior of contract partners makes an opportunistic government weigh the gains from breaching the agreement against the future losses from being sanctioned. The purpose of such a strategy is to provide sufficient incentives for complying with a treaty in cases when a supranational enforcement authority does not exist and other stabilization instruments are not available. Since incentives for cooperation are provided exclusively in terms of abatement activities — which are the core element of an environmental treaty — we refer to this strategy as 'internal stabilization' (Heister et al. 1995). Internal stabilization corresponds to the principle of 'reciprocity' in international law. In order to represent an effective threat, the reactions of observant parties to a breach of the treaty have to be both predictable and credible.

Dynamic games of international pollution control can be divided into models where identical decision problems are repeated (supergames) and models in which not only current emissions matter, but also where depositions accumulate over time (*stock externalities*). With stock pollutants, differential game theory is principally the appropriate theoretical framework. In dynamic games of this type, *open-loop* and *closed-loop* (or *feedback*) strategies are distinguished. With open-loop strategies, countries establish an abatement policy that is pursued for ever because governments expect no new information on the other countries' actions and the aggregate emission level. With closed-loop strategies, countries expect to receive new information as time passes and reformulate their policy on the basis of current information. For both types of strategy it can be shown that the globally efficient (full cooperative) allocation of abatements can be implemented as a subgame perfect Nash equilibrium as long as future pay-offs are not discounted too strongly.[14] The strategies prescribe that a country — when observing emission levels that do not correspond to broad cooperation — terminates its own cooperation. They are thus very similar to trigger strategies in repeated (super)games. In the long run, the periodic emissions in the cooperative and in the open-loop non-cooperative equilibrium are the same. However, the convergence towards the efficient level is faster with coop-

---

[14]See, for example, Dockner and Long (1993) or Mäler (1991).

erative strategies, and they result in a lower stock of externalities (see Mäler 1991).[15]

Decisions on the provision of an international environmental good often resemble a repeated *prisoner's dilemma* type of game.[16] As in differential games (see above), global efficiency can be sustained as a cooperative equilibrium as long as the future is not discounted too strongly. This holds for the infinitely repeated prisoner's dilemma (Folk theorem), but under certain conditions and for a subset of rounds also for the finitely repeated prisoner's dilemma (Kreps et al. 1982; Radner 1908).[17] In both cases, cooperation is sustained by the threat to abort cooperation if one party does not stick to the cooperative strategy. One can distinguish different strategies according to how severe the sanctions are.

The most drastic form of internal stabilization is the *trigger* or *grim* strategy. It implies a return to non-cooperation once and for all if one country defects unilaterally. This is a very strong punishment which effectively deters free-riding behavior, but only as long as renegotiations are ruled out. By contrast, if countries can renegotiate a new agreement after the breakdown of the initial one, announcing a grim strategy is not a credible threat because the sanctioning countries would obviously harm themselves if they returned to a definite state of non-cooperation. In addition, it may be technically impossible or economically too costly to return to non-cooperative emission levels. Hence, to be of practical use, trigger strategies must be both effective and credible.

Credibility may require that countries agree to *re-optimize* their cooperative abatement efforts after a breach of the international environmental treaty. The basic mechanism of this strategy is illustrated by Barrett (1994) for both a one-shot and an infinitely repeated game.[18] In his model, N identical countries suffer from a global environmental bad. A subset of cooperating countries is assumed to act as a Stackelberg leader and to maximize their joint net benefits of abatements. As joint net benefits depend on the size of the coalition, cooperative abate-

---

[15]The subsequent exposition concentrates on models with flow pollutants. For the analysis of transboundary stock pollutants, see, for example, Ploeg and de Zeeuw (1991, 1992), Ploeg and Lighthart (1994), Hoel (1992a) or Kverndokk (1994).

[16]For a different view, see Heal (1994) who considers technological spillovers and fixed costs of abatement policies which have reinforcing effects on the formation of a *minimum critical coalition* in an international environmental agreement. The above assumptions imply a coordination problem in addition to the free-rider problem.

[17]See Fudenberg and Maskin (1986) for cooperation in the infinitely repeated prisoner's dilemma with incomplete information.

[18]The one-shot game also mirrors a dynamic structure of the decision problem, but assumes, for the sake of simplicity, that actions are immediately followed by reactions.

ments are readjusted when a country joins or leaves the coalition. A unilateral breach of the agreement by a single country induces a lower level of cooperative abatements and has a sanctioning effect on the disloyal country. This sanction is credible because it maximizes the coalition's welfare. Joining the coalition is individually profitable because a new member benefits from the additional abatements of the other cooperating countries. On the other hand, a new member increases the incentive to take a free ride on the cooperative abatements of other coalition members and to leave the agreement. Consequently, the number of countries that cooperate remains limited. Barrett shows that a coalition of more than three countries is stable only when marginal abatement benefits decrease with global abatement quantities, implying non-orthogonal best-response functions. In general, a stable coalition with many countries emerges only if the difference in global net benefits between full cooperation and the non-cooperative Nash equilibrium is small, that is, if there is not much to gain from cooperation. If there are large potential gains from cooperation, only very small coalitions of a maximum of three countries are stable, irrespective of the total number of countries involved in the externality.[19] Aside from the inability of the re-optimization strategy to support a full cooperative solution, the model cannot predict which of the N countries cooperate and which do not.[20] Moreover, as the defecting country always gains if another country enters and total abatement activities do not change, an effective re-optimization strategy requires that the coalition refuses the entry of new members and credibly commits to a suboptimal size. The limited ability of this stabilization strategy to secure gains from stable environmental cooperation also remains in the context of a supergame (that is, infinite repitions of an identical game), using renegotiation proofness as a stability concept (Barrett 1994). Although the full cooperative outcome can, for sufficiently small discount rates, be sustained as a subgame perfect equilibrium of the infinitely repeated game, the sanctions that guarantee incentive compatibility may be vulnerable to renegotiation.

A stabilization strategy that avoids the incentive to renegotiate is *modified tit-for-tat*. Under this strategy, countries cooperate until one of them defects. Then the remaining countries exclude the defecting country and readjust their emissions. In addition, they do not readmit the

---

[19] Coalition stability is defined here using the concept of D'Aspremont and Gabszewicz (1986) and Donsimoni et al. (1986) for cartel stability in an oligopoly. In the oligopoly literature, similar results are derived with respect to coalition size.

[20] Of course, this is irrelevant in the case of completely homogeneous countries. The coordination problem can be resolved by introducing asymmetries, for example, with regard to the relative bargaining positions of the countries (see, for example, Barrett 1997a and Chapter 5 of this volume).

defecting country before it has paid damages or has made a front-end abatement concession. The latter serves to compensate the countries in the coalition for the losses they incur by executing the punishment, thereby making the threat of its execution credible. The defecting country will pass under the yoke if it can expect sufficiently high gains in the future after all countries have returned to environmental cooperation. Hence, the above punishment strategy eliminates the gains from non-compliance without inducing the observant parties to renegotiate with the defecting government. This kind of 'stick–carrot' strategy is used by Finus and Rundshagen (1998) in a supergame where asymmetric countries form a coalition to cooperate on abatement efforts that constitute a global public bad.[21] It is shown that international environmental agreements stabilized in this way can reap only small aggregate gains from cooperation if the externality problem is most severe, that is, if many countries suffer from transboundary pollution and if abatement is relatively costly compared to perceived environmental damages. In these cases, only small subcoalitions prove to be stable.

Black et al. (1993) analyse a *minimum ratification clause* as an instrument to create incentives for environmental cooperation. It prescribes that the environmental convention does not come into force until a specified number of countries has ratified it.[22] In this case a rational government must take into account not only the effects its participation or abstention will have on the terms of the agreement, but also the possibility that there may be no cooperation at all if it does not join the agreement. Due to the assumption of incomplete information on the net benefits of environmental protection, it is risky to abstain from the uncertain outcome of the ratification process. This risk of treaty failure must be balanced against the expected free-rider benefits. Although the minimum ratification clause provides for participation incentives, it hinges on the assumption that countries do not renegotiate after failing to reach a minimum number of signatories. Moreover, by assuming that the signatories remain committed to their obligations after the convention has come into force, the problem of reduced compliance incentives is disregarded. In fact, the more successful the minimum ratification clause is in making a large number of countries sign the agreement, the greater are the incentives to breach it afterwards. Thus, such clauses generate a conflict between the provision of participation and compliance incentives.

---

[21] The authors call the stability concept of (weak) renegotiation proofness that they apply and extend to more than two countries 'weak coalition proofness'.

[22] As other forms of 'internal stabilization', minimum ratification clauses make national abatement efforts contingent on the cooperative behavior of other countries. The distinctive feature of such clauses is that they represent a sanction for non-cooperation even before the treaty has come into force.

To summarize, internal stabilization strategies are apt to generate participation and compliance incentives for international environmental cooperation, but only to a limited extent. Although it is easier to provide cooperation incentives when environmental policy decisions are taken under the 'shadow of the future', the requirements for successful sanction strategies are strict and often not fulfilled under real-world conditions. The weight that is put on future benefits — expressed by the discount rate — is crucial for all internal stabilization strategies. The higher the discount rate on national welfare in future periods, the less effective is a stabilization through retaliation in terms of lower future abatement efforts. Imperfect observability of the countries' real internalization efforts and time-lags in the implementation of sanctions are detrimental to internal stabilization as well. Finally, retaliation by adjusting emissions to arbitrary levels may be technically impossible or economically too expensive. New and 'greener' technologies that have been developed and adopted in the course of international environmental cooperation may not be reversed easily.[23] Hence, international environmental agreements have to rely on additional stabilization instruments. These are discussed in the next section.

4.4   External Stabilization

Instruments for an external stabilization of international environmental agreements modify the pay-offs of the players in ways other than pollution reductions themselves. They may be used to provide incentives for compliance as well as for participation and can be implemented in various ways. The two basic methods of external stabilization are transfers and sanctions which are stipulated in an environmental convention and executed according to its terms. Both instruments enhance the incentives for cooperation, but in different ways. While sanctions reduce the individual gains from breaching an agreement, transfers redistribute the gains from cooperation in a way that increases cooperation incentives for certain critical countries. Correspondingly, in an incentive compatible agreement transfers will always be executed, whereas sanctions never will (provided that there are no unforeseen changes to exogenous circumstances). Hence, transfers and sanctions are basically dual approaches to creating incentives for cooperation: an agreed-upon transfer not given to a country because of its non-cooperation represents a sanction for defecting behavior.

---

[23]See, for example, Althammer and Buchholz (1993, p. 294) or Carraro and Siniscalco (1993, fn. 3) for this objection.

We start the discussion of external stabilization instruments with a survey of contributions that analyse the general profitability of compensation schemes (Subsection 4.4.1). Subsequently, various forms of transfers and other external stabilization instruments are presented. As will become clear, a strict distinction is often not possible. Nevertheless, we devote separate subsections to 'issue linkage' (Subsection 4.4.2) and trade sanctions (Subsection 4.4.3) because these instruments are discussed the most in the literature. The section concludes with an evaluation of external stabilization of international environmental agreements (Subsection 4.4.4).

4.4.1 Transfers

International compensations are an important instrument in international environmental cooperation. Their basic purpose is to redistribute the gains and burdens from a cooperative solution in a way that makes it attractive to as many countries as possible to join an environmental agreement. In an early contribution, Markusen (1975a) has shown that, in the face of a transboundary environmental externality, international transfers are in general a necessary and sufficient condition for a cooperative solution that yields a Pareto-optimal allocation of world resources. In contrast, without (or with only limited) transfer payments, international environmental agreements will generally not result in global efficiency, even if one assumes that countries can make binding commitments. The reason is that, in these cases, the cooperative solution depends on the characteristics of the countries involved in transboundary pollution such as their initial endowments with resources. The only way to achieve broad cooperation without additional compensations, then, is the recourse to a less ambitious treaty that does not correspond to the full cooperative solution (see Section 4.2). In other words, the aspects of efficiency and distribution cannot be treated separately and the *burden sharing* between cooperating countries becomes a crucial issue of negotiations.

The question of how to share the burdens from an environmental treaty has been analysed extensively in the framework of cooperative game theory, that is, under the assumption that national governments can make binding commitments. The focus of these contributions is how to attract — by appropriate transfer and burden-sharing schemes — the participation of new members to an existing coalition in order to generate additional gains from environmental cooperation. The analysed regimes often base the burden sharing on the relative intensities of the countries' environmental preferences. In this respect, the proposed cooperative solutions are similar to the 'Lindahl prices' of pure public goods in a

Lindahl equilibrium. Eyckmans (1997), for example, analyses a *proportional cost-sharing* mechanism that distributes the total costs of emission reductions in proportion to the participants' marginal willingness to pay for the international environmental good. The proposed mechanism is shown to have the following properties. First, it yields an efficient (that is, cost-effective) allocation of abatements. Second, its proportionality is widely accepted as a form of fairness in international negotiations. It reflects the idea that countries which benefit more from environmental quality should bear a larger share of the burden. Third, proportional cost sharing can be implemented as a Nash equilibrium under complete information with the help of a simple tax/subsidy mechanism.[24]

The adoption of a burden-sharing scheme is a general problem when the cooperating countries are heterogeneous. As burden sharing will be anticipated by governments that are considering joining a coalition, different cooperative solutions may emerge depending on the adopted scheme. In a numerical simulation analysis calibrated to a data set with five world regions, Botteon and Carraro (1997) compare the outcome of negotiations under burden sharing based on the Nash bargaining solution with the one based on Shapley values.[25] According to the simulations, the latter concept seems to be preferable in an agreement that uses transfers to expand a coalition. The reason is that burden sharing according to the Shapley value provides cooperating countries with a more even distribution of the gains from cooperation. This observation underlines the importance of distributional aspects in comparison with efficiency aspects in international environmental negotiations, as has already been emphasized in Section 4.2. The policy implications of this analysis remain somewhat unclear, though, as the adopted burden-sharing rule depends on the relative bargaining power of the governments which have only their national welfare position in mind when negotiating an agreement.

The above contributions have in common that they apply cooperative game theory to the problem of coordinating environmental policies. Although the results derived in this framework certainly provide valuable insights into potential cooperative solutions, the players are taken to be able to engage in binding commitments, an assumption that does not correspond to the lack of enforcement on the international level. On the other hand, the non-existence of a supranational enforcement authority does not imply the absence of any institutional framework at

---

[24] See also Chander and Tulkens (1995, 1997) and Germain et al. (1997) for transfer schemes in cooperative games of international pollution control.

[25] In an analysis of heterogeneous countries, Barrett (1997a) also employs the Shapley value.

the international level. This, however, is implicitly assumed when modeling the strategic interactions of sovereign states as a non-cooperative game. In the latter framework agreements have to be fully self-enforcing and cooperative solutions without transfers or other additional instruments consist of small subcoalitions that achieve only minor welfare gains.[26] In contrast to the extreme assumptions of most models of non-cooperative and cooperative game theory on enforceability, the existence and widespread use of international environmental institutions calls for the introduction of limited forms of enforcement in theoretic models. One way of doing this is by assuming that binding commitments are possible for certain groups of countries (see Carraro and Siniscalco 1993; Hoel 1994), and to analyse the use of side payments within this framework.

Transfers are an important instrument for making countries not only sign, but also comply with an international environmental agreement. This is shown for the case of homogeneous countries by Carraro and Siniscalco (1993) who consider a one-shot abatement game of complete information where cooperating countries induce the accession of additional countries to the coalition by granting self-financed transfers, that is, side payments that are financed out of the former coalition's gains from enlarging the number of cooperating countries. To sustain broader coalitions by means of transfers it is necessary, though, to introduce a minimum degree of commitment into the game. It is assumed that at least some players cannot deviate from the cooperative strategy they have voluntarily agreed upon and it implies that the agreement is not completely self-enforcing.[27] Carraro and Siniscalco (1993) analyse different forms of commitment which — although limited and less demanding than full commitment by all governments — under certain conditions lead to a stable 'grand coalition' (that is, cooperation of all countries). The achievable gains from cooperation depend strongly on what kind of commitment is assumed[28] and on additional assumptions concern-

---

[26] In most cases, coalitions involving more than three countries are not stable. This result is quite robust with regard to different assumptions on countries' welfare functions (see, for example, Barrett 1994; Carraro and Siniscalco 1993; Hoel 1991, 1992b).

[27] In the scenario of identical countries the new, enlarged coalition would otherwise not be stable as paying transfers reduces the interest of the donor countries in the agreement.

[28] For example, if the group of countries that are pre-committed to cooperation is endogenously determined, the anticipation of receiving transfers reduces the incentive to sign an IEA and to commit to cooperation. In a model of identical countries where social norms influence a national government's participation decision, Hoel and Schneider (1997) show that total emissions may be even higher with side payments than without.

ing the costs and benefits of pollution abatements. The latter remain undetermined in the above analysis.

Self-financing transfers can reap even greater gains from stable cooperation if the countries involved in the coalition formation process are heterogeneous. In such cases, some countries may not benefit from free-riding, but experience a welfare loss from environmental cooperation. Yet, for a pre-existing coalition, the entry of the latter countries is often profitable because it can help to reach a negotiated environmental standard at lower costs. Side payments are the only way to create cooperation incentives for these low-cost countries and to generate additional gains through cost-effective abatement policies (see Hoel 1994; Kverndokk 1993).[29] Using a model of heterogeneous countries, Petrakis and Xepapadeas (1996) show that even the global first-best optimum is implementable as a cooperative solution through appropriate self-financing transfers to initial 'outsiders'. This result corresponds to the analysis of Carraro and Siniscalco (1993) for the case of identical countries and is possible as long as (i) a subgroup of countries (the donor countries) is committed to cooperation, (ii) this group maximizes global welfare, and (iii) the marginal pollution damages of the recipient countries are not too high. Furthermore, Petrakis and Xepapadeas (1996) develop a mechanism which enforces a cooperative solution even if monitoring is difficult in the sense that information on global emissions is public, but information on national emission quantities is not. With this mechanism every country has an incentive to report its true emissions. In the cooperative equilibrium the reporting of national abatement quantities is not necessary, and this enables countries to evade the measurement and reporting costs that they would have to bear otherwise. 'Cheating' on cooperative abatement efforts is not profitable as it would be sanctioned by a refusal of the side payment and generate additional measurement and reporting costs.

A related instrument to transfers employed in the above manner is the deposition with a third party of securities that are lost for a non-observant country. The deposition of securities without recourse to a third party can be accomplished by exchanging 'hostages' or 'pledges' (see Williamson 1983). Hostages are of value only for the depositing country; pledges are also valuable to the country that can dispose of them if the depositing country breaches the contract. The more

---

[29]Kverndokk (1994) simulates the gains from expanding an existing subcoalition that is committed to a joint carbon emission abatement policy (analogous to the scenario of 'internal commitment' in Carraro and Siniscalco 1993) by compensating joining countries for the losses they incur from reducing their emissions to cooperative levels. Even if cooperation is only partial, the simulations show that substantial gains are attainable.

valuable the securities are, the higher are the cooperation gains that can be secured. The exclusive purpose of deposits is to enable credible commitments. In contrast, transfers are paid to create cooperation incentives and may be used additionally to secure compliance. If an environmental agreement includes side payments and a trustee is available, it may thus be easier to agree on depositing these transfers instead of additional securities. The deposition of securities or transfers at an international agency can generate additional compliance incentives if the agreement provides that the retained deposits of defaulting countries are used to compensate observant countries for their costs of additionally sanctioning a non-compliant country, thereby making these additional sanctions credible (Heister et al. 1995, p. 38).

We now turn to the various ways in which welfare transfers between countries are conceivable.[30] The most straightforward form are monetary transfers either flowing directly from a donor to a recipient country or being granted by a common fund of the donor countries. Unfortunately, the fungible character of cash creates incentives for opportunistic behavior if a strict appropriation of compensation payments for their purpose cannot be guaranteed. The risk that received monetary transfers are not used for the purpose they were intended is also given in the context of an agreement on internationally tradable carbon emission permits (see Mohr 1991, 1995). A breach of the contract in the case of an international permit market may occur if a (developing) country sells its excess permits and uses the revenue to boost its economic growth, thereby expanding CO_2 emissions as well. Once the country has sold its excess permits, it loses interest in complying with the agreement and may start to emit without possessing the corresponding permits. Such an opportunistic country may even decide to borrow against future income from (leased) permits and breach the contract later. A similar risk of defection is given in agreements that presently provide side payments to certain countries in advance and grant them a grace period of emission abatement obligations afterwards, as is the case in the Montreal Protocol on substances that deplete the ozone layer.

In order to circumvent potential time-consistency problems arising from the fungible character of monetary transfers, national governments may resort to *in-kind* or earmarked transfers. These cannot be used for purposes other than the one they are granted for without incurring re-trading costs. If these costs cover the value of the in-kind transfer completely, the incentive for opportunistic behavior is entirely eliminated. Hence, in-kind transfers are a superior instrument in situations where

---

[30]The contributions discussed so far treat side payments as *utility* or *welfare* transfers and abstract from the way in which they are given.

institutional arrangements which rule out the abuse of side payments are not available (see Stähler 1992). *Joint implementation* stipulated in the Framework Convention on Climate Change makes use of this concept, as it earmarks side payments for the replacement of 'dirty' by 'clean' energy technologies abroad. The same characteristic of an in-kind transfer possesses compensations given to the development and use of environmentally friendly, irreversible technologies that do not allow for an increase in emissions after the new technology has been implemented. By paying for the introduction of a 'clean' but capital-intensive technology, for example, a switch back to an old and cheap 'dirty' one will become prohibitively expensive. This ratchet effect secures compliant behavior of recipient countries. Stähler (1993) shows that transfers for 'irreversible' abatement technologies provide commitment options which render these technologies superior even if they are more costly than alternative reversible technologies. This form of transfer is the more attractive, the less the recipient country takes the future impact of the irreversibility into account. A low valuation of the future by the recipient favors the donor because it decreases the component of the transfer that compensates the recipient for being locked into an irreversible technology.

4.4.2   Issue Linkage

The linkage of different and otherwise independent issues in international negotiations is another way of engaging in international compensations. In a second-best world where monetary transfers between countries are excluded, issue linkage may work as a substitute and enables cooperative solutions where isolated agreements would not emerge.[31] Concessions in other policy fields that are on the agenda at international negotiations, for example, other international environmental problems, trade policy, international debt, development assistance or the membership in a military alliance, may alter the pay-off structure of the countries in a way that makes the participation in an international environmental agreement profitable. Issue linkage can thus be regarded as an implicit transfer between countries. Accordingly, the withdrawal of existing international privileges can be used as a sanction against non-compliance.

Cesar and de Zeeuw (1996) analyse issue linkage involving two different reciprocal environmental externalities within a dynamic bi-matrix game. For each of the two environmental problems, both countries are simultaneously polluters and victims of pollution. National costs and benefits of abatement efforts, though, are distributed asymmetrically

---

[31] For the merits of issue linkage from a global point of view and general conditions under which Pareto optimality emerges, see Carraro and Siniscalco (1995).

across countries so that one country is worse off under isolated cooperation in comparison to mutual non-cooperation without additional compensations. Depending on the pay-off structure, the initial situation can
be characterized either as an asymmetric 'prisoner's dilemma' or as a
'suasion game'. In the former game both countries have an interest in the
negotiated issue whereas, in the latter, only one country is interested.[32]
For both games, cooperation can be sustained if the games are infinitely
repeated and the discount rates are small enough. However, without side
payments, the cooperative equilibrium will not support global efficiency.
Assuming a second game that represents the exact mirror image of the
game described above, Cesar and de Zeeuw (1996) show that, by linking the two offsetting games, the social optimum can be sustained with
renegotiation-proof trigger strategies where non-compliance of a country
in one agreement can be credibly punished by suspension of cooperation
on the other issue.

Folmer et al. (1993) illustrate the linkage of an environmental issue
with a non-environmental one within an *interconnected game*. They
consider an example with two repeated prisoner's dilemma games: a pollution game with a unidirectional transboundary externality and a trade
game. It is shown that playing the two games independently results in
cooperation only if (i) the games are repeated infinitely, (ii) the discount
factor is not too low so that trigger strategies are successful and (iii) if one
allows for side payments. The resulting aggregate pay-off is lower than
in the case where the two games are strategically linked to each other.
The model demonstrates that issue linkage is especially attractive when
countries are strongly asymmetric with respect to their perceived damage from transboundary pollution and when monetary transfers are not
available. This is most obvious for the case of a unilateral externality,
a scenario that naturally calls for a compensation payment. Issue linkage in this model is optimal even if international transfers are feasible.
The superiority of issue linkage in comparison with a cooperative solution with financial transfers, however, hinges crucially on the assumption
that offering a transfer implies a loss in terms of 'being labeled as a weak
negotiator', that is, damage in reputation.

Carraro and Siniscalco (1997) analyse the linkage of negotiations on
an environmental agreement and on technological cooperation by identical countries. In their model, environmental coalitions are profitable
but unstable, whereas coalitions that cooperate on research and devel-

---

[32] In the two-player suasion game, the pay-off structure is such that non-cooperative
behavior is the dominant strategy for one player, whereas 'cooperation' is dominant
for the other. Thus, in contrast to the prisoner's dilemma, in the non-cooperative
Nash equilibrium of the suasion game, one player behaves cooperatively and the other
does not.

opment (R&D) are both profitable and stable. Linking the two issues increases the number of countries that participate in a stable environmental coalition because the gains from R&D cooperation offset the environmental free-riding incentives. This result is shown for a specific functional form of the pay-off of each country and firm. The decision process consists of three stages. In the first stage, individual countries decide whether to participate in the linked agreement and a stable coalition is formed. In the second stage, optimal abatement levels of cooperating and non-cooperating countries are determined, and, in the last stage, the firms in all countries choose their profit-maximizing output levels and expenditures on R&D. Technological spillovers are modeled as an excludable positive externality between firms in different countries.[33] It is assumed that the degree of innovation spillovers is always larger between countries belonging to the coalition than between outsiders. This assumption is debatable because countries may cooperate on R&D activities independently from environmental cooperation. It is not clear why the latter spillovers should be smaller, at least as long as research activities are not connected in some specific manner with environmental policy. For example, if there are economies of scale in R&D cooperation, these may be realized not only by a coalition that simultaneously cooperates on environmental protection, but also by a sufficiently large coalition of outsider countries. In general, issue linkage is of greater relevance when countries are asymmetric, in which case they have differing interests in the various topics dealt with in international negotiations. Issue linkage in most cases is a bargain on concessions in different policy fields between countries which leads to some kind of 'package deal'.

Mohr and Thomas (1998) analyse the prospects of issue linkage between international debt contracts and environmental treaties in the presence of uncertainty.[34] In their model, they consider the simultaneous existence of an international environmental agreement between a state and a multilateral (or foreign) environmental agency and an existing international debt contract between the same state and a foreign lender, both of them burdened by lack of enforcement. The compliance problem in environmental agreements corresponds to the repayment risk for lenders in international loan contracts and the expropriation risk for direct investments. Uncertainty is given through an exogenous ran-

---

[33]The approach resembles the idea put forward most prominently by Olson (1965) to make access to an excludable *club good* dependent on the individuals' contributions to the supply of a non-excludable public good. For instance, in the case of labor unions, membership is rewarded with extra benefits that are excludable to non-members.

[34]See Mohr (1995) for the strategic linkage of international debt and pollution permit trade in the absence of uncertainties.

dom cost to the country of violating any of the two contracts. It is shown that compliance with both of the two contracts can be guaranteed by a 'cross-default' contract between the environmental agency and the lender so that the government cannot discriminate between complying with the debt and the environmental treaty. Cross-default clauses are often used to stabilize international debt relations. Instead of being a contract between several creditors, the idea here is to pool risks between parties that have different relations with the sovereign. The pooling of sovereignty risks additionally creates incentives to engage in 'debt-for-nature swaps' that would otherwise not exist.[35] Induced swaps provide additional gains for the agency and the lender so that both may accept some loss in terms of higher risk from the cross-default contract. However, several limitations exist with respect to the pooling of sovereignty risks.[36] First, both the creditors and the environmental agency must have an incentive to agree on pooling compliance risks. This is given in some but not all constellations where the respective compliance risks are not too different and not too high. Second, the effect of the cross-default contract on a country's welfare position is indeterminate. Thus, the environmental treaty may have to include a clause which allows the pooling of sovereignty risks even without the consent of the sovereign. Finally, successful risk pooling requires the execution of the cross-default clause itself to be incentive compatible *ex post*. If the compliance risk was the same for all kinds of contracts, the risk pooling strategy would not be effective. Yet, in many cases it may be possible to protect cross-default clauses from the compliance problem if the parties contract under their national law, because the latter is fully enforceable. The advantage of stabilizing environmental treaties in the above manner is that the compliance problem governments face is delegated to the private sector. In contrast to national governments, private firms or institutions are able to engage in binding commitments because they are subject to national law enforcement.[37]

4.4.3 Trade Sanctions

The discussion of cross-default clauses has illustrated that the threat to withdraw some existing preference or to terminate cooperation in another policy field is a special form of issue linkage. The difference

---

[35] A debt-for-nature swap is a trade where a reduction in a country's debt is granted in exchange for undertaking additional environmental policy measures.

[36] See Kirchgässner and Mohr (1996, sect. 4.2), on problems of cross-default clauses.

[37] Of course, this requires the existence of an international agency or other independent party to engage in cross-default contracts.

to the previous approaches is that they represent a sanction instead of a transfer (in terms of national welfare). The most prominent and widely discussed form of sanctions are trade restrictions intended to be a retaliation against non-cooperative behavior on the international level. Like cross-default clauses, they are often stipulated in an environmental treaty so that they can be properly anticipated.[38]

The potential of trade sanctions as a measure to stabilize environmental cooperation is analysed by Barrett (1997b) in a partial equilibrium model with homogeneous countries and intra-industry trade. It is assumed that imperfectly competitive firms produce an identical output but segment their markets. Trade sanctions are used to enforce the cooperative supply of a global public environmental good. The threat to exclude from trade countries that do not cooperate on international pollution control is credible because the sanctioning countries gain from executing the sanction via increased firm profits. The decisions of firms and governments are modeled in a game of several stages. First, governments decide whether the environmental treaty should employ trade sanctions and, if so, under what conditions. Then, countries simultaneously choose to become a signatory or non-signatory of the treaty. In the third and fourth stages, signatories and non-signatories determine their abatement standards, respectively. In the final stage, firms choose their segmented outputs according to Cournot–Nash behavior. Governments that do not cooperate take the abatement standards of other countries as given, whereby cooperating countries are assumed to maximize their collective welfare.[39] Using numerical simulations for agreements with and without trade sanctions, it is shown that, in many (but not all) cases, an agreement with trade sanctions is preferred and that the social optimum can even be sustained. The latter outcome additionally requires the introduction of a minimum participation level to secure coordination on the full cooperative solution. Unfortunately, an intuitive explanation is not given on how the execution of trade sanctions is also made incentive compatible *ex post*, once a violation of the agreement by a single country has occurred. Moreover, the results of the analysis need to be considered carefully due to the specific set-up.

Global environmental policy will also typically be linked to international trade policy without the above stabilization strategy.[40] One rea-

---

[38]The general influence of uncertainty and reputation on the effectiveness of sanctions as a stabilization device is discussed by Heister et al. (1995).

[39]This is not problematic since countries are assumed to be identical and the question of how to distribute the gains from cooperation does not arise.

[40]See Kirchgässner and Mohr (1996) for a general discussion of the effectiveness, efficiency and credibility of trade restrictions to promote international environmental policy.

son for this is the 'leakage' phenomenon which cooperating countries can try to curb by imposing appropriate tax and tariff adjustments.[41] Another reason is problems of implementing regulatory measures in cooperating countries where the externality-generating activity takes place. For example, implementation problems are often caused by administrative difficulties or lack of enforcement in developing countries. Trade policy measures then can principally serve as a second-best instrument for international pollution control. Of course, trade restrictions often also serve protectionist purposes. Moreover, the causes for non-compliance sometimes do not lie in deliberate, but rather in endemic and erratic decisions. Multilateral trading rules should therefore not permit the parties to an (environmental) agreement to impose arbitrary trade restrictions. On the other hand, it can be argued that the political support for trade restrictions due to national protectionist interests can be an advantage in the sense that it increases the credibility of this instrument (see Kirchgässner and Mohr 1996, pp. 210–13).

4.4.4 Evaluation

In sum, the above discussion shows that issue linkage can contribute substantially to the achievement of mutual gains from environmental cooperation. This is especially the case when the welfare-improving removal of trade restrictions is used as a carrot to make countries participate in and comply with international environmental agreements. The general advantage of linking different policy issues consists in its ability to provide participation and compliance incentives for a package deal in cases where isolated agreements would not be signed or would not be stable. On the other hand, linking previously unrelated topics in international negotiations may go along with substantial negotiation and transaction costs. For example, a complication arises when the issues to be linked in an international environmental agreement are already regulated by international law as in the case of trade policy and the rules of the World Trade Organization. In addition, the strategy to substitute many isolated compliance risks with only a few bundled risks may create the danger of a deep crisis in international politics, once a contract violation for whatever (accidental) reason has occurred.

The crucial precondition for the applicability of sanction schemes intended to sustain international environmental cooperation is that they are credible. After a unilateral breach of an environmental convention it must not be rational for the observant parties to continue cooperation with the defecting country. Given that, in most cases, sanctions

---

[41] See Section 4.5 for a sketch of this problem.

will be costly for the punishing country as well, it is not an easy task to fulfill the credibility requirement. This is one major aspect in which transfers differ from sanctions. Self-financing transfers are credible by definition.[42] The basic advantage of external stabilization by transfers is that it allows for a separation of national abatement efforts from related economic burdens. Thereby, larger and stable coalitions with a more efficient distribution of abatement activities across countries are attainable, resulting in a higher degree of internalization.

Even if feasible, transfers also have a number of limitations for the stabilization of international environmental agreements. Side payments may give rise to inefficiencies in so far as they are given by downstream countries to bribe polluting countries to internalize these externalities. For, in this case, they imply the application of the *victim pays principle* rather than the *polluter pays principle*.[43] Although the distribution of property rights makes no difference for global efficiency in a static framework, the polluter pays principle is preferable from a dynamic perspective because it creates appropriate incentives for innovations in abatement technologies (see, for example, Mäler 1990, p. 82). It is true that the polluter pays principle has been adopted by various agreements for domestic implementation by national environmental policy, but its application on the international level is unrealistic given the status quo in which each sovereign state claims the right to pollute for itself. Moreover, countries that are less concerned with environmental quality and thus potential recipients of side payments may reduce their own abatement efforts below non-cooperative levels or even stop abatement altogether if the cooperative measures they are compensated for are sufficient to satisfy their own lower preferences. In such cases, strategic behavior will lead to a *crowding out* of cooperative and non-cooperative abatement efforts (Mäler 1990, p. 99). Especially when abatement technologies are politically chosen, it is difficult to determine the hypothetical scenario that would have been realized without any agreement. In many cases, the anticipation of agreements creates incentives for pre-negotiation behavior that is detrimental to environmental protection. For example, it may be a rational strategy for a national government which anticipates an international environmental agreement to choose deliberately a 'dirty' production technology with high per unit costs of emission reduction, even though a cleaner one with lower per unit costs is available

---

[42] Of course, this requires that donor countries can commit themselves credibly on the *execution* of transfers, an aspect often neglected in the literature.

[43] Implicit transfers from polluted to polluting countries by issue linkage imply the application of the victim pays principle, the payment being made in these cases not in cash but in kind.

(Buchholz and Konrad 1994).[44]

To sum up, instruments for the external stabilization of international environmental agreements are able to contribute substantially to their incentive compatibility. This holds for the incentives to sign international treaties on environmental policy as well as for the willingness to comply with their obligations. Moreover, as the strategies discussed in this section are 'external' to the environmental objective of an international treaty, they may, in principle, be applied to stabilize international cooperation in other policy fields as well. It must be emphasized, though, that in most cases even the combined recourse to all of the instruments that have been presented so far will not suffice to attain globally efficient cooperative solutions in international environmental policy. This is not only a consequence of the second-best character of the discussed strategies in comparison with the enforcement of treaties by a supranational authority, but follows mainly because the maximization of joint welfare is generally not compatible with the pursuit of the individual interests of single countries. Given the diverging interests with respect to national pollution control, the governments of some countries may therefore consider taking additional measures which go beyond what can be achieved through international negotiations. The effects of such unilateral and accompanying policy measures by single countries or subcoalitions on the incentives to participate in and comply with environmental agreements are discussed in the following section.

4.5 Unilateral Measures

Cooperation with other countries is only one option of coping with international environmental problems; each government is free to undertake unilateral measures at any time. This may happen in situations without any agreement but also in different stages of negotiating and implementing a treaty if countries take on the role of a pioneer. Two questions arise if unilateral policies are chosen to internalize transboundary environmental spillovers: (i) What are the motivations for single countries to invest in international environmental improvement? (ii) What accompanying measures can be taken by single governments or subcoalitions of countries to protect their unilateral policies against adverse adaptation processes from abroad?

---

[44]Similar problems arise in the presence of asymmetric information between the donor and the recipient countries. Then, countries have an incentive to report on private information in a distorted manner. Thereby, recipient countries try to receive higher transfers, whereas donor countries try to free ride on the side payments of other donor countries.

The first question refers to motivations to engage in international environmental policy other than those presumed in the previous sections. For example, social norms may play an important role not only for the explanation of individual behavior, but also for the decisions of national governments in the diplomatic arena (Hoel and Schneider 1997).[45] Governments may fear to be seen as opportunistic and non-cooperative and therefore sign and stick to an environmental convention, even if free-riding pays in pure economic terms. In political debates, especially, it is often proposed that particular countries should take the lead and adopt measures for the protection of international environmental resources independently from other countries. By 'setting a good example', they may act as a catalyst and initiate similar behavior from other countries because the latter would otherwise damage their reputation by not being 'cooperative' or because they feel a moral obligation. Unilaterally acting countries may win recognition ('moral leadership') in the international arena.[46] In addition, by implementing unilateral policies (for example, through pilot projects or by promoting new and 'greener' technologies), forerunner countries with a strong concern for the environmental good in question may provide valuable information which facilitates negotiations. Of course, the provision of this information creates a public-good dilemma and is subject to free-rider incentives as well. Nevertheless, the marginal environmental benefit of one dollar invested in providing this information may be greater than from investing in domestic abatements.[47]

Under traditional assumptions regarding the actors' preferences, unilateral actions are often detrimental to the welfare position of the country undertaking these actions. Hoel (1991), for example, shows the negative effects of unilateral abatements on a country's own bargaining position in a cooperative Nash bargaining game. Individual countries suffer welfare losses if they unilaterally abate more before or during international environmental negotiations. In fact, from a national perspective governments will try to maximize their gains from international environmental cooperation by strengthening their position in the negotiations. The possibly detrimental effect of pre-negotiation behavior on environmen-

---

[45] For the role of social norms, intrinsic motivations and altruistic behavior, see, for example, Elster (1989), Holländer (1990) or Sugden (1984).

[46] Taking into account such reputational effects often amounts formally to expanding the set of arguments in the utility functions of the governments to include immaterial values as well.

[47] A motivation not aiming at environmental cooperation could be to obtain a competitive advantage in the development of new (and environmentally friendly) technologies. See Porter and van der Linde (1995) for this argument and Palmer, Oates and Portney (1995) for a critique.

tal protection is shown, for example, by Buchholz and Konrad (1994). In their model, governments anticipate negotiations on the internalization of transboundary externalities. In order to strengthen their own bargaining position, they choose an inefficient technology with high per-unit costs of abatement before negotiations and cooperation start. The choice of technology is also inefficient from a national perspective, but works as a form of commitment for this country and therefore pays off. It is assumed that (abatement) technologies are irreversible once negotiations have started and that the outcome of negotiations is determined by the Nash bargaining solution. Thus, a country with relatively high marginal abatement costs will have an advantage because it is globally efficient to assign a relatively small share of the abatement burden to this country.

Unilateral abatement measures of a single country may not only weaken the bargaining position during negotiations, but they may even *worsen* environmental quality. This is shown by Hoel (1991) in a model where the cooperative equilibrium is determined by the Nash bargaining solution. The result, though, is valid only for increasing marginal abatement costs and depends on the assumption that marginal abatement costs of the unilaterally acting country increase sufficiently more than those of the other countries. Moreover, the economic reason that makes a single country engage in unilateral abatements remains unclear. On the one hand, it is assumed that a unilaterally acting country is not acting according to its 'true' best reply function. On the other hand, the true net benefits of abatements are relevant for the cooperative solution. If intrinsic motivations for unilateral measures are present in the case of non-cooperation, these should also be considered for the cooperative solution. If, however, the exclusive motivation for unilateral action is to manipulate the outcome of negotiations, the true net benefits should be the basis of the decision-making. Finally, it is hard to justify why one does not assume the same behavior for (at least some of) the other players involved. Of course, in that case the result of a deterioration in environmental quality would hardly prevail.

A different approach is taken by Endres and Finus (1998) who analyse the effects of increased environmental awareness (that is, a change in preferences) on the incentives for international environmental cooperation and environmental quality. In this framework, unilateral measures conform with optimizing behavior of national governments. In one part of their analysis, the authors assume that the cooperative solution is characterized by uniform emission reduction quotas — the outcome of many real-world negotiations on international environmental resources. They analyse the ecological effects of unilateral actions before negotiations start as well as of overfulfilling the assumed environmental agreement after it has been signed. As in Hoel (1991), the result is that, in many cases, global emissions will *increase* due to unilateral environmental policy measures. The deterioration in environmental quality in this model is caused by strategically adjusted proposals and reduced abatements of countries that observe or anticipate unilateral measures by others. It is shown that the results depend on the stage at which the commitment of overfulfillment is known to the parties involved and how they react to this knowledge. Both of the contributions cited above assume non-orthogonal reaction functions. Although this assumption is plausible from a theoretical point of view, it remains open as to whether it is also empirically justified. It implies that countries' abatement quantities are interdependent even in the non-cooperative equilibrium.[48]

The second question raised at the beginning of this section refers to the problem of protecting individual or joint efforts to reduce transboundary pollution against detrimental reactions from abroad. This is relevant for the provision of cooperation incentives for subcoalitions of countries because the more the environmental impact of a cooperative strategy is eroded by offsetting adjustment processes of outsider countries, the less attractive it is to participate in an international environmental agreement. Such leakage effects may interfere with national abatement efforts via two channels: (i) directly, if marginal abatement benefits decrease in emission reductions and optimizing behavior leads to an adjustment of marginal abatement costs through higher emissions abroad; (ii) indirectly, if, because of a changed price vector, general equilibrium effects lead to an international reallocation of polluting industries and a change in the demand and supply of polluting goods abroad.[49] In the context of global warming, the latter effect is well known as 'carbon leakage'. Joint efforts of a subcoalition of countries to reduce their consumption of fossil fuels would tend to reduce world market fuel prices and thereby increase fuel consumption in non-signatory countries. In addition, an increased demand for imports of goods whose production is fuel-intensive would tend to increase fuel demand abroad even further.

One can think of different ways which would help to counteract offsetting emission increases in countries that are unconcerned about international environmental problems. In effect, it makes no difference whether such accompanying measures are taken by a single government or by a subcoalition of countries which coordinate their environmental policies. From the perspective of the outsider countries, in both cases they rep-

---

[48] For a critical discussion of this scenario see, for example, Carraro and Siniscalco (1993, pp. 323–5).

[49] See, for example, Felder and Rutherford (1993); Merrifield (1988).

resent 'unilateral' measures. A crowding-out strategy put forward by Bohm (1993a) is to reduce the fuel supply to non-signatories by having signatories buy or lease suitable fossil fuel deposits from producer countries. In the case where the unilaterally acting countries themselves are suppliers of fossil fuels, an alternative option is to reduce the international supply by adopting domestic policies such as a tax on production and/or consumption of fossil fuels. As shown by Hoel (1994), it is often impossible to identify whether a demand or a supply policy is superior for the subcoalition without additional information on the shape of demand and supply functions in the 'carbon market'. In general, some combination of production and consumption taxes will be better than one instrument alone.[50] However, to the extent that a single 'large' country or a group of cooperating countries exerts monopolistic power on the world carbon market, domestic policies not only pursue environmental goals — they are also used to alter the terms of trade in a favorable manner. From the point of view of this optimal tariff argument, the optimal policy mix will be to tax consumption and subsidize production or vice versa, depending on whether the coalition in equilibrium is a net importer or exporter of carbon. Hence, the optimal intervention on supply and demand of fossil fuels from the perspective of the unilateral actor depends on the relative importance of the damages from climate change and the gains from manipulating terms of trade.[51] An alternative strategy would be to induce the cooperation of other countries in order to influence the demand and/or supply abroad. This requires instruments which have already been discussed in the previous sections, in particular the compensation of non-cooperating countries for the free-rider gains they forgo due to cooperation (Bohm 1993a, Hoel 1994).

It remains to be noted that, in contrast to the legal meaning of the term 'unilateral', in effect it makes no difference if the measures discussed above are taken by a single government or if they are the outcome of a coordination among a subgroup of countries. With respect to the external effects of its coordinated measures, a subcoalition faces the same patterns as an individual country. Therefore, no strict separation can be made between cooperative and unilateral internalization strategies, and

---

[50]See Golombek et al. (1994) for the question regarding under what circumstances a tax per unit of carbon should be differentiated across *sectors* from the point of view of a subcoalition on climate protection.

[51]Similar results are obtained by Killinger (1996) in a general equilibrium framework with two countries where one 'large' country uses its market power for an 'indirect internalization' of transboundary externalities from abroad. See Böhringer and Rutherford (1997) for an argument against a unilateral German carbon tax that includes exemptions for energy- and export-intensive industries as a compromise between environmental objectives and employment in these sectors.

the above considerations also apply for subcoalitions.

4.6   Flexibility and Framework Provisions

The last category of instruments which create incentives for stable international environmental cooperation consists of measures which are effective in the long run. Such provisions increase the flexibility of an agreement with regard to adaptations to new and previously unknown circumstances. They may also aim at ameliorating the general framework of international negotiations. At the time of negotiating and signing an environmental treaty, it is often impossible to foresee the future development of all relevant factors. If at some point in the future important parameters such as economic income, technology or the natural situation change in a substantial and not foreseeable way, compliance with an existing agreement may no longer be optimal for some countries. In order not to endanger the whole cooperation, treaty provisions may be included which enable a flexible adjustment in future periods without undermining the substance of the treaty. Examples of such flexibility clauses include the indexation of national obligations to central economic variables such as national (per-capita) income or population size and the concession of *escape clauses* for special circumstances (Heister et al. 1995). More far-reaching adjustments could be arranged by renegotiating the treaty. Renegotiation, however, may have a destabilizing effect and be counterproductive if it does not take place due to unforeseen changes, but in reality is triggered by defecting behavior in the past. Hence, there might be a trade-off between the flexibility and the effectiveness of an international environmental agreement (Kerr 1995).

In the long run, incentives for international environmental cooperation can also be affected by enhancing the fundamental framework conditions of negotiations. One crucial factor for the success of negotiations is the information available to the governments involved. This is especially true for global environmental externalities given the substantial uncertainties over physical and biological regularities and their economic consequences. An important instrument for facilitating environmental cooperation thus consists in improving the relevant information for negotiations and making it accessible to all parties. This is a traditional task of international organizations and research facilities. Another long-run strategy is to pursue a general policy of global integration in order to increase the political and economic interdependencies between national jurisdictions. The latter makes it generally more difficult for a single country to behave in an opportunistic manner. The literature on issue linkage suggests that, in general, the more paths are open to punish non-cooperative behavior, the higher is the degree of integration.

4.7 Conclusions

This chapter has surveyed recent contributions to the rapidly growing theoretical literature on the incentives for international environmental cooperation. We proposed a taxonomy of instruments that create incentives for the participation in and compliance with international environmental agreements. The conceivable strategies for promoting a successful coordination of environmental policies despite an only rudimentary institutional structure on the international level have been grouped into (i) the choice and detailed form of the internalization instrument itself; (ii) carrot–stick strategies which make cooperative abatement efforts dependent on the past behavior of other countries (internal stabilization); (iii) transfers and sanctions in various forms (external stabilization); (iv) unilateral and accompanying measures by single countries or subcoalitions; and (v) long-term provisions to increase the flexibility of agreements and to improve the framework conditions of international negotiations.

The surveyed body of literature on international environmental cooperation has overcome and to some extent replaced the traditional economic theory of environmental policy because it accounts for incentive compatibility and time-consistency problems not being an issue in traditional analyses of environmental policy. Thus, the principal merit of this research is that it systematically addresses the fundamental institutional restrictions which apply to the management of international environmental resources. The second-best character of international environmental policy is mirrored by the common feature of numerous models that international environmental cooperation will be only partial. Moreover, due to the lack of first-best lump-sum transfers, the focus is often not on mere efficiency aspects but on the distributional implications of international environmental policy. Despite these limitations, the discussed contributions show that, in theory, there are quite a variety of instruments available to provide incentives for stable environmental cooperation. In practice, though, the requirements (for example, on intertemporal discount rates) for these strategies to be successful are often not fulfilled.

The limitations of the discussed body of literature must not be overlooked. Although game theory is the appropriate theoretical framework to analyse the strategic interactions of national governments in international environmental policy, it nevertheless abstracts from many factors that are important for the outcome of international environmental negotiations in practice. One striking simplification in game-theoretic models of transboundary pollution is assumptions on the enforceability of international treaties. It is true that the surveyed literature considers different scenarios regarding the ability of sovereign countries to engage in binding commitments credibly. Recent contributions not only look at international environmental agreements which are completely self-enforcing, but also analyse cases of restricted enforceability where some but not all countries can make binding commitments. Both approaches, however, neglect the institutional dimension of environmental cooperation. Concerning the former variant, the lack of a supranational authority does not imply the absence of any institutional framework on the international level. This, however, is implicitly assumed when we analyse international environmental agreements which are fully self-enforcing. In the latter case a limited degree of commitment (and enforceability) is usually simply assumed without explaining how this is achieved. It seems to be more appropriate to model explicitly the institutional structure on the international level. This allows us to analyse how credible commitments of sovereign countries can be achieved and to illustrate the usefulness of particular international institutions. A step in this direction is taken in the next chapter by assuming the existence of an international institution that works as an intermediary.

Another shortcoming of most models on international environmental cooperation is that they start out with quite strong assumptions on the rationality and the capacities of the 'players'. Crucial aspects of real-world decisions on environmental policy are thus often neglected. Among other aspects,[52] uncertainties and informational imperfections certainly play an important role in environmental decision-making, especially in the case of global environmental problems such as the anthropogenic greenhouse effect and the depletion of the ozone layer. Up to now, most studies on international environmental agreements have neglected such problems because of informational shortcomings. Usually it is assumed that national governments have perfect information both on their own costs and benefits of environmental policy and on those of all other countries affected by transboundary pollution. In the real world, national governments neither know exactly the characteristics of all other countries, nor are they able to identify precisely their own costs and benefits of emission abatements. As countries may have an incentive as well as the opportunity to conceal their true characteristics, incomplete

---

[52]For example, phenomena like reputation or bounded rationality have been introduced in formal economic models of international environmental policy only rarely. Another crucial assumption is that governments and the populations they represent are treated as 'unit actors', neglecting conflicting interests within a country.

information enlarges the strategy space and generates new and potentially inefficient outcomes. The question therefore arises whether and
how mechanisms and bargaining processes can be designed in order to
make reporting true information incentive compatible and to achieve
the utmost mutual gains from international environmental cooperation.
This issue is taken up in Chapter 6 in the context of cost-effectiveness
and 'joint implementation'.

Chapter 5

Enforcement and Side Payments

5.1 Introduction

A successful international environmental agreement has to take into account two key features of transboundary pollution problems, as the preceding discussion has shown: (i) the non-existence of a supranational authority which could force the contracting parties to fulfill their obligations, and (ii) the fact that most countries differ considerably with respect to numerous characteristics. It is often argued that such asymmetries are detrimental to the successful negotiation of international environmental agreements (see, for example, Barrett 1992b). By contrast, this chapter argues that the reverse might be true as soon as we allow for side payments. The theoretical analysis of this chapter shows how international transfers can be used to take into account both of the above aspects and to support stable cooperative solutions in international environmental policy. A game structure is proposed that uses self-financing transfers and sequential moves in the implementation of the agreement to induce the voluntary participation *and* compliance of heterogeneous countries with an international environmental agreement (IEA), even though enforcement by a supranational authority is not available. We consider two types of asymmetries between countries: national differences in abatement costs and benefits as well as different relative bargaining positions of the national governments. We shall analyse how these asymmetries influence the welfare gains which are attainable through the proposed enforcement mechanism.

We have argued in the previous chapter that the lack of a supranational authority does not imply the absence of any institutional framework on the international level. The existence and widespread use of international environmental institutions suggests that we should introduce at least a limited degree of enforcement in a theoretic model on international environmental cooperation. One way of doing this is to assume that binding commitments are possible for certain subgroups of countries (Carraro and Siniscalco 1993, Hoel 1994). An alternative route — which is followed in the present chapter — is to model explicitly the underlying institutional structure. This allows us to analyse how credible commitments of sovereign countries can be achieved and to illustrate the usefulness of particular international institutions. The results demonstrate that substantial gains from international environmental cooperation are enforceable even without assuming binding commitments of single countries if existing institutions are properly used.

The practicability of (monetary) transfers between countries is often disputed (see, for example, Finus and Rundshagen 1998). This skepticism must be acknowledged but does not rule out side payments completely. Therefore in this chapter we consider self-financing transfers of the type analysed by Carraro and Siniscalco (1993), but we also consider side payments which are further restricted: transfers serve to compensate the country with lower marginal abatement costs for its higher (incremental) abatement costs under cooperation. Financing a foreign country's abatement efforts is often attractive for certain governments because it would be more costly to achieve the same environmental effect with domestic policy measures. In fact, it is the mandate of international institutions such as the Global Environment Facility to administer international compensation payments to enhance cost-effectiveness in international environmental policy. The approach to compensate for the *incremental abatement costs* of environmental protection projects is an operational principle of these agencies and also eventually for future 'joint implementation' activities under the Framework Convention on Climate Change.[1]

The chapter is organized as follows. In Section 5.2 we outline the basic two-countries, two-goods model that is formulated in terms of abatement costs and benefits and we describe the properties of the non-cooperative Nash equilibrium as well as the full cooperative (that is, globally efficient) solution. In Section 5.3, a cooperative abatement game using side payments and sequential moves in the implementation of the agreement is introduced. We derive analytically the gains from stable cooperation that can be achieved with this enforcement mechanism under three alternative scenarios and illustrate the results using numerical simulations. Section 5.4 discusses a generalization of the model to more than

---

[1] See, for example, King (1993) for the incremental cost concept; for an overview on the concept of 'joint implementation', see Pearce (1995).

two countries and presents simulation results for the three-country case. Section 5.5 concludes with a summary and possible implications for international environmental policy.

5.2 The Model

Consider the same general framework as in Section 3.2. The governments of two countries A and B decide upon emission reductions of a flow pollutant that constitutes a pure public bad and national abatement quantities add up to equation (3.7). Net abatement benefits π of country k are given by equation (3.8). As in Section 3.2, abatement costs and benefits have to be specified further in order to analyse different scenarios of asymmetry and to compare national welfare levels in the subsequent analysis. Again, we assume linearly increasing marginal costs of abatements

$$C'_k = c_k \, q_k, \quad c_k > 0, \tag{5.1}$$

where c_k is a country-specific exogenous parameter. The values of c_k may differ across countries due to different abatement technologies, substitution possibilities for energy production, or the impact of a country's base-year emission level on its marginal abatement costs (Barrett 1992a). A less expensive abatement technology or a higher base-year emission level implies, *ceteris paribus*, a lower value of c_k.

In contrast to the specification in Section 3.2, it is assumed here that the marginal benefit from the reduction of pollution by one unit is constant:

$$B'_k = b_k, \quad b_k > 0, \tag{5.2}$$

where b_k is an exogenous country-specific parameter. For some environmental problems this specification has been regarded as empirically better justified than assuming decreasing marginal abatement benefits (Carraro and Siniscalco 1993, pp. 323-5). Global warming, for example, is not linear but logarithmic in CO_2 concentrations so that marginal damages that rise in temperatures may well be constant in CO_2 emissions and concentrations (Nordhaus 1991b, p. 148). Therefore, assuming constant marginal benefits is justified at least for some pollutants and over a certain range of abatement quantities.[2] In the case of carbon emissions, marginal abatement benefits differ across countries because

---

[2] See also Cline (1992a, 1992b). The assumption is made here for analytical convenience. Assuming (linearly) decreasing marginal abatement benefits does not change the qualitative results concerning side payments as enforcement mechanisms.

of different regional impacts of climate change, different economic damages in terms of lost income and differing valuations of environmental quality. Assuming that the cost of the first unit of abatement in the absence of any environmental concern is (close to) zero and integrating marginal abatement benefits and costs, the national net benefit function is given by

$$\pi_k = b_k\, Q - c_k/2\, q_k^2, \quad b_k > 0,\ c_k > 0,\ k = A, B. \qquad (5.3)$$

Global net benefits of abatements Π are the sum of national net benefits π_A and π_B:

$$\Pi = (b_A + b_B)\, Q - (c_A/2)\, q_A^2 - (c_B/2)\, q_B^2. \qquad (5.4)$$

Balancing marginal benefits against costs determines the optimal abatement level q_k of country k. In the following we compare the non-cooperative equilibrium with the central planner (or full cooperative) solution.

Let us first look at the properties of the non-cooperative equilibrium when national governments exhibit Nash behavior.[3] In this case each government chooses the abatement level that is *nationally* optimal and maximizes (5.3). From a single country's perspective, national abatement quantities are optimal when marginal benefits equal marginal costs for this country:

$$\partial \pi_k / \partial q_k = b_k - c_k\, q_k \overset{!}{=} 0 \quad \Leftrightarrow \quad q_k^N = b_k/c_k. \qquad (5.5)$$

Note that the 'best response' of country k according to (5.5) is independent from the abatement level of the other country. This is due to the assumption of constant marginal benefits and implies that the reaction functions are orthogonal to each other. The intersection of the reaction curves determines the non-cooperative Nash equilibrium N.[4] Substituting equilibrium abatement levels (5.5) into the global net benefit function (5.4) gives global net benefits under Nash behavior, denoted by $\Pi^N \equiv \Pi(q_A^N, q_B^N)$.

National abatement levels that are *globally* optimal can be derived by maximizing global net benefits (5.4) with respect to q_A and q_B:[5]

$$q_k^* = \frac{b_A + b_B}{c_k}, \quad k = A, B. \qquad (5.6)$$

---

[3] Alternatively, one could consider a Stackelberg game. See Section 3.2 for a comparison of the Nash and Stackelberg cases with respect to their efficiency properties.

[4] The equilibrium is unique and stable because reaction curves (5.5) are linear with a slope of 0.

[5] Note that uniqueness of globally efficient abatements is no longer given once one departs from the simplifying assumptions made here. Chander and Tulkens (1997, pp. 381–2) derive the conditions for uniqueness in a general setting.

Comparing the globally efficient allocation (5.6) with the non-cooperative allocation of abatements (5.5) reveals the two basic sources of inefficiency analysed in Section 3.2. First, aggregate abatements are too low ($Q^N < Q^*$), and second, the distribution of abatement efforts across countries is not cost-efficient. Since marginal abatement costs are not equalized between A and B, the same global environmental standard could be achieved at lower global costs. The two ratios $q_A^*/q_B^* = c_B/c_A$ and $q_A^N/q_B^N = (b_A c_B)/(b_B c_A)$ coincide, marginal abatement costs are equalized, and cost-effectiveness is reached even in the non-cooperative equilibrium, *only* in the special case of $b_A = b_B$.

The potential welfare gains from full cooperation are measured by comparing global net benefits Π^N with Π^*. For this purpose we can use the welfare loss ratio (3.22) which we evaluate for different parameter constellations. Substituting for the optimal abatement levels under Nash and full cooperative behavior we get

$$
\Delta^N = \frac{\Pi^* - \Pi^N}{\Pi^*} = \frac{b_A^2 c_A + b_B^2 c_B}{(b_A + b_B)^2 (c_A + c_B)} = \frac{1 + \beta^2 \gamma}{(1 + \beta)^2 (1 + \gamma)}, \quad (5.7)
$$

where $\beta \equiv b_A/b_B$ and $\gamma \equiv c_A/c_B$ can be interpreted as asymmetry parameters. Note that index Δ^N depends solely on the heterogeneity of the countries, and not on the levels of b_k and c_k. The relationship between asymmetry and welfare losses due to non-cooperation may be monotonous or non-monotonous, depending on the values of β and γ. For high degrees of asymmetry, however, the more heterogeneous the countries, the smaller the welfare losses. This holds because with very asymmetric countries, the importance of one of the two countries' actions on global welfare is negligible. It corresponds to the results derived in Section 3.2 for the case of two countries that differ in population size, and assuming decreasing marginal abatement benefits (see Figures 3.3 and 3.4).[6] For the benchmark case of identical countries, equation (5.7) simplifies to $\Delta = 1/4$, irrespective of c_k/b_k. Hence, under the present model specification and with completely symmetric countries, non-cooperative behavior always implies that 25 per cent of global welfare is lost, irrespective of how severe the environmental problem at stake is. Of course, this result only holds for the two-countries case. In general, the more countries are involved, the more severe are the welfare losses from non-cooperation (Barrett 1994). In the extreme case, a single country's abatement efforts only incur costs but have almost no impact on global environmental quality so that no abatement efforts will

---

[6] As the relationship between the countries' asymmetry and welfare losses from non-cooperation has already been analysed in Section 3.2, we do not discuss it in more detail here.

be undertaken by any country.

For the rest of the chapter we define country A to be the country with higher net benefits under global efficiency ($\pi_A^* \geq \pi_B^*$) and hence higher potential gains from cooperation. A sufficient condition is that both marginal abatement benefits and costs are higher (or equally high) for country A: $b_A \geq b_B \land c_A \geq c_B \Rightarrow \pi_A^* \geq \pi_B^*$. We can show this by substituting efficient abatement quantities (5.6) in (5.3). Simplifying and rearranging gives

$$
\begin{aligned}
\pi_A^* - \pi_B^* &= b_A Q^* - \frac{c_A}{2} q_A^{*\,2} - \left(b_B Q^* - \frac{c_B}{2} q_B^{*\,2} \right) \qquad (5.8) \\
&= (b_A - b_B)Q^* - \frac{(b_A + b_B)^2}{2c_A} + \frac{(b_A + b_B)^2}{2c_B} \\
&= (b_A - b_B)Q^* + (c_A - c_B)\frac{(b_A + b_B)^2}{2c_A c_B}.
\end{aligned}
$$

The first term is positive for $b_A > b_B$ and the second is positive for $c_A > c_B$. Hence, a sufficient condition for $\pi_A^* > \pi_B^*$ is $b_A > b_B \land c_A > c_B$.

5.3   An Enforceable Agreement with Side Payments

This section explores the role of side payments in an international environmental agreement that is enforceable. For that purpose we use a game structure involving an international institution and sequential moves of the parties. Assume that the starting-point for negotiations is the non-cooperative Nash equilibrium.[7] An environmental treaty stipulates a certain vector of abatement quantities and side payments from a donor country i to a recipient country j. As additional institutional structure we presume the existence of an independent third party where the side payments are deposited before they flow to the recipient country.[8] This provision guarantees that side payments are paid and transferred according to the terms of the IEA and that the commitments with respect to international transfers are always credible. The sequence of the game is as follows:

1. Countries A and B negotiate the terms of the IEA with regard to cooperative abatement levels q_k^C of both countries and a transfer T_{ij} from country i to j.

---

[7] Hence, pre-negotiation strategic behavior as, for example, in Buchholz and Konrad (1994), is ruled out.

[8] The third party could be an international agency such as the Global Environment Facility.

2. The donor country i moves first. It raises abatements to the level q_i^C and deposits the transfer T_{ij} agreed in stage 1.
3. The recipient country j moves second. It raises its abatements to the cooperative level q_j^C or defects and abates q_j^D.
4. Country j receives the side payment T_{ij} if it cooperates or T_{ij} is refunded to country i if j has defected.

When negotiations start it is open which country will take the part of the donor and which that of the recipient country. The assignment of roles is determined by negotiations in stage 1 and will crucially depend on the governments' bargaining positions. Therefore in the following we consider two countries that differ not only with respect to abatement benefits and/or costs, but also with respect to their bargaining power, expressed by parameter δ in equation (5.9). In any case, the agreement has to be individually rational for both countries by guaranteeing the reservation level of utility in the non-cooperative equilibrium, see equations (5.10) and (5.11).[9] To be incentive compatible as well, countries must be worse off if their governments deviate from the agreed measures. For the recipient country, incentive compatibility of the IEA is secured if the gain from defecting is not greater than the sanction of the refused side payment, see equation (5.12). This sanction is credible because denying the side payment does not harm the donor country. Compliance of the donor country is secured by the provision that it moves first in the cooperative abatement game. Thereby, defection of the donor country is not possible as cooperation starts only when the donor country fulfills its obligations.[10] The above sequence of moves thus ensures compliance of the donor without requiring an incentive compatibility constraint corresponding to the one for the recipient, see equation (5.12).

According to the above game structure, the terms of the international environmental agreement are the outcome of the following optimization problem:

$$\max \left[\pi_A(q_A^C, q_B^C) + \delta \, \pi_B(q_A^C, q_B^C) \right], \quad \text{s.t.} \tag{5.9}$$

$$\pi_i(q_i^C, q_j^C) - T_{ij} \geq \pi_i(q_i^N, q_j^N) \tag{5.10}$$

$$\pi_j(q_i^C, q_j^C) + T_{ij} \geq \pi_j(q_i^N, q_j^N) \tag{5.11}$$

$$\pi_j(q_i^C, q_j^C) + T_{ij} \geq \pi_j(q_i^C, q_j^D). \tag{5.12}$$

---

[9]It is assumed that if a country is indifferent between cooperating or not, it cooperates.

[10]Alternatively, with simultaneous moves of the governments, the loss of the transfer deposited by the donor country would not constitute a sanction as the transfer is paid under cooperation as well. In fact, if the donor could also defect from paying the transfer, its incentive to act non-cooperatively would be even stronger.

Parameter δ ($0 \leq \delta \leq 1$) denotes the bargaining strength of country B's government. It is defined as the extent to which country B's government succeeds in pushing through its interests during the negotiations that determine the optimization problem.[11] The relative bargaining positions of the negotiating governments are crucial for the cooperative outcome because they determine which objective function is maximized by the negotiated IEA and which country is going to be the donor i and which the recipient j. Transfer T_{ij} is defined in terms of transferable utility rather than monetary units or units of a representative private good. The transfer mechanism differs from the Kaldor–Hicks compensation principle in two ways: to yield incentive compatibility, side payments have to actually be undertaken instead of just being possible; they also have to provide sufficient incentives to comply with the treaty in addition to creating incentives to sign it. Abatements q_j^D maximize j's net benefits when defecting unilaterally from the agreement. Since we have assumed constant marginal abatement benefits, the best response functions are orthogonal to each other and non-cooperative abatements do not depend on abatement efforts in the rest of the world ($q_j^D = q_j^N$).[12]

The outcome of negotiations in stage 1 basically depends on two factors: (i) the relative bargaining positions of the negotiating governments and (ii) the extent to which international side payments are feasible. Concerning the first factor we restrict the analysis to two extreme scenarios: either country has the same bargaining power and both are able to push through their national interests ($\delta = 1$), or country A has the power to dictate the terms of the agreement in line with its national interests, whereas B can only accept or reject it ($\delta = 0$). In the latter scenario, the government of country A is able to submit a 'take-it-or-leave-it' offer to country B. The case of equal bargaining positions where both countries agree to maximize joint net benefits of abatements is treated in Section 5.3.1, the opposite benchmark of a take-it-or-leave-it offer is analysed in Section 5.3.2. With respect to the feasibility of international side payments we consider two scenarios as well: in Sections 5.3.1 and 5.3.2 it is assumed (as, for example, in Carraro and Siniscalco 1993) that transfers must be self-financing (that is, paid out of the donor country's welfare gains from cooperation), but are otherwise unrestricted. In Section 5.3.3 we analyse self-financing transfers which are further restricted: side payments serve exclusively to compensate the

---

[11] As only relative bargaining positions matter, we define country A to be at least as powerful as country B during negotiations and assume that country A's interests are always taken into account completely during negotiations. The same could be presumed for country B without changing the general results.

[12] In the case of non-orthogonal reaction functions q_j^D is calculated by substituting q_i^c into j's best response.

country with lower marginal abatement costs for its higher abatement efforts under cooperation in order to reach a cost-effective allocation of international abatements.

5.3.1 Equal Bargaining Positions

Assume that governments dispose of identical bargaining positions and that they agree to maximize joint net benefits of cooperative abatements ($\delta = 1$).[13] Side payments under the environmental treaty must be self-financing, that is, they are restricted by the welfare gains from cooperation a potential donor country could realize through the agreement. Moreover, as the transfers influence how the global welfare gains from environmental cooperation are shared among the countries, they are determined by the relative bargaining positions of the negotiating governments. With equal bargaining power, the governments may agree on transfers so that the total welfare gains from cooperation are shared in equal amounts.[14] Under these assumptions the optimization problem (5.9)–(5.12) transforms to

$$\max \ \Pi^C(q_i^C, q_j^C), \quad \text{s.t.} \tag{5.13}$$

$$\pi_i(q_i^C, q_j^C) - T_{ij} \geq \pi_i(q_i^N, q_j^N) \tag{5.14}$$

$$\pi_j(q_i^C, q_j^C) + T_{ij} \geq \pi_j(q_i^N, q_j^N) \tag{5.15}$$

$$\pi_j(q_i^C, q_j^D) - \pi_j(q_i^C, q_j^C) \leq T_{ij} \tag{5.16}$$

$$\pi_i^C - T_{ij} - \pi_i^N = \pi_j^C + T_{ij} - \pi_j^N, \tag{5.17}$$

where subscript i (j) stands for the donor (recipient) country. The assignment of roles, that is, which of the two countries A and B will be the donor and which the recipient of transfers, is endogenously determined by the negotiations in stage 1. Given the gain-sharing rule (5.17), the individual rationality constraints (5.14) and (5.15) of the donor and the recipient country are identical and equivalent to $\Pi^C \geq \Pi^N$.[15] The latter constraint is never binding because global welfare is always higher under cooperation than in the non-cooperative equilibrium, by definition. Hence, with transfer scheme (5.17) *both* countries will gain by

---

[13] Assuming that the bargaining process takes place in order to achieve a Pareto-optimal outcome allows us to compare the results of the present analysis with those of the related literature (Barrett 1994, Carraro and Siniscalco 1993).

[14] The rule of 'equal absolute gains' is used here because it corresponds to the modus of sharing gains in the Nash bargaining solution. Of course, other rules such as sharing according to equal *relative* gains are also possible.

[15] This is seen by substituting equation (5.17) into the constraints (5.14) and (5.15) and rearranging.

cooperating compared to their welfare in the non-cooperative Nash equilibrium. Omitting $\Pi^C \geq \Pi^N$ and substituting equation (5.17) into incentive compatibility constraint (5.16), the Lagrangian of optimization problem (5.13)–(5.17) simplifies to

$$L(q_i, q_j, \lambda) = \Pi(q_i, q_j) + \lambda \left[\Pi(q_i, q_j) + \pi_j^N - \pi_i^N - 2\pi_j^D \right], \quad (5.18)$$

with $\pi_l^N = \pi_l(q_i^N, q_j^N)$, $l = i, j$, and $\pi_j^D = \pi_j(q_i, q_j^N)$. Differentiating and using the Nash abatement levels (5.5), the Kuhn–Tucker conditions for a maximum of Π^C are

$$\frac{\partial L}{\partial q_i} = b_i + b_j - c_i q_i + \lambda(b_i + b_j) - \lambda c_i q_i - 2\lambda b_j \leq 0 \quad (5.19)$$

$$\frac{\partial L}{\partial q_j} = b_i + b_j - c_j q_j + \lambda(b_i + b_j) - \lambda c_j q_j \leq 0 \quad (5.20)$$

$$\frac{\partial L}{\partial \lambda} = (b_i + b_j)(q_i + q_j) - \frac{c_i}{2} q_i^2 - \frac{c_j}{2} q_j^2 - 2b_j q_i \quad (5.21)$$

$$- \frac{b_j(2b_i + b_j)}{2c_j} + \frac{b_i(2b_j - b_i)}{2c_i} \geq 0 \quad (5.22)$$

$$0 = q_i \, \partial L / \partial q_i$$

$$0 = q_j \, \partial L / \partial q_j \quad (5.23)$$

$$0 = \lambda \, \partial L / \partial \lambda \quad (5.24)$$

$$q_l \geq 0, \quad l = i, j \quad (5.25)$$

$$\lambda \geq 0. \quad (5.26)$$

In general, two solutions are possible depending on whether the incentive compatibility constraint of the recipient country is binding or not. Obviously, if neither the individual rationality nor the incentive compatibility constraints are binding, the full cooperative outcome and global efficient allocation can be sustained (Case 1: $\lambda = 0$). Globally efficient abatement levels and sharing the gains from cooperation according to equation (5.17) are attainable as long as the country with higher potential gains from cooperation (country A) is the donor and $b_A^2 c_A \geq 3b_B^2 c_B$. We can show this by setting $i = A$ and $j = B$, substituting gain-sharing rule (5.17) into constraint (5.16), inserting the respective abatement quantities and simplifying to

$$1/2 \left[\pi_A^* - \pi_A^N - (\pi_B^* - \pi_B^N) \right] \geq \pi_B^D - \pi_B^* \iff b_A^2 c_A \geq 3b_B^2 c_B, \quad (5.27)$$

with $\pi_k^* = \pi_k(q_A^*, q_B^*)$, $k = A, B$, and $\pi_B^D = \pi_B(q_A^*, q_B^N)$. Thus, if countries are sufficiently asymmetric with respect to abatement benefits and/or costs, both governments will voluntarily agree in stage 1 on the agreement

$$q_A^C = q_A^*, \quad q_B^C = q_B^*, \quad T_{AB} = \frac{3b_A^2 c_A - 3b_B^2 c_B}{4 c_A c_B}, \tag{5.28}$$

where country A is the donor and moves first and country B is the recipient and moves second. Since cooperation gains are shared equally and enforcement is ensured, the assignment of roles makes no difference from the perspective of the single governments. For global efficiency to be enforceable, however, it is necessary that the country with a higher interest in the treaty, that is, country A, takes up the role of the donor. Therefore, both countries will voluntarily agree on the above assignment of roles.

In scenarios of only moderate asymmetry $(b_A^2 c_A < 3b_B^2 c_B)$ the recipient's incentive compatibility constraint (5.16) is binding. For the enforcement mechanism to work and with side payments according to (5.17), governments then agree on a treaty that is only second best (Case 2: $\lambda > 0$):

$$q_A^C = \frac{b_A - b_B}{c_A} + \frac{\sqrt{b_A^2 c_A + b_B^2 c_B}}{c_A \sqrt{c_B}} < q_A^*, \quad q_B^C = q_B^*. \tag{5.29}$$

Hence, under this agreement both countries will intensify their abatement efforts, but only recipient country B abates globally efficient quantities, implying that under the second-best treaty cost-effectiveness is not reached $(q_A^C / q_B^C \neq q_A^* / q_B^*)$. The governments agree on the same assignment of roles as in case 1 $(i = A,\ j = B)$ because both countries would be worse off if the country with a lower interest in environmental cooperation were the donor.

To summarize, whether the incentive compatibility constraint is binding or not, there always exists an enforceable international environmental agreement where the welfare gains from environmental cooperation are shared equally between the two countries. Accordingly, the governments voluntarily agree that the country with higher potential welfare gains from cooperation grants a transfer to the other country. A coordination problem over the assignment of roles does not arise. When the countries are sufficiently heterogeneous with respect to abatement benefits and/or costs, global efficiency can be attained as an enforceable cooperative solution, whereas in cases of moderate asymmetry only a second-best agreement emerges. Hence, under the above game structure the countries' heterogeneity is *favorable* to the cooperative outcome. This result, however, hinges crucially upon the assumption of equal bargaining positions where the negotiating parties agree to maximize joint net benefits of abatements. Therefore, in the following section we analyse the opposite benchmark concerning the distribution of bargaining power between the two governments.

5.3.2 A 'Take-it-or-leave-it' Offer

As in the previous section, we consider negotiations on an international environmental agreement which includes self-financing transfers. Assume now, however, that country A is able to dictate the terms of the agreement, whereas country B can only accept or refuse to cooperate ($\delta = 0$). Country A then submits a take-it-or-leave-it offer to B that solely reflects A's interests. It may either choose to be the donor and offer an optimal transfer T_{AB} or to be the recipient and offer T_{BA}. In either case, A's offer obviously prescribes side payments so that the maximum (if not all) of the attainable welfare gains from cooperation are reaped by country A, whereas country B is just indifferent between cooperating or not. Therefore, either the individual rationality constraint or the incentive compatibility constraint of B or both will be binding, whether it is the recipient or the donor country.

Given that country A opts to be the donor of transfers, optimization problem (5.9)–(5.12) simplifies to

$$\max \ (\pi_A^C - T_{AB}), \quad \text{s.t.} \quad T_{AB} = \pi_B^D - \pi_B^C, \tag{5.30}$$

with incentive compatibility constraint (5.12) binding for country B. Individual rationality constraint (5.11) cannot be the sole constraint binding for B because if it were, $\pi_B^N - \pi_B^C > \pi_B^D - \pi_B^C \Leftrightarrow \pi_B(q_A^N, q_B^N) > \pi_B(q_A^C, q_B^N) \Leftrightarrow q_A^C < q_A^N$, that is, the IEA would prescribe that donor A *reduces* its abatements. However, this is not possible because with a transfer $T_{AB} = \pi_B^N - \pi_B^C$, country A's offer would be the outcome of maximizing $(\Pi^C - \pi_B^N)$, with π_B^N being exogenously given. Cooperative abatements would thus correspond to globally efficient quantities ($q_A^C = q_A^*$) which is in contradiction to $q_A^C < q_A^N$. Finally, individual rationality constraint (5.10) of country A is never binding because $\pi_A^C - \pi_A^N > \pi_B^D - \pi_B^C \Leftrightarrow \Pi^C > \pi_A^N + \pi_B^D$ by definition. The first-order conditions for optimization problem (5.30) yield an agreement with

$$q_A^C = q_A^N, \quad q_B^C = q_B^*, \quad T_{AB} = b_A^2/(2\,c_B). \tag{5.31}$$

Hence, under the environmental treaty with a transfer from A to B only country B increases its abatements and global efficiency is not attained.

As country A is able to prescribe the terms of the agreement it will compare its pay-off from offering agreement (5.31) with its pay-off from offering a cooperative solution where country B is the donor and A

the recipient of transfers. Transfers T_{BA} are optimally chosen by A so that individual rationality constraint (5.10) of country B is binding and holding with equality. The gains from cooperation then go entirely to country A.[16] The optimization problem (5.9)–(5.12) thus simplifies to

$$\max \ (\pi_A^C + T_{BA}), \quad \text{s.t.} \quad T_{BA} = \pi_B^C - \pi_B^N, \tag{5.32}$$

which is equivalent to maximizing $(\Pi^C - \pi_B^N)$, with π_B^N being exogenously given. Cooperative abatements in this case thus correspond to globally efficient quantities and the agreement offered by A stipulates

$$q_A^C = q_A^*, \quad q_B^C = q_B^*, \quad T_{BA} = b_B^2/c_A - b_A^2/(2\,c_B). \tag{5.33}$$

Comparing country A's national net benefits under the offers (5.31) and (5.33) shows that it is always superior for country A to be the recipient country.[17] However, for the enforcement mechanism to work, transfers T_{BA} have to be positive. Otherwise country A would have an incentive to defect and B, knowing this, would not cooperate either. From (5.33) follows that side payments are positive when $b_A^2 c_A < 2 b_B^2 c_B$ holds. Hence, only if countries are sufficiently homogeneous with respect to abatement benefits and/or costs, are globally efficient abatements compatible with positive side payments of the country that is in the unfavorable bargaining position. By contrast, when countries are considerably asymmetric, the government which has a higher interest in environmental cooperation and is able to dictate the terms of the agreement decides to be the donor. Global efficiency is not reached in this case because only recipient country B raises its abatements. Taken together, introducing unequal bargaining positions in the form of a take-it-or-leave-it offer reverses the results of the preceding section with regard to the impact of the countries' heterogeneity. Only if the countries are sufficiently homogeneous, will a cooperative solution be offered which implements the globally efficient allocation of abatements. Otherwise, the fact that national but not global welfare is relevant from a single government's perspective leads to cooperative solutions that are suboptimal from a global point of view. Thus, in this case the general conjecture that the players' asymmetries are detrimental to cooperative solutions is supported.

---

[16]The incentive compatibility constraint (5.12) of recipient A is not binding because $T_{BA} = \pi_B^C - \pi_B^N > \pi_A^D - \pi_A^C \Leftrightarrow \Pi^C > \pi_A^D + \pi_B^N$, which is fulfilled by definition.

[17]Inserting the respective values of the variables gives $\pi_A^* + T_{BA} > \pi_A^C - T_{AB} \Leftrightarrow b_B^2 c_B > 0$.

5.3.3   Compensations for Cost-effectiveness of Abatements

In the following, we analyse an IEA with self-financing transfers that are restricted to compensate for higher, cost-effective abatements of countries with relatively low marginal abatement costs. As before, transfers can be used not only as an instrument to make countries sign an IEA, but also to enforce it. We can think of such an agreement first as negotiating an increase in abatements by equal percentages, resulting in intermediate cooperative quantities q_k^P, and then reallocating them in a cost-effective way towards q_k^C, which minimizes aggregate abatement costs, leaving the global amount of cooperative abatements unchanged ($Q^P = Q^C$). This may be seen as a rule of fairness and is the approach used in many environmental negotiations. The resulting transfer scheme determines not only the size, but also the direction of side payments in the cooperative equilibrium. Since we have assumed that marginal abatement costs are, *ceteris paribus*, lower for country B ($c_B < c_A$), it is the recipient of transfers $T^{CE} \equiv C_B(q_B^C) - C_B(q_B^P)$.[18] Hypothetical quantities q_k^P which reduce national emissions proportionally are allocated as in the Nash equilibrium ($q_A^P/q_B^P = q_A^N/q_B^N = b_A c_B/b_B c_A$). Reallocating those quantities cost-effectively implies $q_A^C/q_B^C = q_A^*/q_B^* = c_B/c_A$. Using the above relationships, we get the restriction for transfers

$$T^{CE} = s\,\frac{c_B}{2}\,q_B^2, \quad s \equiv \left[1 - \frac{\left(1 + \frac{c_B}{c_A}\right)^2}{\left(1 + \frac{b_A c_B}{b_B c_A}\right)^2}\right], \tag{5.34}$$

where s denotes the share of B's total cooperative abatement costs that is financed by the high-cost country A ($0 \leq s < 1$). Assuming as in Section 5.3.1 that the negotiating parties agree to maximize joint welfare gains,[19] the optimization problem is

$$\max \Pi^C(q_A^C, q_B^C), \quad \text{s.t.} \tag{5.35}$$

$$\pi_A(q_A^C, q_B^C) - T_{AB} \geq \pi_A(q_A^N, q_B^N) \tag{5.36}$$

$$\pi_B(q_A^C, q_B^C) + T_{AB} \geq \pi_B(q_A^N, q_B^N) \tag{5.37}$$

$$\pi_B(q_A^C, q_B^D) - \pi_B(q_A^C, q_B^C) \leq T_{AB} \tag{5.38}$$

$$T^{AB} = T^{CE}. \tag{5.39}$$

---

[18]Similar results with respect to the enforceable cooperation gains are obtained if side payments to finance *gross* incremental abatement costs ($T^g \equiv C_B(q_B^C) - C_B(q_B^N)$) are specified.

[19]Considering a take-it-or-leave-it offer would not be compatible with the present transfer scheme because the latter does not maximize the donor's gains from the IEA.

Inserting equation (5.39) into constraints (5.36)–(5.38), the Lagrangian is

$$L(q_A, q_B, \lambda_1, \lambda_2, \lambda_3) = \Pi(q_A, q_B) \qquad (5.40)$$
$$+\lambda_1 \left[\pi_A(q_A, q_B) - s\, C_B(q_B) - \pi_A^N \right]$$
$$+\lambda_2 \left[\pi_B(q_A, q_B) + s\, C_B(q_B) - \pi_B^N \right]$$
$$+\lambda_3 \left[\pi_B(q_A, q_B) + s\, C_B(q_B) - \pi_B^D \right],$$

with $\pi_k^N = \pi_k(q_A^N, q_B^N)$, $k = A, B$, and $\pi_B^D = \pi_B(q_A, q_B^N)$. Differentiating and using the Nash abatement levels (5.5), the Kuhn–Tucker conditions for a maximum of Π^C are

$$\frac{\partial L}{\partial q_A} = b_A + b_B - c_A q_A + \lambda_1 b_A - \lambda_1 c_A q_A + \lambda_2 b_B \leq 0 \quad (5.41)$$

$$\frac{\partial L}{\partial q_B} = b_A + b_B - c_B q_B + \lambda_1 b_A - \lambda_1 s c_B q_B + \lambda_2 b_B \qquad (5.42)$$
$$+ \lambda_2(s-1)c_B q_B + \lambda_3 b_B + \lambda_3(s-1)c_B q_B \leq 0$$

$$\frac{\partial L}{\partial \lambda_1} = b_A(q_A + q_B) - \frac{c_A}{2}q_A^2 - s\frac{c_B}{2}q_B^2 \qquad (5.43)$$
$$- \frac{b_A(b_A c_B + b_B c_A)}{c_A c_B} + \frac{b_A^2}{2c_A} \geq 0$$

$$\frac{\partial L}{\partial \lambda_2} = b_B(q_A + q_B) + (s-1)\frac{c_B}{2}q_B^2 \qquad (5.44)$$
$$- \frac{b_B(b_A c_B + b_B c_A)}{c_A c_B} + \frac{b_B^2}{2c_B} \geq 0$$

$$\frac{\partial L}{\partial \lambda_3} = b_B q_B + (s-1)\frac{c_B}{2}q_B^2 - \frac{b_B^2}{2c_B} \geq 0 \qquad (5.45)$$

$$0 = q_k\, \partial L/\partial q_k, \quad k = A, B \qquad (5.46)$$

$$0 = \lambda_l\, \partial L/\partial \lambda_l, \quad l = 1, 2, 3 \qquad (5.47)$$

$$q_k \geq 0, \quad k = A, B \qquad (5.48)$$

$$\lambda_l \geq 0, \quad l = 1, 2, 3. \qquad (5.49)$$

Three types of cooperative outcomes are possible. Depending on parameter values, either the full cooperative solution (Case 1), a second-best agreement with constraint (5.38) binding (Case 2), a second-best IEA with constraint (5.37) binding (Case 3), or no cooperation at all can be enforced. In the following, we provide the analytical results for the three cases and illustrate each type of outcome using a numerical example.[20]

---

[20] Numerical simulations are taken out with the software package GAMS. Computed values are rounded.

To compare aggregate welfare under a second-best agreement with global welfare under global efficiency we define analogously to (5.7) a welfare loss ratio for cooperative solutions $\Delta^C \equiv (\Pi^* - \Pi^C)/\Pi^*$ which we can evaluate for different types of agreements. Figure 5.1 summarizes the

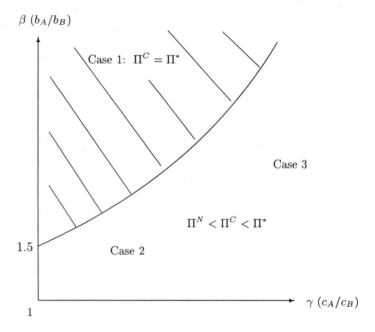

Figure 5.1: Agreements with compensations for cost-effectiveness

results. It shows that the gains from stable environmental cooperation using compensations for cost-effectiveness depend on how heterogeneous countries are with respect to abatement benefit and cost parameters, indicated by β and γ, respectively.

Case 1 ($\lambda_l = 0$, $l = 1, 2, 3$): Obviously, if neither the individual rationality nor the incentive compatibility constraints are binding, the globally efficient allocation of abatements is implemented and the terms of the agreement are

$$q_A^C = q_A^*, \quad q_B^C = q_B^*, \quad T^{CE} = \frac{s(b_A + b_B)^2}{2c_B}. \quad (5.50)$$

The full cooperative solution is attainable if compensations for cost-effectiveness (5.34) are sufficiently high so that incentive compatibility constraint (5.38) is not binding.[21] Substituting transfer rule (5.34) into

---

[21]Individual rationality constraints (5.36) and (5.37) are not binding in this case,

constraint (5.38), inserting the respective abatement quantities and re-arranging yields

$$T^{CE}(q_B^*) \geq \pi_B^D - \pi_B^* \Leftrightarrow \frac{(1+\beta)^2}{\beta} \geq \frac{\left(1 + \frac{\beta}{\gamma}\right)^2}{\left(1 + \frac{\beta}{\gamma}\right)^2 - \left(1 + \frac{1}{\gamma}\right)^2}, \quad (5.51)$$

with $\pi_B^D = \pi_B(q_A^*, q_B^N)$ and $\pi_B^* = \pi_B(q_A^*, q_B^*)$. We see immediately that condition (5.51) depends solely on the heterogeneity of the countries and not on the levels of b_k and c_k. The more heterogeneous countries are with respect to benefit parameter b_k and the less heterogeneous they are with respect to cost parameter c_k, the more likely it is that condition (5.51) holds and the full cooperative solution can be attained. This outcome is indicated by the shaded area in Figure 5.1.[22] When condition (5.51) does not hold, compensations for cost-effectiveness are so low that either constraint (5.37) or constraint (5.38) is binding and only a second-best agreement is enforceable (unshaded area in Figure 5.1).

Table 5.1 provides a numerical example for Case 1 which represents a benchmark: country B's abatement benefits are (close to) zero. This

Table 5.1: Unidirectional pollution

$b_A = 10,$	$b_B \to 0,$	$c_A = 2,$	$c_B = 2$		
$q_A^N = 5.0$	$q_B^N = 0$	$Q^N = 5.0$	$\pi_A^N = 25.0$	$\pi_B^N = 0$	$\Delta^N = 0.5$
$q_A^C = 5.0$	$q_B^C = 5.0$	$Q^C = 10.0$	$\pi_A^C - T = 50.0$	$\pi_B^C + T = 0$	$\Delta^C = 0$
$q_A^* = 5.0$	$q_B^* = 5.0$	$Q^* = 10.0$	$\pi_A^* = 75.0$	$\pi_B^* = -25.0$	$T = 25.0$

mirrors the scenario of a unidirectional externality where only one country is interested in environmental protection (country A), but both pollute (for example, pollution of a river). The country not harmed by pollution will participate only if it receives a compensation that is high enough to make it at least indifferent to non-cooperation. As there are no free-rider incentives for B in this case, the increase in net benefits that B can achieve by defecting is equal to B's reduction in abatement costs. According to (5.34), country B is compensated for these higher costs, implying that the gains from cooperation go in total to the donor country. In general, the full cooperative solution can always be enforced with the present transfer scheme when the recipient country pollutes but

---

either.

[22] Due to our asymmetry assumptions ($b_A \geq b_B \wedge c_A \geq c_B$) only the first quadrant is of interest. In the case of $c_A = c_B \Leftrightarrow \gamma = 1$, (5.51) simplifies to $\beta \geq 3/2$ (see Figure 5.1).

is not harmed by pollution. This holds regardless of how inefficient the initial non-cooperative equilibrium is (in Table 5.1, $\Delta^N = 0.5$).

Case 2 ($\lambda_3 > 0$, $\lambda_l = 0$, $l = 1, 2$): In the case of only moderate asymmetry the potential gains of recipient country B from defecting (5.38) constitute the constraint that restricts the terms of the agreement and cooperative abatement quantities are determined by $T^{CE} = \pi_B^D - \pi_B^C$, yielding an agreement[23]

$$q_A^C = \frac{b_B(1 + \sqrt{s})}{c_A(1 - s)}, \quad q_B^C = \frac{b_B(1 + \sqrt{s})}{c_B(1 - s)}, \quad T^{CE} = \frac{b_B^2\, s\,(1 + \sqrt{s})^2}{2\, c_B\,(1 - s)^2}. \quad (5.52)$$

The extent to which this second-best cooperative solution falls short of welfare under global efficiency is given by

$$\Delta^C = 1 - \frac{(1 + \beta)(1 + \sqrt{s})(1 - s) - (1 + \sqrt{s})^2}{(1 + \beta)(1 - s)^2}. \quad (5.53)$$

Welfare loss ratio (5.53) does not depend on c_k/b_k, but only on asymmetry parameters β and γ. Aggregate cooperative welfare is the higher, *ceteris paribus*, the more heterogeneous countries are with respect to marginal abatement benefits and the less asymmetric they are with respect to the slope of the marginal cost function. Table 5.2 illustrates

Table 5.2: Incentive compatibility constraint binding

$b_A = 11,$	$b_B = 10,$	$c_A = 1,$	$c_B = 1$			
$q_A^N = 11.0$	$q_B^N = 10.0$	$Q^N = 21.0$	$\pi_A^N = 170.5$	$\pi_B^N = 160.0$	$\Delta^N - 0.25$	
$q_A^C = 14.4$	$q_B^C = 14.4$	$Q^C = 28.8$	$\pi_A^C - T = 203$	$\pi_B^C + T = 194$	$\Delta^C = 0.10$	
$q_A^* = 21.0$	$q_B^* = 21.0$	$Q^* = 42.0$	$\pi_A^* = 241.5$	$\pi_B^* = 199.5$	$T = 9.6$	

that in this case both countries increase their abatements and substantial gains from cooperation are attainable.

Case 3 ($\lambda_2 > 0$, $\lambda_l = 0$, $l = 1, 3$): In the case of strong asymmetry with respect to cost parameter c_k an agreement stipulating a reduction in A's and a sharp increase in B's abatements is negotiated. Given that high-cost country A *reduces* its abatements under cooperation, defecting behavior by country B is not profitable. Too high cooperative abatements would make B worse off than in the Nash equilibrium because compensations for cost-effectiveness would not suffice for constraint (5.11)

---

[23] Due to the quadratic functional form of $T^{CE} = \pi_B^D - \pi_B^C$, there are two solutions for the cooperative abatements q_B^C, only the positive one being economically meaningful.

to hold.[24] Hence, cooperative abatement quantities are determined by $T^{CE} = \pi_B^N - \pi_B^C$, yielding an agreement[25]

$$q_A^C = \frac{r}{c_A(s-1)}, \quad q_B^C = \frac{r}{c_B(s-1)}, \quad T^{CE} = \frac{r^2 s}{2 c_B (1-s)^2}, \quad (5.54)$$

$$r \equiv -b_B \left(1 + \frac{c_B}{c_A}\right) - \sqrt{b_B^2 \left(1 + \frac{c_B}{c_A}\right)^2 + b_B \left(2 b_A \frac{c_B}{c_A} + b_B\right)} (s-1).$$

The extent to which agreement (5.54) falls short of welfare under global efficiency is given by

$$\Delta^C = 1 - \frac{2(b_A + b_B)(s-1)r - r^2}{(b_A + b_B)^2 (s-1)^2}. \quad (5.55)$$

As before, welfare loss ratio Δ^C does not depend on c_k/b_k, but only on the ratios b_A/b_B and c_A/c_B. For a numerical example where constraint (5.11) is binding and country A reduces its abatements in the cooperative solution, see Table 5.3. The example illustrates that the

Table 5.3: Individual rationality constraint binding

$b_A = 10,$	$b_B = 1,$	$c_A = 10,$	$c_B = 1$		
$q_A^N = 1.0$	$q_B^N = 1.0$	$Q^N = 2.0$	$\pi_A^N = 15.0$	$\pi_B^N = 1.5$	$\Delta^N = 0.75$
$q_A^C = 0.5$	$q_B^C = 5.5$	$Q^C = 6.0$	$\pi_A^C - T = 48.1$	$\pi_B^C + T = 1.5$	$\Delta^C = 0.25$
$q_A^* = 1.1$	$q_B^* = 11.0$	$Q^* = 12.1$	$\pi_A^* = 114.9$	$\pi_B^D = 1.0$	$T = 10.4$

welfare losses from non-cooperation are especially large when countries are strongly asymmetric with respect to benefit as well as cost parameters ($\Delta^N = 0.75$), and that substantial gains are enforceable with compensations for cost-effectiveness ($\Delta^C = 0.25$).

In the benchmark case of identical countries, marginal abatement costs do not differ in the Nash equilibrium. Thus, no gain can be made from cost-effectiveness of cooperative abatements which could be used as enforcement mechanism for the environmental treaty. The same holds for scenarios where the countries are heterogeneous, but in a way that does not influence the cost-effectiveness of non-cooperative abatements. This

---

[24]This can be seen from (5.34): compensations for cost-effective abatements increase at a lower rate ($\partial T^{CE}/\partial q_B = s c_B q_B$, $0 \leq s < 1$) than marginal abatement costs of recipient country B ($C_B' = c_B q_B$).

[25]Due to the quadratic functional form of $T^{CE} = \pi_B^N - \pi_B^C$, there are two solutions for the cooperative abatements q_B^C, only the positive one being economically meaningful.

is the case when the slopes of marginal abatement cost functions differ ($c_A \neq c_B$), but marginal abatement benefits do not ($b_A = b_B$).[26] In all other cases heterogeneities allow substantial cooperation gains to be enforced through compensations for cost-effectiveness. In the case where marginal abatement benefits differ strongly across countries, but costs do not, even the full cooperative outcome is enforceable.

5.4   The Case of Three Countries

The two-country model of the previous section could be interpreted as two groups of countries acting like single agents and engaging in international environmental cooperation. One may think of a club of industrialized countries jointly undertaking side payments to a group of developing countries. This approach, however, cannot explain how such coalitions emerge as a result of individual optimizing behavior. Moreover, it ignores the incentives for strategic behavior *within* coalitions. In agreements with heterogeneous parties the problem of how to arrange the 'burden sharing' becomes predominant. This is especially relevant when side payments are funded jointly by a group of donors.[27] In the multiple-country case, the free-rider problem is manifest not only in the incentive to defect from an existing agreement, but also in the incentive to abstain from environmental cooperation right from the beginning. As the abstention of one single country does not necessarily lead to a collapse of negotiations and cooperation, each government will try to free ride on the intensified abatement efforts of cooperating countries. This strategy is the more promising, the more countries are involved and the smaller the impact of a single government's behavior on the cooperative solution is. As a result, in most cases not only is partial cooperation by a subgroup of governments the best that can be achieved (Barrett 1994), but also an additional coordination problem arises concerning who cooperates and who stays outside.

To investigate the participation decision of single countries and potential coordination problems we extend the model in this section to the three-country case. This is the simplest possible framework to address the questions raised above. The impact of the participation decision on the cooperative equilibrium is illustrated for each of the two scenarios

---

[26]To see this compare the efficient distribution of abatements $q_A^*/q_B^* = c_B/c_A$ with that in the Nash equilibrium $q_A^N/q_B^N = (b_A c_B)/(b_B c_A)$. All such scenarios lie on the horizontal axis of Figure 5.1.

[27]In Carraro and Siniscalco (1993) these aspects are disregarded by restricting the analysis to identical countries and by assuming that a specified subgroup of countries is already committed to cooperation.

of Sections 5.3.1 and 5.3.3 using numerical simulations of the model specified in Section 5.2.[28] In the following, first we show that the enforcement mechanism of Section 5.3 is also working for three (and more) countries. Subsequently, we investigate the prospects for stable environmental cooperation with self-financing transfers (Section 5.4.1) and with compensations for cost-effectiveness (Section 5.4.2) when joint benefits are maximized. The results are illustrated by showing for a given parameter combination the pay-off matrix for the critical cooperative solutions (Tables 5.4 to 5.6 below). All agreements indicated are enforceable.

Consider three countries A, B and C involved in transboundary pollution. Costs and benefits of abatements are distributed across countries as before ($b_A \geq b_B \geq b_C \wedge c_A \geq c_B \geq c_C \Rightarrow \pi_A^* \geq \pi_B^* \geq \pi_C^*$). First it has to be shown that the game structure introduced in Section 5.3 to ensure enforcement of the IEA is also applicable for three (as well as for n) countries. From Section 5.3.1 we know that in the two-country case global efficiency is reached when joint net benefits are maximized and the country with higher potential gains becomes the donor. When three countries are involved in pollution, the globally optimal agreement must obviously include all three of them. In this 'grand coalition' side payments can either be paid by only one country, say A, to two recipient countries (B and C), or jointly by two countries, say A and B, to the third country (C).[29] In the first case, incentive compatibility is ensured when country A moves first. The recipient countries execute the IEA simultaneously and will comply as long as side payments are sufficiently large. Hence, the sequence described in Section 5.3 can be used. However, in contrast to the two-country case, the potential gains from cooperation of the single donor country may not suffice to finance the necessary transfers to make all of the recipients comply with the full cooperative solution.[30] If so, the individual rationality constraint for A is binding and only a second-best cooperative solution is enforceable (Table 5.5). This potential problem is avoided in the second case when two countries share the burden of side payments to the third country. Then, however, the simultaneous execution of the agreement by donors A and B in stage 2 is not incentive compatible because unilateral defection

---

[28] In total, 45 pay-offs of the three countries resulting from 15 different possible agreements have to be compared in order to identify the cooperative equilibria for each of the two scenarios in Sections 5.4.1 and 5.4.2. Therefore, we abstain in this section from an analytical exposition of the results.

[29] We do not consider other possible assignments of roles (for example, C paying transfers to A and B) that may be the outcome of uneven bargaining positions because the focus here is on the maximal *aggregate* welfare gains being enforceable.

[30] This is more likely, the more homogeneous the countries and the greater the number of recipients that have to be bribed to stick to the IEA by one single country.

always pays off. To make a cooperative solution with two donor countries enforceable one therefore has to introduce *sequential transfers* and modify the game structure introduced in Section 5.3 as follows:

1. Countries A, B and C negotiate the terms of the IEA with regard to cooperative abatements q_k^C and transfers T_{AB} and T_{BC}.
2. Country A moves first. It raises its abatements to the level q_A^C and deposits with a third party the transfer T_{AB} agreed in stage 1.
3. Country B moves second. If it cooperates, it raises its abatements to q_B^C, deposits the agreed transfer T_{BC}, and receives the side payment T_{AB}.
4. Country C moves last. If it cooperates by raising its abatements to q_C^C, it receives the side payment T_{BC}.

Country B is both a recipient and a donor of side payments. The transfer it receives from A serves as a carrot to make it sign and comply with the agreement.[31] The transfer it grants to C ensures C's compliance. This transfer scheme accomplishes two purposes: it enables the enforcement of an agreement signed by all three countries and ensures that country A does not bear the entire burden of the required side payments. In the scenario of compensations for cost-effectiveness, it prescribes in addition the flows of transfers when more than two countries with differing marginal abatement costs cooperate. In spite of the fact that the full cooperative solution is enforceable it may not be an equilibrium, as we show in the following. This is because in addition to the decision problem as described in Section 5.3, each government also decides whether to join the IEA or to abstain from it, given that the other two governments cooperate.

5.4.1   Self-financing Transfers

Table 5.4 shows a scenario where the heterogeneity with respect to marginal abatement benefits is sufficiently large for global efficiency to be attainable. The letter P stands for 'participation' and O for 'staying outside' the agreement. The numbers in brackets denote the individual pay-offs (π_A, π_B, π_C) and the number in square brackets indicates the extent to which welfare under global efficiency is reached $[\Pi/\Pi^*]$. NC stands for the non-cooperative Nash equilibrium; the other solutions describe agreements where a transfer is paid from the country on

---

[31]The relevant compliance constraint for B is $\pi_B^C(q_A^C, q_B^C, q_C^C) + T_{AB} \geq \pi_B^D(q_A^C, q_B^N, q_C^N)$. Numerical simulations show that in most cases country B is a net donor of transfers $(T_{AB} < T_{BC})$.

the left of the arrow to the country on the right.[32] The pay-off matrix

Table 5.4: Strong asymmetry with respect to b_k

		P	country B	O	
		P country C O		P country C O	
A	P	$A \to B$ and C: (46,34,17) [1.0] $A \to B \wedge B \to C$: (66,14,17) [1.0]	$A \to B$: (38,18,15) [0.73]	$A \to C$: (40,26,9) [0.77]	NC
	O	$B \to C$: (43,14,10) [0.69]	NC	NC	NC: (28,14,8) [0.51]

Parameter values: $b_A = 5 > b_B = 2 > b_C = 1$, $c_A = c_B = c_C = 1$.

shows that there is a unique cooperative equilibrium where A is granting side payments to B and C ($A \to B$ and C) and the social optimum is reached. Country A prefers the other full cooperative solution where — according to the game described above — country B is both a donor and a recipient of transfers (66 > 46). However, this agreement is not an equilibrium as country B in that case would rather prefer to abstain from cooperation at all (26 > 14). Hence, in this scenario of asymmetry the cooperative solution is both globally efficient and unique.

When countries differ only slightly with respect to benefit and costs parameters, global efficiency is only enforceable when B is a donor as well as a recipient of side payments (Table 5.5). In this case A's potential gains from cooperation do not suffice to bribe both countries B and C to stick to efficient abatement levels. In contrast to the scenario of Table 5.4, the efficient IEA is no longer supported by all countries: given that country B cooperates with C, country A would rather prefer not to participate in the IEA (45 > 36); and given that A and C cooperate, country B favors the other grand coalition where A is the only donor (52 > 41 > 37). The only cooperative equilibrium is a subcoalition of countries B and C: given that these countries cooperate, A can do no better than stay outside; and given A's optimal strategy, B and C will cooperate. Table 5.5 illustrates that aggregate gains from environmental cooperation are substantial even if not all three countries cooperate. In the benchmark case of identical countries there are six such partial cooperative equilibria in total and an additional coordination problem

---

[32]For clarity of the exposition we do not indicate in the pay-off matrices cooperative solutions that are dominated. Values are rounded.

Table 5.5: Modest asymmetry with respect to b_k and c_k

		P country B O			
		P country C O		P country C O	
	P	$A \to B$ and C: (25,52,44) [0.98] $A \to B \wedge B \to C$: (36,37,50) [1.0]	$A \to B$: (26,31,36) [0.76]	$A \to C$: (27,41,28) [0.78]	NC
A	O	$B \to C$: (45,24,27) [0.78]	NC	NC	NC: (25,23,20) [0.55]

Parameter values: $b_A = 10 > b_B = 9 > b_C = 8$, $c_A = 10 > c_B = 9 > c_C = 8$.

arises.[33] This situation can be described as a 'chicken game' where each player tries to make the others believe that he/she will not 'give in' and cooperate (see, for example, Althammer and Buchholz 1993 or Carraro and Siniscalco 1993, p. 322).

5.4.2   Compensations for Cost-effectiveness of Abatements

In the case where side payments are restricted to compensations for cost-effectiveness of abatements, the enforcement mechanism loses the ability to enforce the full cooperative solution, even if countries are considerably asymmetric (Table 5.6). The grand coalition is even Pareto-dominated by any agreement of only two countries. This is because the higher the potential for transfers (and thereby for enforceability), the larger the asymmetries and thus the gains from emissions trading. Therefore, global welfare is highest under the IEA where the two most heterogeneous countries (A and C) cooperate [$\Pi^C/\Pi^* = 0.81$]. In the numerical example of Table 5.6, all three partial cooperative solutions are an equilibrium, again giving rise to a coordination problem. However, in a game with a great number of countries, the coordination problem would be resolved to some extent as several pairs of strongly asymmetric countries could engage in bilateral agreements.

---

[33]The cooperative equilibria are $A \to B$, $B \to A$, $A \to C$, $C \to A$, $B \to C$ and $C \to B$.

Table 5.6: Strong asymmetry with respect to b_k and c_k

| | | P   country B | | O | |
		P country C O		P country C O	
	P	$A \to B$ and C: (44,22,4) [0.35] $A \to B \wedge B \to C$: (49,19,5) [0.37]	$A \to B$: (50,25,9) [0.42]	$A \to C$: (86,70,5) [0.81]	NC
A	O	$B \to C$: (90,31,6) [0.64]	NC	NC	NC: (37,19,4) [0.30]

Parameter values: $b_A = 10 > b_B = 5 > b_C = 1$, $c_A = 5 > c_B = 3 > c_C = 1$.

5.5   Conclusions

This chapter has demonstrated how self-financing transfers can help to overcome the time-consistency problem of enforcing international environmental agreements. Within the framework of specific abatement cost and benefit functions a model contract has been developed which uses conditional transfers and sequential moves of the contracting parties to stabilize an international environmental agreement. Self-financing transfers prove to be powerful instruments for earning substantial welfare gains from stable environmental cooperation, even if transfers are paid only to compensate for incremental abatement costs. If the exclusive restriction on transfers is that they must be self-financing and if countries agree to maximize their joint net benefits of abatements, the full cooperative solution can always be enforced in the two-country-case. However, it has been shown that substantial gains from cooperation — if not the social optimum — are enforceable even if transfers are restricted to compensations for cost-effectiveness of abatement efforts and if more than two countries are involved. The three-country case illustrated, however, that with multiple countries involved in environmental cooperation, a coordination problem may arise in addition to the enforcement problem.

In the analysed game structure the influence of the countries' heterogeneity on global welfare is ambiguous. On the one hand, the prospects for environmental cooperation rise with greater asymmetry regarding abatement costs and benefits because they increase the potential for transfers being used as an enforcement mechanism. Moreover, uneven bargaining positions may help to overcome coordination problems that arise during negotiations on an international environmental treaty. On the other hand, we have illustrated in Section 5.3.2 that with uneven bargaining positions, joint net benefits from international environmental policy are generally *not* maximized. Rather, the outcome of negotiations in these cases is an agreement that reflects only individual interests of single countries or some weighted sum of national net benefits. Consequently, from a global welfare point of view this type of asymmetry generally has an adverse effect.

The results of this chapter cannot claim generality due to the simple functional relationships which are presumed to represent a country's environmental decision-making. In particular, uniqueness of the efficient allocation is no longer given in a more general setting. The purpose of the model, however, is not to address this fundamental problem, but rather to identify new welfare-improving cooperative strategies by using the common assumptions in the related literature. It also has to be stressed that an IEA executed according to the proposed game structure is not completely self-enforcing. Its successful implementation relies on the existence of a third party that works as an intermediary for international side payments. This assumption, however, not only seems to be more realistic than to exclude any form of enforcement on the international level, but it also illustrates how at least limited binding commitments can be reached by the use of existing institutions. The agency's only competence needed is to collect and distribute side payments according to the rules previously determined by the IEA. Any own discretionary power is not necessary. Of course, insurance against non-compliance by the deposition of a mortgage is always possible, if only the deposited amounts are high enough. However, this is a stronger requirement than depositing only those transfers which are paid in accordance to an agreement anyway.

The general policy implication of this chapter's analysis is that sovereign countries are able to coordinate their environmental policies successfully if they fall back on existing international institutions and use them in an innovative way. Whenever side payments are available as an instrument in international environmental cooperation, these should be used not only to make national governments sign an environmental treaty, but also to comply with the obligations to which they have committed. Moreover, the beneficial role of international transfers is the more distinct the more the cooperating parties differ. In a world of many more or less heterogeneous countries one can therefore make a case for a bundle of (bilateral) environmental treaties in which asymmetric countries join together and cooperate (see, for example, Section 5.4.2).

In the special case where an environmental treaty stipulates compensations for incremental abatement costs, there is an additional implication for international environmental policy. Governments should not engage in the international cost-effectiveness of their environmental policies before an IEA is successfully negotiated. Every measure which improves the cost-effectiveness of abatement efforts across countries even before the successful ratification of the environmental treaty reduces the cost-savings that can be reached within the agreement itself and which may be used to enforce it. From this perspective, the concept of 'joint implementation' stipulated in the Framework Convention on Climate Change and the Kyoto Protocol, for example, should be linked closely to the success of the Protocol itself.

Chapter 6

Financing Incremental Abatement Costs under Asymmetric Information

6.1 Introduction

Like the majority of studies on international environmental agreements, the previous analysis of cost-effective and incentive compatible international environmental policy was restricted to situations of perfect information.[1] It was assumed that national governments have perfect knowledge both on their own costs and benefits of environmental policy and on those of all other countries involved in a transboundary pollution problem. This assumption is relaxed in the following. It is a stylized fact that in most cases international environmental policy is confronted with problems of imperfect information. In the real world, national governments neither know exactly the characteristics of all other countries involved in an international environmental problem, nor can they easily identify their own costs and benefits of pollution reduction. This is especially true for environmental problems with a dynamic character. However, even under perfect foresight the fundamental problem remains that information on environmental preferences (that is, on marginal willingness to pay for the environment) is private by nature.

In this chapter we investigate the influence of asymmetric information on an international environmental agreement which provides for

---

[1] Barrett (1994), for example, analyses IEAs that are self-enforcing, but considers identical countries, assumes perfect information and rules out the possibility of side payments. Carraro and Siniscalco (1993) allow for international side payments, but assume perfect information and identical countries as well. See Mäler (1990) for aspects of international environmental policy under perfect and imperfect information.

side payments between the contracting parties. International environmental agreements increasingly make use of transfers. Recent examples are the Framework Convention on Climate Change, the Montreal Protocol on the protection of the ozone layer or the biodiversity convention. An important purpose of transfers in these agreements is to improve the international cost-effectiveness of pollution reduction efforts, that is, to reach the negotiated environmental standard at lowest overall costs. This is the mandate of the Global Environment Facility (GEF) and the Montreal Protocol Multilateral Fund (MPMF) which both grant financial support for activities of developing countries to protect global environmental resources. The available funds are provided by industrialized countries who believe that the same environmental effect could be achieved through domestic measures but at higher costs. Another example for the practical relevance of international compensation schemes is the concept of 'joint implementation' which was elaborated in the course of the Rio process and which has recently been confirmed in the Kyoto Protocol.

In general, perfect information is one of the crucial underlying assumptions for the validity of the Coase theorem, as stated in Chapter 2. When relevant information is in the private domain, decentralized bargaining often results in inefficient outcomes. As national governments may take actions to conceal their true preferences and characteristics, incomplete information enlarges the strategy space and generates new and potentially inefficient outcomes. Beside additional negotiation costs such as costs of delay, *ex post* efficiency may be incompatible with the individual *ex ante* incentives of the bargaining parties (Myerson 1979).[2] Such incentives for inefficient strategic behavior are especially strong when side payments are on the agenda of environmental negotiations. National governments may try to manipulate the amount of transfers stipulated in an environmental treaty by concealing their own damage and abatement costs and by giving false information that supports their own position. Similarly, when side payments are financed jointly by a group of donor countries, each of them may try to lower its own share of the burden by releasing biassed information. By analogy to the optimal regulation of environmental externalities in a purely national context (see, for example, Kwerel 1977), efficient solutions on the management of international environmental resources require that the true national benefits of international environmental policy are revealed. The question therefore arises as to how mechanisms and bargaining processes can be designed in order to achieve the utmost mutual gains from interna-

---

[2] For an overview on bargaining problems under imperfect information, see Kennan and Wilson (1993).

tional environmental cooperation. Apart from the enforcement problem — which was the focus of the previous chapter — there is thus another natural route of departure from the traditional framework of Coasian bargaining.

Given the above observations and the focus on compensation payments in the present study, a model contract for international environmental problems has to address the question of how asymmetric information influences the transfer scheme that is adopted in an international environmental agreement. Therefore, in the following we compare compensations for net versus gross incremental abatement costs and analyse the respective incentives for truth-telling or false-reporting, the preferred transfer scheme and potential cooperative solutions. The notion of 'incremental abatement costs' prescribes that recipient countries are compensated for the extra costs they incur if they participate in an environmental agreement. Under the net incremental cost rule, project-induced extra benefits that accrue to the host country of an environmental protection project are deducted from the payment that compensates this country for its gross incremental abatement costs. The extra benefits may be given in terms of an increased quality of the international environmental resource at stake, in terms of local environmental benefits or in terms of other, non-environmental side-benefits (for example, technology transfer or capacity building in developing countries). The incremental cost concept is an operational guideline to promote cost-effectiveness in global environmental policy for institutions such as the Global Environment Facility (see, for example, King 1993) and the Montreal Protocol Multilateral Fund as well as for 'activities implemented jointly' (Art. 4 Para. 2a FCCC) and potentially for the 'Clean Development Mechanism' of the Kyoto Protocol.

The framework of the analysis is a static signaling game on emission abatements. Two heterogeneous parties negotiate an environmental treaty to reduce globally harmful emissions. To this end, countries with relatively high marginal abatement costs grant transfers to low-cost countries. It is assumed that the two groups of countries act like single agents and that the parties can credibly commit themselves to their treaty obligations.[3] Information is imperfect in the sense that national abatement costs are public knowledge, but information on abatement benefits is private.[4] This assumption reflects the fact that the

---

[3] In the context of the negotiations that led to the creation of the GEF and the MPMF, the formation of subcoalitions, the presence of outsider countries and enforcement problems have been relatively insignificant compared to other issues (see, for example, DeSombre and Kauffman 1996 and Fairman 1996).

[4] See Chillemi (1997) for a similar model with multiple countries that also allows for international side payments. Bac (1996) analyses a repeated game of two countries

economic costs of environmental protection measures abroad are relatively well known in comparison to the environmental preferences of a
foreign country. The signaling device is emission abatements in the non-
cooperative Nash equilibrium. Based on this information the parties
negotiate agreements that either include differentiated transfers for each
type the recipient may take (separating equilibria) or uniform transfers
to compensate for net or for full incremental abatement costs (pooling
equilibria).

The structure of the chapter is as follows. Section 6.2 briefly reviews
the basic model which has been introduced in Section 5.2 and describes
possible agreements under perfect information. In Section 6.3 we introduce asymmetric information and derive the signaling incentives under
the two alternative incremental cost concepts. Section 6.4 analyses the
terms of the agreement in the separating equilibrium and in Section 6.5
we derive the properties of pooling equilibria where transfers compensate either for net or for full incremental abatement costs. We investigate
which of the transfer schemes is favored by each of the two coalitions.
Section 6.6 discusses possible extensions and implications of the results
for 'joint implementation' projects to protect global environmental resources.

6.2 Agreements under Perfect Information

Consider a world divided into two groups of countries who act like single agents.[5] Assume the same basic model and functional specification
of abatement costs and benefits as in Chapter 5 (that is, orthogonal
best-response functions), with subscripts A and B being replaced by D
and R, respectively. As in Section 5.2, national abatement quantities
in the non-cooperative Nash equilibrium[6] are $q_k^N = b_k/c_k$, $k = D, R$
and in the central planner (full cooperative) solution they are $q_k^* = (b_D + b_R)/c_k$, $k = D, R$, see equations (5.5) and (5.6). Marginal abatement benefits and costs are both taken to be higher for the donor coali-
tion D: $b_D > b_R \wedge c_D > c_R$. In addition, we define the group of recipient

---

under imperfect information about environmental valuations. Steiner (1997a, 1997b)
considers IEAs including transfers in the presence of asymmetric information on
abatement costs. Asymmetric information in JI projects is analysed by Hagem (1996).

[5] For simplicity, we disregard heterogeneities and diverging interests within each
group of countries and ignore free-riding by third countries that do not belong to any
of the two groups.

[6] By treating the two groups as single agents it is implicitly assumed that the (perfectly homogeneous) members of each group coordinate their environmental policies
even in the non-cooperative equilibrium, resulting in higher abatement efforts than
without any cooperation.

countries R to be worse off in the full cooperative solution compared to non-cooperation: $\pi_R^* < \pi_R^N \Leftrightarrow b_D^2 \, c_D > 2 \, b_R^2 \, c_R$. This asymmetry between the two groups of countries implies that marginal abatement costs are higher for countries D in the non-cooperative Nash equilibrium. Moreover, it requires positive side payments from D to R in order to make countries R cooperate voluntarily.

The parties negotiate on an international environmental agreement prescribing emission reductions and including a transfer from donor countries D to recipients R. The side payments serve to induce the cooperation of those countries which have relatively little interest in pollution control but are able to reduce emissions at smaller marginal costs. The starting-point for negotiations is the non-cooperative Nash equilibrium. As in Section 5.3.1, we assume that governments agree to maximize joint net benefits of cooperative abatements.[7] The agreement has to be individually rational for both parties, that is, it has to guarantee at least the same utility as in the non-cooperative equilibrium.[8] We assume that the enforcement of the agreement is assured once it has been signed.[9] There are thus no incentive compatibility constraints but only individual rationality constraints in optimization problem (6.1)–(6.3):

$$\max \Pi(q_D^C, q_R^C), \quad \text{s.t.} \tag{6.1}$$

$$\pi_D(q_D^C, q_R^C) - T \;\geq\; \pi_D(q_D^N, q_R^N) \tag{6.2}$$

$$\pi_R(q_D^C, q_R^C) + T \;\geq\; \pi_R(q_D^N, q_R^N). \tag{6.3}$$

Writing constraints (6.2) and (6.3) together and rearranging to $\pi_D^C - \pi_D^N \geq T \geq \pi_R^N - \pi_R^C$ shows that there always exists a positive transfer so that both conditions are fulfilled with inequality. Since, by definition, aggregate net benefits are higher under cooperation than in the non-cooperative Nash equilibrium, we have: $\Pi^C > \Pi^N \Leftrightarrow \pi_D^C + \pi_R^C > \pi_D^N + \pi_R^N \Leftrightarrow \pi_D^C - \pi_D^N > \pi_R^N - \pi_R^C$. Hence, without additional restrictions on T the individual rationality constraints are never binding. The first-order conditions of (6.1)–(6.3) yield $q_k^C = q_k^*$, $k = D, R$, that is, the globally efficient allocation of emission abatements can be implemented as a cooperative solution. The structure of the above cooperation problem, however, does not suffice to identify a unique cooperative solution

---

[7] Assuming that the bargaining process takes place in order to achieve a Pareto-optimal outcome allows us to compare the results of the present analysis with those of the related literature.

[8] It is assumed that if a coalition is indifferent towards cooperation, it will cooperate.

[9] Allowing for binding commitments seems to be not too problematic in the context of 'joint implementation' because related projects can be delegated to private agents (companies or non-governmental agencies) and are monitored by an international institution which administers the financial funds.

with respect to the amount of transfers T. Any positive transfer which satisfies $\pi_D^C - \pi_D^N > T > \pi_R^N - \pi_R^C$ is compatible with the full cooperative solution. To yield uniqueness an additional assumption concerning the side payments thus has to be made. As the latter determine how the aggregate welfare gains from environmental cooperation are distributed among donor and recipient countries, this assumption reflects to a large extent the relative bargaining strengths of the negotiating parties.

For illustrative purposes, let us consider as in Chapter 5 two extreme scenarios with respect to the distribution of aggregate gains from international environmental cooperation. The first scenario is that the gains are shared in equal amounts between the two coalitions (see Section 5.3.1). Transfers T in optimization problem (6.1)–(6.3) are then unambiguously determined by $\pi_D^C - T - \pi_D^N = \pi_R^C + T - \pi_R^N \Leftrightarrow T = 1/2\left[(\pi_D^C - \pi_D^N) - (\pi_R^C - \pi_R^N)\right]$, see equation (5.17). The other benchmark is that the gains from environmental cooperation go entirely to the potential donor countries D, the recipients' welfare remaining unchanged. This cooperative solution emerges if one party (the donor coalition) is able to dictate the terms of the agreement and submits a 'take-it-or-leave-it' offer, whereas the other party can only accept or reject it.[10] In this case, the individual rationality constraint of the recipients (6.3) is binding and the transfer is given by

$$
\begin{aligned}
T &= \pi_R^N - \pi_R^C & (6.4) \\
&= \left[C_R(q_R^C) - C_R(q_R^N)\right] - \left[B_R(Q^C) - B_R(Q^N)\right] \equiv T^n.
\end{aligned}
$$

Transfer (6.4) covers the *net* incremental abatement costs incurred by the recipient. The first term in square brackets represents R's *gross* incremental abatement costs due to its cooperation,

$$
T^g \equiv C_R(q_R^C) - C_R(q_R^N), \qquad (6.5)
$$

the second term stands for its incremental benefits from reduced pollution. R's welfare gains from a higher environmental quality are subtracted from the side payments it receives as a compensation for higher abatement costs under cooperation. Transfer scheme (6.4) suggests that countries R have an incentive to understate their true environmental preferences when they possess private information on their benefits from a cleaner environment. If such a signaling strategy is successful they can avoid the transfer cut through their incremental benefits from environmental cooperation. In the following, we discuss R's incentives (not) to

---

[10]The optimization problem for the donor coalition then is to maximize $\pi_D(q_D^C, q_R^C) - T$ with $T = \pi_R^N - \pi_R^C$ which is equivalent to maximizing $\Pi^C - \pi_R^N$. The donors optimal offer thus stipulates globally efficient abatement quantities, analogously to equations (5.32) and (5.33) in Section 5.3.2.

reveal its true type under the two transfer schemes (6.4) and (6.5), that is, compensations for net and for gross incremental abatement costs.

6.3   Signaling Incentives

We examine a scenario with asymmetric information on environmental preferences (that is, abatement benefits) and perfect information on abatement costs. The analysis focusses on the incentives of recipient countries to disguise their true environmental preferences strategically in order to induce higher side payments. For simplicity, it is therefore assumed that only the abatement benefits of the recipients are imperfectly known, whereas those of the donors are common knowledge. Information is asymmetric on marginal abatement benefits, expressed by the benefit parameter b_R. For simplicity, we assume that the set of values b_R may take consists of only two elements: $\theta = \{b_R^-, b_R^+\}$. In other words, countries R have either high (b_R^+) or low (b_R^-) marginal abatement benefits, the true type being known only by themselves.

The signaling device that allows for a strategic reporting of R's marginal abatement benefits b_R is the emission reduction level in the non-cooperative Nash equilibrium. As abatement quantities q_k, cost parameters c_k and the characteristics of the Nash game are common knowledge, donor countries can infer from the abatement level in the Nash equilibrium ($q_k^N = b_k/c_k$) the marginal abatement benefits of the recipients. However, they can only observe the type that is *signaled* by R via q_R^N. For example, by abating less than optimal Nash quantities, countries R of the high type b_R^+ can signal that they are of the low type b_R^-. The donors are aware of this possibility, but cannot detect the fraud. The only way out is to try to reach a solution which makes 'truth telling' (that is, non-cooperative abatement quantities that correspond to R's true type) rewarding for countries R. In either case, the fact that the recipient countries have private information on their marginal abatement benefits is an asset for them in the cooperation game which produces a rent and thus modifies the cooperative solution compared to the case of perfect information.

Before investigating the properties of an agreement in the presence of asymmetric information it has to be established if and under what conditions countries R have an incentive not to report their true type. Signaling false abatement benefits is costly for coalition R because of two reasons. First, in the non-cooperative Nash equilibrium it has to choose an abatement level that is inferior to its true optimal quantities. Second, cooperative abatement quantities are not calculated on the basis of R's true environmental preferences but on the basis of the given signal. When deciding on the optimal signal, countries R therefore have to weigh the costs in terms of a suboptimally chosen environmental standard against the gains in terms of the amount by which the transfer can be increased.

6.3.1   Financing of Net Incremental Abatement Costs

Consider a take-it-or-leave-it offer by donor countries D which prescribes globally efficient abatements and the adoption of transfer scheme (6.4) in an international environmental agreement. Countries with relatively low marginal abatement costs are compensated for their net incremental abatement costs of cooperation. In this case, we can define the potential net gain of R by a false reporting of its type (indicated by $\tilde{b}_R$) and call it R's 'information rent' I^n:

$$I^n = \left[\pi_R^N(\tilde{b}_R) - \pi_R^N(b_R)\right] + \left[T^n(\tilde{b}_R) - T^n(b_R)\right] \tag{6.6}$$
$$+ \left[\pi_R^C(\tilde{b}_R) - \pi_R^C(b_R)\right].$$

The first term in square brackets is the welfare loss incurred by the strategically chosen abatement level in the Nash equilibrium which deviates from the true optimal quantity. The second term is the change in the transfer induced by the wrong signal. It is positive (negative) when R is type $\theta = b_R^+$ ($\theta = b_R^-$) but signals that it is of the low type (high type). The third term represents the change in welfare due to cooperative abatement levels $q_k^C = q_k^*$ which do not correspond to the quantities calculated on the basis of R's true type. The sign of the third term is generally ambiguous, but positive when the countries are sufficiently asymmetric. Understating, for example, decreases both cooperative abatement costs and benefits, the net effect depending on parameter values. Inserting cooperative abatement quantities $q_k^C = q_k^*$, $k = D, R$ and simplifying yields a positive change in R's cooperative net benefits when R is 'lying' if

$$2b_D c_D(b_R - \tilde{b}_R) - 2b_R c_R(b_R - \tilde{b}_R) - c_D(b_R - \tilde{b}_R)^2 > 0 \tag{6.7}$$
$$\Leftrightarrow 2(b_D c_D - b_R c_R) > (b_R - \tilde{b}_R)c_D.$$

Hence, only in cases in which the countries are fairly homogeneous and when the difference between b_R^+ and b_R^- is sufficiently large,[11] does R lose in terms of cooperative net benefits by not revealing its true type.

---

[11] For $c_D \approx c_R$, a sufficient condition for the above inequality to hold is $2(b_D - b_R) > b_R - \tilde{b}_R$.

In all other cases the third term of equation (6.6) is positive and 'lying' pays off, regardless of R's true type. A greater difference between the low and the high value of θ works, *ceteris paribus*, against R's incentive for understating because understating is costly for R in terms of suboptimally low cooperative (and non-cooperative) abatement quantities. These costs increase with the difference between b_R^+ and b_R^-.

As there are only two types of θ, the question of whether 'false reporting' pays off is answered by checking for each of the two types if I^n is positive.[12] We find that for the low type ($\theta = b_R^-$) overstating never pays off, whereas for the high type ($\theta = b_R^+$) understating always pays off, given that $b_D > b_R$. We can see this by inserting into equation (6.6) the equilibrium quantities for non-cooperative and full-cooperative abatement quantities. Simplifying yields

$$
\begin{aligned}
I^n &= [\pi_R^N(\tilde{b}_R) - \pi_R^N(b_R)] + [\tilde{\pi}_R^N(\tilde{b}_R) - \tilde{\pi}_R^C(\tilde{b}_R)] && (6.8) \\
&\quad - [\pi_R^N(b_R) - \pi_R^C(b_R)] + [\pi_R^C(\tilde{b}_R) - \pi_R^C(b_R)] \\
&= \tilde{B}_R(\tilde{Q}^N) + B_R(\tilde{Q}^N) - 2\,B_R(Q^N) + B_R(\tilde{Q}^C) \\
&\quad - \tilde{B}_R(\tilde{Q}^C) + 2\,C_R(q_R^N) - 2\,C_R(\tilde{q}_R^N) \\
&= \frac{b_R - \tilde{b}_R}{c_D c_R} \left[(b_D - b_R)c_D + \tilde{b}_R(c_D + c_R) \right].
\end{aligned}
$$

The sign of I^n for the two possible types can be determined from the last line: for $\theta = b_R^+$ ($\theta = b_R^-$), the term before the square bracket is positive (negative), while the first term in the square bracket is positive for $b_D > b_R$ which is fulfilled by assumption. Hence, overstating never pays off, whereas a sufficient condition for understating to pay off is $b_D > b_R$. To sum up, whenever the marginal abatement benefits of the donor countries are relatively higher, the recipients will signal that they are of the low type, regardless of their true marginal abatement benefits ($\tilde{b}_R = b_R^- \,\forall\, \theta$).

6.3.2 Financing of Gross Incremental Abatement Costs

Consider an international environmental agreement which stipulates globally efficient abatement levels and a transfer scheme according to equation (6.5), that is, recipient countries are compensated for their gross incremental abatement costs of environmental cooperation. As in equation (6.6), we can define R's potential net gain of misrepresenting

---

[12]If equation (6.6) were a continuous function, the optimal value of $\tilde{b}_R$ would be determined by setting the first derivation of I^n equal to zero.

its true type (indicated by $\tilde{b}_R$) as R's 'information rent' I^g:

$$I^g = \left[\pi_R^N(\tilde{b}_R) - \pi_R^N(b_R) \right] + \left[T^g(\tilde{b}_R) - T^g(b_R) \right] \tag{6.9}$$
$$+ \left[\pi_R^C(\tilde{b}_R) - \pi_R^C(b_R) \right].$$

As before, the first term in square brackets is the change in welfare incurred by the strategically chosen abatement level in the Nash equilibrium which deviates from the true optimal quantity, the second term is the change in the transfer induced by the wrong signal, and the third term represents the change in welfare due to cooperative abatement levels $q_k^C = q_k^*$ which do not correspond to the quantities calculated on the basis of R's true type. The first term of equation (6.9) is unambiguously negative, the second term is positive (negative) for $\tilde{b}_R = b_R^+ > \theta$ ($\tilde{b}_R = b_R^- < \theta$), and the third term is positive when countries are sufficiently asymmetric, the net effect being ambiguous. Thus for the high type ($\theta = b_B^+$) understating never pays off, whereas for the low type ($\theta = b_B^-$) a sufficient condition for overstating to pay off is

$$\frac{b_R}{\tilde{b}_R - b_R} > \frac{c_D}{c_R}. \tag{6.10}$$

We can see this by inserting into equation (6.9) the respective equilibrium quantities for non-cooperative and cooperative abatements, which yields

$$\begin{aligned} I^g &= [\pi_R^N(\tilde{b}_R) - \pi_R^N(b_R)] + [C_R(\tilde{q}_R^C) - C_R(\tilde{q}_R^N)] \tag{6.11}\\ &\quad - [C_R(q_R^C) - C_R(q_R^N)] + [\pi_R^C(\tilde{b}_R) - \pi_R^C(b_R)]\\ &= B_R(\tilde{Q}^N) - B_R(Q^N) + B_R(\tilde{Q}^C) - B_R(Q^C)\\ &\quad + 2\,C_R(q_R^N) - 2\,C_R(\tilde{q}_R^N)\\ &= \frac{\tilde{b}_R - b_R}{c_D c_R} \left[b_R c_R - (\tilde{b}_R - b_R)c_D \right]. \end{aligned}$$

Inspection of the last row yields that for $\theta = b_R^+$ ($\theta = b_R^-$) the term before the square brackets is negative (positive), while the term in square brackets is positive (positive for $b_R/(\tilde{b}_R - b_R) > c_D/c_R$). Hence, under the gross rule understating never pays off for R, whereas a sufficient condition for overstating to pay off is $b_R/(\tilde{b}_R - b_R) > c_D/c_R$ (that is, for $c_D \approx c_R$, $b_R^+ < 2b_R^-$).

The intuition for the incentive of low-type countries to signal high marginal abatement benefits is that by such a strategy, recipient countries can induce higher cooperative abatement quantities. As they are entirely compensated for the corresponding incremental costs, the extra gain may overcompensate the loss incurred when suboptimally large non-cooperative abatement quantities work as the signal towards the donors. These losses increase with the difference between b_R^+ and b_R^-. Interestingly, strategic signaling in this case leads to higher non-cooperative emission reductions and therefore counteracts to some extent the inefficiency of non-cooperative behavior.

A comparison of the signaling incentives under the two alternative transfer schemes shows that under the financing of net incremental costs, overstating never pays off and R always signals low environmental preferences, whereas under the financing of gross incremental costs, understating never pays off and R always signals high environmental preferences (Table 6.1). Given these signaling incentives, the question arises as to

Table 6.1: Signaling incentives

	$\theta = b_R^+$	$\theta = b_R^-$	
T^n	$\tilde{b}_R = b_R^- < \theta$	$\tilde{b}_R = b_R^- = \theta$	
T^g	$\tilde{b}_R = b_R^+ = \theta$	$\tilde{b}_R = b_R^+ > \theta$ $\quad$ for	$\frac{b_R}{\bar{b}_R - b_R} > \frac{c_D}{c_R}$
		$\tilde{b}_R = b_R^- = \theta$	$\frac{b_R}{\bar{b}_R - b_R} < \frac{c_D}{c_R}$

how the negotiating parties can ensure that the recipients of transfers reveal their true type. It is known from the theory of environmental regulation under imperfect information that this can be achieved by differentiated (separating) agreements. In the next section we therefore discuss the properties of an agreement that corresponds to a separating equilibrium.

6.4   Transfers in the Separating Equilibrium

In this section we look at the separating equilibrium which ensures that revealing the true type is rational for the recipients of compensation payments. This is possible if the parties agree on differentiated (separating) agreements, depending on the type of the recipients. In our simplified framework two different agreements will be offered, one for each type.

Maintaining the assumption that the parties maximize joint net benefits of cooperative abatements, the optimization problem being solved for each of the two possible types θ is:

$$\max \Pi \left[q_D^C(\theta), q_R^C(\theta) \right], \quad \theta = \{ b_R^-, b_R^+ \}, \quad \text{s.t.} \tag{6.12}$$

$$\pi_D^C(\theta) - T(\theta) \geq \pi_D^N(\theta) \tag{6.13}$$

$$\pi_R^C(\theta) + T(\theta) \geq \pi_R^N(\theta) \tag{6.14}$$

$$\overset{-}{\pi_R^N} (b_R^-) + \overset{-}{\pi_R^C} (b_R^-) + T(b_R^-) \geq \overset{-}{\pi_R^N} (b_R^+) + \overset{-}{\pi_R^C} (b_R^+) + T(b_R^+) \tag{6.15}$$

$$\overset{+}{\pi_R^N} (b_R^+) + \overset{+}{\pi_R^C} (b_R^+) + T(b_R^+) \geq \overset{+}{\pi_R^N} (b_R^-) + \overset{+}{\pi_R^C} (b_R^-) + T(b_R^-). \tag{6.16}$$

The additional incentive compatibility constraints (6.15) and (6.16) ensure that coalition R is at least as well off under truth telling as under false reporting. Condition (6.15) ensures that revealing its true type is incentive compatible for the low type, while constraint (6.16) does the same for the type with high marginal abatement benefits. Given that the transfers do not restrict the maximization of Π^C, the resulting agreement implies for both types of θ globally efficient abatements. The requirements on the size of the transfers, however, are more restrictive than under perfect information because they must be high enough to make the recipients at least indifferent between revealing and misrepresenting their true type.

The undifferentiated application of the net or gross incremental cost concept does not guarantee that the true type is revealed. For example, consider compensations for net incremental abatement costs that would be optimal for the donors under perfect information. From Section 6.3.1 we know that, under this rule, R always has an incentive to signal low environmental preferences, irrespective of its true type. To ensure that revealing the true type is also incentive compatible when $\theta = b_R^+$, transfers to high-type R must be greater than the net incremental abatement costs. The separating equilibrium that is optimal for the donors is

$$q_D^C = q_D^*(b_R^-), \ q_R^C = q_R^*(b_R^-), \ T(b_R^-) = T^n(b_R^-) \quad \text{for} \quad \theta = b_R^-; \tag{6.17}$$

$$q_D^C = q_D^*(b_R^+), \ q_R^C = q_R^*(b_R^+), \tag{6.18}$$

$$T(b_R^+) = T^n(b_R^-) + [\pi_R^N(b_R^-) - \pi_R^N(b_R^+)] + [\pi_R^C(b_R^-) - \pi_R^C(b_R^+)] \text{ for } \theta = b_R^+.$$

When countries R are of the low type, transfers compensate for the net incremental abatement costs of R and the cooperation gains go entirely to the donors (that is, individual rationality constraint (6.14) is binding). In the case where countries R are of the high type, part of the gains go to R even if D is able to dictate the terms of the IEA. The transfer chosen in (6.18) makes R just indifferent between revealing its true type and understating its environmental preferences (that is, incentive compatibility constraint (6.16) is binding). Transfer (6.18) granted in case R is of the high type is greater than it would be under financing R's true net incremental costs:

$$T = T^n(b_R^-) + [\overset{+}{\pi_R^N} (b_R^-) - \overset{+}{\pi_R^N} (b_R^+)] \tag{6.19}$$

$$+ [\overset{+}{\pi_R^C} (b_R^-) - \overset{+}{\pi_R^C} (b_R^+)] > T^n(b_R^+).$$

We see this by inserting the equilibrium quantities for non-cooperative and full-cooperative abatement quantities, using equation (6.4) and simplifying which yields

$$2\tilde{b}_R c_R (b_R - \tilde{b}_R) + 2 b_D c_D (b_R - \tilde{b}_R) - 2 c_D (b_R - \tilde{b}_R)^2 > 0 \tag{6.20}$$

$$\Leftrightarrow \tilde{b}_R (c_D + c_R) + c_D (b_D - b_R) > 0,$$

where $\tilde{b}_R = b_R^-$ and $\theta = b_R^+$. Hence, a sufficient condition for the transfer to exceed the net incremental costs is that marginal abatement benefits of the donors are higher than those of the recipients ($b_D > b_R$), which has been assumed.

In a more general setting where information on type θ is characterized by a continuous probability distribution function, the offered transfers will — except for the type with the lowest possible value of b_R — always exceed net incremental abatement costs. By inducing countries R to reveal their true (high) type, the donors circumvent the inefficiency losses from suboptimal abatement quantities otherwise chosen by R in order to exploit their informational advantage. Generally, there is no undifferentiated (pooling) agreement that would make the donors better off than under an agreement which discriminates between types.[13] However, often it may not be possible to negotiate complex differentiated agreements. In the next section we therefore investigate which uniform transfer scheme would be preferable from the perspective of the individual countries if based either on the net or on the gross incremental cost concept.

6.5 Transfers in the Pooling Equilibrium

Real-world negotiations on international environmental policy often lead to simple, uniform solutions. For example, the policy instruments chosen

---

[13]This is shown, for example, by Ellis (1992) in the context of environmental regulation of polluting firms that have private information on their abatement costs.

for the internalization of transboundary externalities in most cases are not market based but of the command-and-control type (for example, an agreement on equal percentage emission reductions by all signatories). This may be true all the more under imperfect information, as agreeing on differentiated terms for each possible type on which information is imperfect will generally be connected with high negotiation costs. Environmental negotiations are more likely to lead to uniform cooperative solutions that apply to all possible types (that is, pooling equilibria). Such solutions not only may be associated with lower negotiation and implementation costs; they also may work as a 'focal point' during negotiations when agreement on one of multiple possible equilibria is difficult. Furthermore, they may reflect the bargaining positions when a uniform solution is in the interest of certain parties. In the context of our model, pooling equilibria that compensate either for net or for gross incremental abatement costs are of particular interest. In the following, first we describe the properties of these cooperative solutions and then we analyse which of the two uniform transfer schemes is endogenously chosen during negotiations.

Assume that the parties agree to maximize aggregate gains from environmental cooperation, but that in contrast to equations (6.12)–(6.16) the agreement does not differentiate between the possible types of R. Consider first the case where transfers compensate for net incremental costs, see equation (6.4). We know from Section 6.3.1 that under the financing of net incremental costs, recipient countries will always signal that they have low marginal abatement benefits, irrespective of their true type ($\tilde{b}_R = b_R^- \forall \theta$). To make cooperation individually rational for low-type countries R as well, the uniform agreement has to be calculated for b_R^-:[14]

$$q_D^C = q_D^*(b_R^-), \quad q_R^C = q_R^*(b_R^-), \quad T^n = b_D^2/2c_R - b_R^{-2}/c_D. \quad (6.21)$$

Alternatively, the transfer scheme may be given by equation (6.5). With compensations for gross incremental costs, recipient countries will signal high (low) marginal abatement benefits in the case of either $\theta = b_R^+$ or $\theta = b_R^-$ and $b_R/(\tilde{b}_R - b_R) > c_D/c_R$ (otherwise). Therefore, the respective pooling equilibria under this rule are

$$q_D^C = q_D^*(\tilde{b}_R), \quad q_R^C = q_R^*(\tilde{b}_R), \quad T^g = b_D^2/2c_R + b_D\tilde{b}_R/c_R, \quad (6.22)$$

with $\tilde{b}_R = b_R^+, b_R^-$.

---

[14]Note that agreements (6.21) and (6.22) will not lead to globally efficient abatement quantities if they are calculated for the wrong type. Cooperative abatements calculated for the low type in (6.21) are inefficiently low if R in reality is of the high type, abatements according to (6.22) are too high in the reverse case.

Given the signaling incentives and the cooperative outcomes for the two types of pooling equilibria, which transfer scheme is favored by each of the two parties when side payments in an international environmental agreement are to be based on either of the two incremental cost concepts? The answer will be given in two steps. First we derive which of the two concepts is preferred by each coalition, given the signaling incentives summarized in Table 6.1; then we must check whether the optimal (and possibly unanimous) choice of the transfer scheme is in fact implemented, that is, if it is time consistent. The first part of the answer is given by comparing both the donors' and the recipients' welfare under the net incremental cost concept with their welfare under the gross rule. The comparison is done separately for each of the two types that R's marginal abatement benefits may take in order to determine which concept would have been optimal *ex post*, after the game has been played. On the basis of this information it is then possible to deduce the optimal transfer scheme *ex ante* and to check whether the interests of the two parties regarding the preferred incremental cost concept are in harmony or in conflict with each other.

We start with the case where R has high-type marginal abatement benefits ($\theta = b_R^+$). Given that the donor coalition has to choose between either of the two incremental cost concepts irrespective of the recipients' possible types, it faces a trade-off: on the one hand, transfers according to the gross rule may eliminate strategic signaling incentives; on the other hand, this implies that part of the aggregate cooperation gains are shifted from D to R. Bearing in mind the signaling incentives of R and taking into account that the chosen rule influences abatement quantities and welfare in the non-cooperative Nash equilibrium (via the signaling behavior of R), the gross concept is superior for donors D if

$$\pi_D^N(b_R^+) + \pi_D^C(b_R^+) - T^g(b_R^+) > \pi_D^N(b_R^-) + \pi_D^C(b_R^-) - T^n(b_R^-). \quad (6.23)$$

Inserting the relevant values of equations (5.5) and (5.6) into equation (6.23) and simplifying shows that donors prefer compensations for gross incremental abatement costs over the net incremental cost concept if

$$2b_D b_R^+ c_D - 4b_D b_R^- c_D - b_R^{+2} c_R - b_R^{-2} c_R > 0 \quad (6.24)$$

$$\Leftrightarrow \left[b_D(b_R^+ - 2b_R^-)c_D - b_R^{+2} c_R \right] + \left[b_D(b_R^+ - 2b_R^-)c_D - b_R^{-2} c_R \right] > 0.$$

From the left-hand side of the last row we see that for the gross concept to be favored, $b_R^+ > 2b_R^-$ is necessary. A sufficient condition for the inequality to hold is $b_D(b_R^+ - 2b_R^-)c_D > b_R^{+2} c_R$ which is fulfilled when the countries are sufficiently asymmetric. Hence, under the conditions that

(i) the donors' marginal abatement benefits and/or costs are sufficiently higher than those of the recipients (that is, when the countries differ strongly) and (ii) the difference between the low and the high value of R's type is substantial (that is, when the knowledge on R's marginal abatement benefits is poor), the donors will be better off by compensating the recipients for their *gross* incremental abatement costs of cooperation.[15] The reason for this outcome is that under the above parameter constellations, D's losses due to a misrepresentation of R's type are particularly high so that the gains of making countries R reveal their true (high) type more than compensate the distributional disadvantage of the gross concept.

Recipient (high-type) countries R prefer compensations for gross incremental abatement costs over the net incremental cost concept if

$$\overset{+}{\pi_R^N}(b_R^+) + \overset{+}{\pi_R^C}(b_R^+) + T^g(b_R^+) > \overset{+}{\pi_R^N}(b_R^-) + \overset{+}{\pi_R^C}(b_R^-) + T^n(b_R^-). \quad (6.25)$$

Inserting the equilibrium abatement quantities in equation (6.25) and simplifying yields

$$b_R^{+2}c_D + b_R^{-2}c_D - 2b_R^+b_R^-c_D + b_R^{+2}c_R \quad (6.26)$$
$$+ b_R^{-2}c_R - b_R^+b_R^-c_R + b_Db_R^-c_D > 0$$
$$\Leftrightarrow \quad (b_R^+ - b_R^-)^2(c_D + c_R) + b_R^+b_R^-c_R + b_Db_R^-c_D > 0.$$

Hence, when recipients R are of the high type, they always prefer the gross over the net incremental cost concept.

Consider now that R in reality possess low-type marginal abatement benefits ($\theta = b_R^-$). Under the net incremental cost concept, recipient countries signal that they are of the low type ($\tilde{b}_R = b_R^-$). Under the gross rule, R will overstate and signal $\tilde{b}_R = b_R^+$ if $b_R^-/(b_R^+ - b_R^-) > c_D/c_R$, that is, if the difference between b_R^+ and b_R^- is not too large. Otherwise, R reveal their true low type. As the donors in the latter case can infer from the recipients' differentiated signaling R's true low type (see Table 6.1), they favor the net incremental cost concept. If the recipients overstate their environmental preferences ($\tilde{b}_R = b_R^+ > \theta$), the condition for the gross incremental cost concept to be favored by the donors is identical to equation (6.23). In particular, $b_R^+ > 2b_R^-$ is necessary (see above). This, however, is in conflict with the necessary condition for R's incentive to overstate and signal $\tilde{b}_R = b_R^+$ (for $c_D \approx c_R$

---

[15] As stated in Section 6.2, donor countries will of course always favor the net rule given that they know R's true type. Here, however, the question is which rule turns out to be superior when D learns R's true type only after the game has been played.

and $\tilde{b}_R = b_R^+$, $b_R/(\tilde{b}_R - b_R) > c_D/c_R$ becomes $b_R^+ < 2b_R^-$). Hence, with $\theta = b_R^-$ the donors always favor the net over the gross concept.

Low-type recipient countries always prefer compensations for gross incremental costs. Given that R signal their true low type, they favor the gross over the net incremental cost concept because their domestic environmental benefits are not subtracted from the granted transfer under the gross rule. If low-type recipients have an incentive to overstate their environmental preferences (see equation 6.10), they always favor the gross rule, too, as overstating is only rational under the gross rule (see Table 6.1). Hence, (low-type) recipients always favor the gross incremental cost concept regardless of their signaling behavior.

Which transfer scheme is preferred by the donors at the stage where they do not know R's true type depends on the prior probabilities of R's type. *Ex ante*, D favors the gross incremental cost concept if[16]

$$p \quad [\pi_D^N(b_R^+) + \pi_D^C(b_R^+) - T^g(b_R^+) \quad (6.27)$$
$$-\pi_D^N(b_R^-) - \pi_D^C(b_R^-) + T^n(b_R^-)] >$$
$$(1-p) \quad \left[\pi_D^N(b_R^-) + \pi_D^C(b_R^-) - T^n(b_R^-) - \pi_D^N(\tilde{b}_R) - \pi_D^C(\tilde{b}_R) + T^g(\tilde{b}_R)\right],$$

where p stands for D's belief in the probability that $\theta = b_R^+$ $(0 < p < 1)$ and $\tilde{b}_R = b_R^+, b_R^-$. A given profitability of the gross incremental cost concept increases with the probability that R is of the high type. Depending on the values of the benefit and cost parameters and on the probability that R is of the high type, the donors will favor either the gross or the net incremental cost concept *ex ante*.

The results for the different cases are summarized in Table 6.2. Although the countries' preferences for either of the two alternative transfer schemes are generally not in harmony, scenarios exist where both parties favor *ex ante* financing of the recipients' gross incremental abatement costs. This is the case if the countries are sufficiently asymmetric and the donors conject a high probability that the recipients possess high-type marginal abatement benefits. The two basic reasons for the outcome where both parties prefer the gross incremental cost concept are that this transfer scheme (i) avoids the inefficiencies due to strategically understating the true environmental preferences and (ii) counteracts the inefficiencies due to too low non-cooperative abatement efforts when signaling behavior leads to overstating the true environmental preferences.

However, it has already been pointed out that we must check whether opting for the gross rule is also optimal once the true type of the recipients is revealed, that is, if it is time consistent. From Section 6.2 we

---

[16]Inequality (6.27) mirrors condition (6.23) in that it is relevant for both types of θ, where both cases are weighted by their probabilities.

Table 6.2: The preferred incremental cost concept

	$\theta = b_R^+$	$\theta = b_R^-$
D	$T^g \succ T^n$ for $b_D(b_R^+ - 2b_R^-)c_D > b_R^{+2} c_R$	$T^n \succ T^g$
R	$T^g \succ T^n$	$T^g \succ T^n$

Note: $T^g \succ T^n$ stands for a party's preference for the gross concept compared with the net concept.

know that this is obviously not the case for the donors and that instead the net incremental cost concept is optimal for them, given knowledge on R's true type. The recipients, anticipating D's inclination for the net concept in the case of truth telling, will therefore not reveal but understate their environmental preferences in the non-cooperative game. If this time-consistency problem cannot be solved, the pooling equilibrium with the net rule and the potentially false representation of R's type emerges although it may be inferior to the gross concept from the perspective of both parties.

One possible solution to the above time-consistency problem could be that the donor countries credibly commit themselves to the application of the gross incremental cost concept *before* the recipients decide on non-cooperative abatement quantities which are used for strategic signaling. This commitment could be a unilateral obligation; it could also be the outcome of environmental negotiations that proceed in several steps and result in subsequently amended agreements.[17] Another solution both to the time-consistency problem and to the question of which incremental cost concept is in fact applied when the transfer scheme has to be based on simple, uniform rules lies in the relative bargaining strengths of the negotiating parties. Agreement on compensations for gross incremental abatement costs may simply be because the recipient countries — given they favor this rule — are able to push through their interests during

---

[17]Of course, potential donor countries could try to infer the other party's characteristics from the observation of pollution reduction efforts even before a future agreement is on the agenda. In that case, the precommitment on the gross incremental cost concept would not be necessary from the perspective of the donors.

negotiations.[18] Paradoxically, the bargaining strength of the recipients is also to the benefit of the donors if it helps to overcome the time-consistency problem described above. In any case, the application of the gross incremental cost concept results in a more equitable distribution of the gains from environmental cooperation between (industrialized) donor and (developing) recipient countries.

6.6 Conclusions

The analysis of this chapter has shown that in the presence of asymmetric information on environmental preferences, the approach whereby recipient countries are compensated for their net incremental costs of emission abatements in an international environmental agreement is in general no longer optimal for the donor countries. This holds even if the donors are in a position to submit an offer that is optimal for themselves and where the terms of the agreement are differentiated for each possible type of the recipients (that is, a separating equilibrium). The mark-up of transfers in this case serves to render truth telling incentive compatible for the recipients and can be regarded as 'informational rent'. Also in cases where international transfers have to be based on simple, uniform rules (that is, a pooling equilibrium), scenarios exist in which donor as well as recipient countries will favor the application of the gross over the net incremental cost concept. Although the former transfer scheme shifts part of the cooperation gains from the donors to the recipients, it reduces the inefficiencies through strategic pre-negotiation behavior and may therefore also be beneficial for the donors.

The parameter constellations for which financing gross incremental abatement costs is favored by both parties are exactly those that one has in mind when international environmental negotiations between industrialized and developing countries take place: marginal abatement benefits and costs are both considerably higher for the industrialized donor countries (that is, the asymmetries between countries, expressed by the benefit and cost parameters in our model, are substantial) and knowledge on the true environmental preferences in developing countries (expressed by the difference between the high- and the low-type parameters) is relatively poor (see Table 6.2). Furthermore, agreement on the full incremental cost concept supports the conjecture that developing (recipient) countries are in a better bargaining position than often presumed and that asymmetric information compensates for the generally

---

[18] A similar result is derived by Mohr (1996) in a dynamic model of complete information where industrialized and developing countries bargain over the protection of an international environmental resource (rain forests) and accompanying transfers.

weak bargaining position of these countries. Paradoxically, in the case of a pooling offer, a strong bargaining position of the recipients can also be to the benefit of the donors because it helps to overcome the time inconsistency in the choice of the superior full incremental cost rule.

Of course, the results have to be considered with care because of the restrictive assumptions and the specific nature of the model. There are a number of straightforward extensions that would also enable us to check the validity of the results in a more general context. One important aspect is to consider a situation where negotiations do not lead to a maximization of joint gains from cooperation. Another simplification of the model is that only recipients dispose of private information but donors do not. It remains to be seen which agreement and transfer scheme emerges when both parties are able to pursue signaling strategies. Furthermore, other signaling devices than pre-negotiation behavior in the form of non-cooperative emission abatements may also be possible.

A model extension that seems to be particularly relevant in the context of joint implementation is to allow for local environmental and/or economic benefits in recipient countries. Such extra gains undoubtedly often exist in developing countries. It has sometimes been argued that these should be subtracted from the transfers that compensate for the incremental abatement costs a project generates. However, considering private information on local benefits entails that the recipients may again have an incentive to signal low environmental preferences. It is possible that the incentive would prevail even if global emissions are barely (or, in the case of pure emission trading, not at all) reduced by a single project, as long as global and local pollution are closely related to each other. Strategic signaling behavior would harm donor countries in this case, too, given that the signal is set in terms of inefficiently low abatements of the global pollutant. The superiority of the gross rule then may still be valid.

In any case, an important model extension would be to relax the assumption of two homogeneous groups of countries and to regard the parties as two single countries that agree on a bilateral transaction under a multilateral framework treaty. A single project then has a negligible impact on global pollution and will only aim to redistribute international abatement efforts cost-effectively. This is the relevant scenario for the analysis of joint implementation projects and transactions within a possible future tradable permit system under the Framework Convention of Climate Change. In this respect, the present analysis is only a first step towards the analysis of cost-effective global environmental policy in the presence of imperfect information.

Chapter 7

Institutions for the Global Environment

Given highly varying national costs and benefits from any action to protect global environmental resources, the idea of side payments between countries and institutional arrangements to implement this instrument is straightforward. The preceding theoretical analysis has shown that international transfers are a crucial element of global environmental policy with regard to both cost-effectiveness and incentive compatibility. It is thus not surprising that they have gained importance in recent proposals for international agreements and institutions to protect the global environment. This chapter describes the most important international institutions that have been established to support cost-effectiveness in global environmental policy and discusses to what extent they fulfill the mandate for which they have been created. We consider the Global Environment Facility, the Montreal Protocol Multilateral Fund, as well as the concept of 'joint implementation' elaborated under the Framework Convention on Climate Change.

According to the focus of the present study, the criteria being applied in the evaluation of the international environmental institutions are cost-effectiveness and incentive compatibility. Cost-effectiveness is a straightforward criterion since it constitutes the core mandate of the institutions discussed below. Incentive compatibility is a supplementary criterion, as it constitutes a necessary condition for any project where two or more parties cooperate to achieve gains from cost-effectiveness. The evaluation is related both to the operational guidelines and principles stipulated in the underlying legal texts and to the de facto practice which may or may not be in accordance with the operational guidelines.

7.1   The Global Environment Facility

7.1.1   Mandate and History

In the late 1980s, a growing number of international environmental problems received attention. Given the widespread consensus that developing countries had scarce information about pollution and also little interest or capacity to take action on these problems, the industrialized countries explored options for financing developing countries' actions in this field of environmental policy. In November 1990, the Global Environment Facility (GEF) was established as a pilot program to finance policy measures of developing countries concerning the following four global environmental problems: climate change, biodiversity, international water pollution, and depletion of the ozone layer. Subsequently, the GEF has become one of the most prominent examples of an institution exclusively designed to promote cooperation on the global environment. Its general purpose is to finance environmental 'programs and activities for which benefits would accrue to the world at large while the country undertaking the measures would bear the cost, and which would not otherwise be supported by existing development assistance or environment programs.' (World Bank 1990). The support relates to developing countries' actions on global environmental problems that they would not undertake without the financial means granted by developed countries.

From its creation, the GEF has received considerable attention from governments of developed and developing countries, from the international public community as well as in the academic world. Diverging national conceptions on its mandate, however, caused major difficulties in implementing this financial mechanism during its pilot phase and dominated the discussion on the institutional status of the GEF from its creation to its actually restructured form (Table 7.1). For the group of industrialized and potential donor countries, it was crucial to retain control over the general policy of the GEF and its financial decisions. As a consequence, these countries pushed hard for a leading role of the World Bank in the management of the GEF. It was also essential for the developed countries that the GEF focuses on the 'global commons'. On the other hand, developing countries equally wanted to have considerable influence on the decisions concerning which environmental projects would be supported. Generally, there has been much more concern about local environmental problems such as desertification in these countries. Those problems were addressed by UNCED's 'Agenda 21' in Rio in 1992. Developing countries wanted the GEF to be a finacial mechanism for this class of environmental problems as well or, alternatively, called for the creation of a new 'green' fund for sustainable development. Another reason for difficulties in implementing the GEF during the pilot phase was that it was seen by both groups of countries to have a precedent-setting role. This is also mirrored in the development of the organizational structure of the GEF before and after its restructuring in 1994.

Table 7.1: History of the Global Environment Facility

Sept. 1989	French and German governments propose that the World Bank is asked to design an international environmental aid facility
Nov. 1990	GEF is established as a three-year (1991–93), US$1 billion pilot program
Spring 1992	Sharp disagreement between developed and developing countries about the relation of the GEF to conventions on (a) climate change, (b) biodiversity, and (c) sustainable development (Agenda 21)
June 1992	Agreement during UNCED to restructure the GEF and to use it as an interim financial transfer mechanism for global environmental problems
Spring 1993	Negotiations on restructured GEF concentrate on (a) independence of GEF chairman and secretariat from World Bank and other implementing agencies; (b) inclusion of non-global environmental problems (desertification etc.) identified in Agenda 21; (c) the balancing of representation and decision-making authority between donor and recipient countries
March 1994	GEF is restructured, established as a permanent facility and provided with US$2 billion for the next three years (1994–96)

Source: Fairman (1996, pp. 58–69).

7.1.2   Organization and Operation

National governments participating in the GEF include most of the OECD countries and about 140 developing countries. These countries form the participants' assembly, which reviews the GEF's work program and makes operational decisions. General program priorities and eligibility criteria are determined directly by the parties of the conventions on climate change and on biodiversity. The new, restructured GEF further consists of an executive council, an independent secretariat and a chairman. The executive council has 32 members, 16 from developing countries, 14 from industrialized countries, and two from countries in transition. The council usually takes decisions by consensus, otherwise by weighted qualified majority.[1] The GEF is jointly administered by the World Bank, the United Nations Development Program (UNDP) and the United Nations Environment Program (UNEP). These institutions are the 'implementing agencies'. The World Bank takes the role of a lead administrator; it manages the financial resources and is in charge of investment projects. According to their respective comparative advantages, the UNDP administers technical assistance projects and coordinates GEF projects with national environmental programs in recipient countries, whereas UNEP provides the connection with UNCED and the convention process. It is also responsible for the 'independent scientific and technical advisory panel' (STAP).

As of summer 1995, the GEF has authorizised US$736 million in grants for 115 projects in 63 countries. However, less than US$100 million had been disbursed at that time. The funds collected at the GEF are assigned to provide grants for investment projects, technical assistance and applied research. Additionally, small grants are given to non-governmental organizations in developing countries. The financing of projects to protect the stratospheric ozone layer is organized by the Montreal Protocol Multilateral Fund, although the ozone problem is explicitly incorporated in the initial design of the GEF and represents a natural field of application.[2]   The GEF finances ozone protection projects only in former socialist countries that are not eligible for transfers from the MPMF, since they belong to the group of donor countries under the Montreal Protocol. The bulk of GEF funds is dedicated to greenhouse gas reduction projects (40–50 per cent) and biodiversity protection (30–40 per cent). Projects for international water protection (10–20 per cent) and

---

[1]The majority rule is 60 per cent of the represented countries and 60 per cent of donation-weighted votes.

[2]See the next section for the MPMF. In 1991/92 there were unsuccessful attempts by some European governments to reintegrate the financing of ozone projects into the GEF.

the protection of the ozone layer (5 per cent) play a minor role in the allocation of funds.

The international environmental treaties on climate change, the protection of the ozone layer and biological diversity all stipulate that financial assistance shall compensate the recipient countries for the *incremental costs* they bear by such additional environmental action. Originally, the concept had been elaborated within the World Bank for application to projects of global environmental protection, then was codified by international environmental agreements and was incorporated into the mandate of the GEF. The concept of incremental costs (and benefits) stems from cost–benefit analysis and is clear-cut in theory. The GEF defines incremental costs as the difference between the total costs of an environmental preferable alternative and the cost of the baseline project that yields the same domestic benefits (Ahuja 1993, p. 7). In practice, the challenge is to develop methods for making incremental cost estimates that take into account all relevant aspects of a funding decision.[3] This is a crucial task since the overall amount of financial transfers needed, the distribution of the gains from environmental cooperation and the cost-effectiveness of abatement projects initiated by the GEF all depend on how incremental costs are determined.

Beside the GEF, joint implementation under the FCCC also aims at cost-effectiveness in international measures to protect the global climate (see below). It is expected that a future mechanism for JI projects within the FCCC will not be incorporated into the GEF. Hence, many abatement projects in developing countries may become potential candidates for both mechanisms. It is not clear yet in which way abatement projects will then be allocated between these alternative institutional frameworks.

7.1.3 Evaluation

Cost-effectiveness

To minimize aggregate costs of environmental protection, abatement measures have to be distributed cost-effectively not only between industrialized donor and developing host countries, but also between different projects in different recipient countries. Without a binding financial constraint on GEF project funding, all projects for which the resulting global environmental benefit is higher than the related incremental costs could be carried out and it would not be necessary to compare the attractiveness of different projects. However, since funding is lim-

---

[3] For a discussion of the incremental cost concept within the operation of the GEF, see King (1993).

ited, those beneficial projects should be implemented first for which the cost per unit of global environmental benefit obtained is minimal. The GEF takes these considerations into account by calculating the ratio of environmental benefits a project generates over its incremental costs relative to the baseline and by ranking potential projects according to this ratio (Mintzer 1993, p. 22). This project-ranking by cost-effectiveness, though, is not strictly applied for the actual selection of projects by the GEF. First, explicitly calculated indices of cost-effectiveness are only of limited reliability because they are very sensitive to base-line assumptions. These assumptions are only hypothetical and have to deal with many uncertainties. Second, cost-effectiveness also competes with other economic considerations such as the incentive compatibility of alternative projects, and non-economic goals such as preferences for an equal regional distribution of GEF projects.

The attractiveness of GEF projects should be determined not only on the basis of the present situation, but also with regard to dynamic cost-effectiveness. Projects should also take into account the leverage they may have for the reduction of abatement costs in the long run. For example, if it is possible to support the emergence of markets for cleaner energy production technologies (for example, solar energy) which reduce unit production costs and make less environmentally harmful energy production competitive, they may be chosen in the future even without funding by the GEF. In the long run such projects may be substantially more cost-effective (and demand fewer financial transfers) than those which achieve the same environmental benefit at lower costs today. The problem is, however, to assess which technologies will be most marketable in the future and should be supported. The approach of the GEF here is to pick a limited number of those options which seem to be the most promising and to spread the risk, but nevertheless to generate sufficient leverage through the amounts of transfers given.

A number of critical aspects of the incremental cost concept as the core operational guideline of the GEF have to be stated. The most important problem is the high informational requirements to measure the incremental costs of very different environmental protection projects on the basis of a common, comparable standard. Aiming at cost-effectiveness is a tremendous task, especially in the case of global warming since there are manifold options for achieving the same environmental goal with different measures and per unit abatement costs. Besides the general choice between mitigation and adaptation options for climate change, interventions are possible not only in different economic sectors (energy, forestry, agriculture, industry, public sector), but also within these at

different stages of production and consumption.[4] Finally, global engineering interventions or measures of population stabilization are possible
alternatives. Because of the many factors which are specific to each
potential project and which have an impact on incremental costs, the
calculation of and agreement on incremental costs have to be done on
a case-by-case basis. This, however, makes comparison across different
projects and a ranking of projects with respect to the cost–benefit ratios
problematic.

A related critical aspect of the incremental cost concept is the question
whether to deduct domestic benefits and cost savings of a GEF project
from the incremental costs when determining the amount of transfers
granted. The FCCC and the convention on biological diversity are vague
in this respect as they stipulate that developed countries are to meet the
'agreed full incremental costs' incurred by the developing countries in
complying with the conventions. Although the incremental cost rule is
a political and not an economic decision there seems to be a general
tendency within the GEF to compensate only for the net incremental
costs (King 1993, p. 16). One explanation for this inclination for the net
rule may be that it requires a lower amount of total funding. Indeed, if
for example the domestic benefits of a given project exceed the related
incremental costs, then there is a 'win–win' strategy that is attractive
even without outside financing and hence should not be eligible for GEF
funding. However, in some cases these alternatives are not chosen by
developing countries because of institutional constraints or limited access
to capital markets. It can be argued, then, that incremental costs should
incorporate the costs to remove these barriers (King 1993, p. 21).

A problem connected with the application of the net incremental cost
concept is that it may produce incentives for inefficient strategic behavior of the host countries. Under the net incremental cost concept,
recipient countries have an incentive to release biassed information in
order to decrease the deduction that accounts for the domestic benefits
of a project. The same incentive is present with respect to the reporting
of the baseline. By strategically manipulating the baseline of a project
it is possible to extract higher transfers. According to officials of the
GEF, there is not much opportunity for this strategy since the baseline is mostly known, for example, through public energy supply plans.
However, these plans and projections are susceptible to manipulation
themselves if the incentives to do so are strong enough. The theoretic
analysis of Chapter 6 has demonstrated that in the presence of asymmetric information on domestic environmental (or other) benefits in recipient

---

[4]See Ahuja (1993, Table 1.1) for a taxonomy of interventions in the energy and
non-energy sectors and an illustration of various examples of different project types.

countries, it may be profitable both for the donors and for the recipients of transfers to opt for the gross incremental cost rule in order to avoid inefficient strategic behavior of recipient countries. In general, problems due to informational imperfections have not been sufficiently taken into account in the present guidelines and operation of the GEF.

According to the guidelines of the GEF, the initiative for project proposals is with the recipient country. If the compensation according to the incremental cost rule is such that host countries are indifferent between implementing a project or not, why should they make the effort and incur the costs of taking this initiative? The answer is that either the incremental costs and thereby transfers are generously calculated and exceed true net incremental costs, or there are indirect side benefits from GEF projects (training, domestic political reasons and so on) which make it worthwhile for a developing county's government to propose a GEF project. A related problem that may arise due to the initiative role of the host country is that the host country may not propose the project that yields the highest global environmental benefit for a given incremental cost when there are several alternative projects feasible. Instead, it may propose the one with highest *domestic* benefits. Although this reduces the net incremental costs and increases a project's attractiveness from the perspective of the GEF, nevertheless another project that has not been proposed may be even more cost-effective (King 1993, p. 10). To include those projects into the portfolio of potentially sponsored abatement measures which are not proposed by national governments of developing countries but which are very attractive with regard to cost-effectiveness, the GEF should therefore also be given the right to take the initiative and to propose projects.

The choice of the financing principle distributes the gains from cost-effectiveness in a certain manner. Financing only the net incremental abatement costs makes the recipient countries indifferent between the status quo (the baseline) and a GEF project (see Chapter 6). Consequently, the gains from executing GEF projects under this rule go entirely to the (rich) donor countries. Moreover, although GEF funds are claimed to be additional to existing national budgets of donor countries for environmental and development issues, this assertion is not consistent with rational policy decisions in donor countries. Given that industrialized countries have in fact provided resources for the creation and operation of the GEF, it follows from a revealed preference argument that they would also have allocated resources for the same environmental purpose in the absence of this institution. Hence, at least part of the money granted for the funding of the GEF would be spent for the same purpose if the GEF did not exist — funding then is *not* entirely additional to existing budgets. In fact, if some of the financial resources devoted to GEF projects would otherwise have financed development aid or regional environmental problems such as desertification in developing countries, the operation of the GEF may even aggravate the welfare position of these countries. Developing countries which are aware of this possibility may not support or even obstruct the GEF's mandate altogether. In other words, problems of incentive compatibility may arise due to the repercussions of the donor countries' funding of the GEF with their other financial assistance to developing countries.

Incentive compatibility

It was argued above that incentive compatibility is a second important criterion against which the GEF's success has to be measured, as it constitutes a necessary condition for any GEF project to increase the cost-effectiveness of global pollution reduction. Besides the incentives of single governments to participate in the GEF's operation and to propose or to sponsor projects (see the last two paragraphs above), it is essential that the governments also have an interest in actually executing the approved projects. The public-good character of national abatement efforts and the long time horizon of many projects, though, also endanger sustainable cooperation in the special context of GEF projects. Non-compliance due to time-consistency problems is an important problem, given the incentives for opportunistic behavior both of recipient as well as of donor countries.

To the extent that emission abatement projects are additional to other abatement obligations or the induced abatement quantitites are not (fully) credited, there is an incentive for donor countries to take a free ride on the donations of other countries to the GEF's financial resources.[5] Such free-riding behavior is especially tempting in the case of GEF funding because fixed contributions are not negotiated, every country rather arbitrarily determines its own share of the total financial means and it does not have to fear serious sanctions even when postponing the payment of announced amounts.

For the recipients of GEF grants, non-compliance may also be tempting when the grants given in connection with a certain project are fungible (for example, cash money, see Section 4.4.1) or when technical equipment transferred for environmental protection measures is not used in a way that produces the intended emission reduction quantities. This is true especially for small and/or long-term projects where monitoring

---

[5] If the abatements are not additional but merely traded among countries, the global level of pollution remains unchanged and free-riding on the other countries' grants does not occur. Then there is competition for the 'cheapest' JI projects.

the fulfillment of the abatement obligations is rather difficult. A successful reforestation project, for example, requires that the land remains reforestated *for ever*, unless the wood which works as a carbon sink is not conserved in some way (for example, as furniture). Until recently, the GEF lacked institutionalized mechanisms of oversight and monitoring over the performance of projects during and after implementation. Although a special organizational unit has been installed at the GEF for this purpose, monitoring will probably become a core problem in the future, given the great variety of projects eligible for funding and the limited capacities of the GEF to survey the host countries' actions.

In general, the extent to which welfare gains from cost-effectiveness in the protection of global environmental resources can be achieved through the GEF depends on the scale of its mandate. This instrument is less effective, the fewer the financial resources and the more the political restrictions on the selection and execution of its projects. According to a statement of Bert Bolin, the former president of the IPCC, an effective climate policy would require financial resources of about 50 to 70 billion US dollars in the next 20 years. In this light, the current annual resources of the GEF available for JI projects of about US$500 million are only about one-tenth of what would be necessary. But even if sufficient funding were available, the gains that can be achieved by a centralized mechanism such as the GEF have to be compared with more decentralized institutional arrangements such as 'true' emission permits trading, bilateral projects outside the framework of a multilateral agreement or even unilateral measures. In the long run, a tradable permit market clearly leads to greater cost-effectiveness because the market allows and encourages innovation in production and in the successful contracting of international pollution reduction projects. It can be argued, though, that an international fund like the GEF is appropriate as an interim measure until property rights on the global environment are clearly defined and monitoring and enforcement problems are sufficiently solved (Kerr 1995). From this perspective, the GEF's guidelines should be designed to facilitate the switch to a future comprehensive permit market.

One innovative role the GEF could play in the long-term development towards a market-oriented global environmental policy is that of a trustee for a global emission stock market. The theoretical analysis of Chapter 5 has demonstrated that payments being granted for abatement activities can be used to solve the compliance risk if they are deposited with a neutral 'third party'. Given that the market for international emission permits will one day also be opened to private agents such as companies or interest groups, it would be of great advantage for these agents (which mostly do not have any significant threat potential on the international arena) if they could fall back on an intermediary who is specialized in global emission trading and who ensures the execution of contracts.

7.2 The Montreal Protocol Multilateral Fund

The Montreal Protocol on substances that deplete the ozone layer was a landmark agreement in global environmental policy. Developing countries initially showed very little interest in an agreement that would preclude them from a class of inexpensive industrial chemicals. They were only willing to cooperate under the condition that developed countries granted comprehensive financial and technical assistance in this field. As a result, in 1990 the Montreal Protocol Multilateral Fund (MPMF) was established in London (see Table 2.6). Its mandate is to administer the financial funds provided by the industrialized countries to assist developing countries in the phase-out of ozone-depleting substances.[6]

7.2.1 Organization and Operation

The MPMF consists of an executive committee (ExCom) with 14 members (seven from developing and seven from industrialized countries) and an independent secretariat.[7] It operates with the help of four implementing agencies: the UNDP, UNEP, UNIDO and the World Bank. Investment projects are implemented by the World Bank, the UNDP and UNIDO. UNEP runs technical information programs and is the treasurer of the fund. The executive committee governs the fund and surveys the implementation of the projects. Decisions in the ExCom are usually taken by consensus or, if this is not possible, by a double-majority voting system.[8] The secretariat is located in Montreal, Canada. It plays an active role in the preparation and approval of project proposals.

Like the GEF, the MPMF applies the concept of 'agreed incremental costs' for the determination of grants to member countries. In 1990, the total incremental costs of changing to ozone-friendly substances in developing countries had been estimated to amount to US\$1.5–5 billion over

---

[6]Developing countries eligible for financial assistance are specified in Article 5 MP as those that use less than 0.3 kg of ozone-depleting substances per person per year. The parties to the MP are often divided into 'Article 5 countries' (developing countries) and 'other countries' (industrialized countries).

[7]For an overview on institutions to protect the ozone layer, see Parson and Greene (1995, p. 35).

[8]The majority rule is overall majority of two-thirds, simultaneously with a majority of both Article 5 (developing) and non-Article 5 (industrialized) countries.

the following 10–18 years. According to a 'country program' prepared by the government of each eligible country, the implementing agencies propose investment projects to the ExCom and implement them after approval. So far, the greatest contributors to the MPMF's financial funds have been the EU (35 per cent), the USA (25 per cent) and Japan (13 per cent). By mid-1995, the ExCom had approved US$292 million and more than 830 activities, but only 39 investment projects and two-thirds of the training programs had been completed. At that time, only 5 349 tons of controlled substances had been phased out, where implementation of the remaining approved projects should lead to a reduction of an additional 44 680 tons (being less than one-third of 1995 consumption of ozone-depleting substances of Article 5 countries). In 1996, the fund was replenished with financial resources. From 1997 to 1999, developing countries that renounce the use of substances which destroy the ozone layer will receive US$540 million from the MPMF.

The reasons for the slow progress in the implementation are diverse. First, the MPMF works through a set of pre-existing institutions which causes a complex administration process from project formulation to execution.[9] Second, technological innovations require an adjustment of the projects, but they also trigger controversial debates about which technologies to switch to. Moreover, there is a substantial lack of capacity in recipient countries to comply with the rules and operations of the MPMF. Finally, the strategic incentives underlying the whole ozone regime give rise to continuous bargaining and renegotiation even within the MPMF.

7.2.2 Evaluation

Compared to projects financed by the GEF, cost-effectiveness can be attained much more easily through the MPMF mechanism for several reasons. The ultimate environmental standard is a complete phase-out of harmful emissions, it involves a shorter time horizon with better-known technological options, the MPMF mandate is better funded and there are fewer countries and economic sectors involved. All these factors facilitate the task of allocating abatements in a cost-effective way. Consequently, cost-effectiveness in the MPMF's operation is not as critical an issue as it is for the protection of environmental goods managed by the GEF and the FCCC because incremental costs are easier to determine and abatement costs do not differ as much between alternative abatement

---

[9]This is expecially true for the World Bank because of its careful, multistage review processes that are designed for large investment projects and its lack of experience in engineering tasks.

options.

Altogether, the creation of the MPMF as part of international cooperation on the protection of the ozone layer can be regarded as a success. The MPMF has worked quite effectively with relatively few conflicts about the general policy target and with a high degree of control over the projects that are financed by it and taken out by the implementing agencies. The high degree of cooperation is due not only to the specific characteristics of the environmental problem at hand (a high degree of scientific knowledge, relatively low abatement costs combined with clear benefits, a favorable distribution of costs and benefits across countries), but also to the negotiation of an issue- and time-bounded funding mechanism that reduces uncertainty over future payment obligations. Conflicts may arise in the future, though, as the operation of the MPMF becomes more demanding with the end of the grace period for the developing countries' abatement obligations. Although the financial contributions of industrial countries are explicitly voluntary, they will be indispensable if the obligations of Article 5 countries to phase out ozone-depleting substances are to be met. Already, the amounts pledged will probably not cover the estimated full incremental costs of all developing countries' phase-outs. In addition, many donor countries have been paying late with the result that not all projects could be funded at the time of their approval.

7.3   Joint Implementation

The use of fixed quotas in international environmental agreements may give rise to substantial cost-inefficiencies, as we pointed out in Section 3.4. In order to avoid the cost-inefficiencies of uniform solutions to some extent, certain governments have pushed for at least a limited possibility of trading emission rights internationally. The most prominent example for this attempt are the 'activities implemented jointly' put down in the Framework Convention on Climate Change. This concept stipulates that two (or more) parties to the convention have the right to implement emission abatement measures jointly if they find it in their interest. According to this provision, contracting parties with relatively high marginal abatement costs can fulfill (part of) their abatement obligations by purchasing abatement activities in countries with low marginal abatement costs. Achieving emission reductions jointly implicitly introduces international transfer payments and is a rudimentary form of trading emission rights. Under ideal conditions with perfect foresight and in the absence of transaction costs, a quota agreement which allows for 'joint implementation' projects would lead to international cost-effectiveness.[10]

Originally, the notion of 'joint implementation' goes back to a common proposal of seven large electric utilities[11], whereby an international climate convention would allow them to fulfill their emission reduction obligations by erecting new, energy-efficient power plants in other countries which have an old and dirty energy sector. It is not necessary that JI is part of an international environmental agreement where the investing country receives a credit for the resulting abatement although the JI discussion focusses on this context. A country may trade emission reductions with another country simply to lower its own non-cooperative abatement costs (Pearce 1995). It was the Framework Convention on Climate Change, though, that stipulated the JI principle for the first time in a formal environmental agreement.

The Kyoto Protocol has taken up the concept of joint implementation by allowing for flexibility in the implementation the individual countries' obligations. It codifies three instruments to support international cost-effectiveness of GHG emission reductions: 'Emissions Trading' (Art. 17 FCCC), 'Joint Implementation' (Art. 6 FCCC) and the 'Clean Development mechanism' (Art. 12 FCCC). Article 3 of the KP stipulates that under any of these instruments, the emissions obligations traded are to be fully credited and charged to the obligations being assigned to the countries by the protocol. The three instruments all follow the same principle and differ only with respect to the parties they are targetting: JI according to Article 6 allows joint projects between Annex I countries,[12] whereas the CDM (Art. 12 FCCC) has been created for projects between industrialized (Annex I) and developing countries; ET according to Article 17 FCCC is the broadest approach as it is not restricted to certain countries and is not necessarily project based. To a limited extent, the KP also provides for intertemporal flexibility in the form that overfulfillment in one commitment period will be creditable to future periods (Article 3 No. 13 FCCC).

Although incorporating the right to trade emissions is in principle a very important step toward a cost-effective, market-based global climate policy, the KP remains rather vague as to the precise modalities under which the above instruments may be employed. All crucial questions that

---

[10]Basically, the concept of JI takes up the Baumol/Oates approach of setting a global environmental standard first and then selecting a cost-minimizing instrument to achieve this target (see Section 4.2).

[11]This group has been called the 'E7' and consists of the French *Electricité de France*, *Hydro Quebec* and *Ontario Hydro* from Canada, *Tokyo Electric Power Co.* and *Kausai Electric Power Co.* from Japan, the Italian *Ente Nazionale per l'Energia Elettrica* and the German *Rheinisch-Westfälische Elektrizitätswerke*.

[12]Annex I countries are industrialized countries and countries in transition.

may give rise to incentive and implementation problems are postponed to later conferences of the parties. To these open issues belong

- how to determine the appropriate baseline;
- how to ensure a reliable verification and reporting system;
- how to sanction non-compliant behavior;
- how to share the gains from CDM and to combine it with development assistance; and
- to what extent is ET still to be judged as 'supplemental'?

A principal problem of the JI concept is how transaction costs can be minimized. With only a few cooperating countries and projects, the supplied project sizes may not be compatible with those demanded. Moreover, search and monitoring costs for bilateral JI projects may be high, even in a situation with a large number of buyers and sellers of emission reduction projects. A possible way to reduce transaction costs would be to channel all JI projects through a clearing-house which could act as a buyer cooperative on the market for such projects. The GEF, for example, could exert this function by collecting all JI offers from developing (seller) countries and and by letting an aggregate supply of abatement quantities meet the demand from industrialized (buyer) countries. This would have the advantage of determining a market clearing price for perfectly divisible emission reduction units (Bohm 1994b).

In general, JI is often seen as the 'thin end of the wedge' towards a full tradable obligations scheme (Pearce 1995, p. 16). Even if it involves in its initial form trades among only a few countries, one may easily imagine a state where JI has evolved to a wholesale trading system in which a multitude of agents participate. A similar development has taken place in the market for acid rain pollution permits under the Clean Air Act in the USA. Nevertheless, critical aspects concerning the ability of JI to work as a precursor to a comprehensive global carbon permit market cannot be overlooked.

The common perception about JI projects is that in most cases industrialized countries will finance emission reduction projects in developing countries. However, developing countries are not yet obliged to commit to any own emission ceilings. Because of this it is very difficult to quantify their counterfactual emission levels without JI projects. But determining the so-called 'baseline' is crucial since it is the basis for determining the actual emission reduction quantity which can be credited to a country's reduction obligation. Determining appropriate baselines hence will be a core problem of any form of JI or emissions trading. Given the difficulties of estimating a developing country's counterfactual baseline, one may argue that JI projects between industrialized and developing countries should be limited to demonstration projects, as long as the latter countries have not made any own commitments on emission quantities (Bohm 1994b).[13] Generally, any emissions trading involving outsider countries without own national emission targets endangers the implementation of an agreed-upon environmental standard by the contracting parties. Buying emission rights from developing countries without an own emission ceiling rather can be seen as a 'selling of indulgences'. In this light, the immediate inclusion of developing countries into a global system of JI as presently demanded by the USA is ecologically counterproductive.

Another objection against the idea of using JI as a preliminary stage for a comprehensive global tradable permit system is that the former may reduce the interests of developing countries (or other countries without any precise national emission target) to participate in the latter. For example, assume that initial emission obligations of developing countries under a tradable permit system would equal an internationally agreed estimate of their expected emissions for the relevant target year. Then, to the extent that JI projects precede the introduction of the permit system and lead to lower emissions in a developing country, the initial emission ceiling (abatement target) for this country would be lower (higher). As a consequence, the developing countries would gain less from joining the tradable permit system in comparison to the situation without prior JI projects. The larger the scope of JI, including countries which have not yet committed to any own emission reduction efforts, the more difficult it may get in the long run to make these countries participate in a broad — and thereby cost-effective — global tradable permit system (Bohm 1994b). An analogous argument has been derived from the theoretical analysis in Chapter 5 where we showed how the combined use of transfers and a cost-effective reallocation of national abatement efforts could be used to provide the necessary incentives both for participation and for compliance.

Taken together, the requirement of incentive compatibility is crucial in the context of JI as it is for all market-based internalization instruments applied on the international level. It remains unclear, though, why there should be incentives for sustainable JI projects when it was not possible to sign a contract including a market-based internalization instrument in the first place. Rather, there is every reason to suspect a trade-off between short-term cost-effectiveness and long-term incentive compatibility (and long-term cost-effectiveness). So far, this aspect has not been sufficiently addressed in the existing institutional arrangements for joint implementation.

---

[13] For a comparison of tradable carbon permits and JI, see also Bohm (1994a).

Chapter 8

Summary and Outlook

8.1 The Scope and Results of the Study

This study has been concerned with the issues that arise from the interdependency between cost-effectiveness and incentive compatibility in international environmental policy. We investigated the prospects for international environmental cooperation in the face of only poorly developed international institutions, focussing on the following questions:

- How does the heterogeneity of countries involved in transboundary pollution problems influence the welfare losses from uncoordinated national environmental policies, the chances of voluntary and stable agreements and the attractiveness of alternative policy instruments?
- What is the general role of transfers in IEAs and how are they best designed in order to overcome the severe incentive problems national governments are confronted with?
- How can international institutions be used to foster an efficient management of international environmental resources; and to what extent are cost-effectiveness and incentive compatibility taken into account by presently operating agencies?

These questions were analysed in three steps. First, we clarified the relevance of cost-effectiveness and incentive compatibility for international environmental policy; then, we investigated the above questions in the light of specific contractual provisions designed to deal with enforcement problems and asymmetric information; finally, we described and evaluated existing international institutions created to support cost-effectiveness in global environmental policy. The first and the last part of the analysis were applied to the anthropogenic greenhouse effect and the destruction of the stratospheric ozone layer.

Chapter 2 of the study introduced the natural scientific background of 'global warming' and the 'ozone hole'. We also reviewed the political attempts of countermeasures undertaken so far and reported on the current state. Furthermore, the basic theoretical concepts that provide the methodological framework of the analysis were outlined.

In Chapter 3, we discussed the concept and the empirical relevance of cost-effectiveness in international environmental policy. It was found that — despite its limitations — this concept offers a useful tool for identifying potential efficiency gains in international environmental policy. Using a simple non-cooperative model of two countries that differ in size we compared the welfare losses resulting from underprovision and from cost-inefficiency. Conditions were derived under which not equalizing marginal abatement costs is a more important source of inefficiency than free-riding. We also compared the non-cooperative Nash and Stackelberg equilibria. Although cost-inefficiencies under Stackelberg behavior are generally lower than under Nash behavior, underprovision is always greater in the Stackelberg case and dominates the first source of inefficiency. In a somewhat broader setting with multiple countries and using current economic data, we calculated the annual excess costs of different carbon reduction scenarios by means of numerical simulations. Although the cost-inefficiencies which accompany proportional emission reductions are important, they differ only slightly from the non-cooperative benchmark. Moreover, the pattern of national emissions that equalizes marginal abatement costs indicates that important factors are missing in the specification of national abatement costs underlying the simulations. The results of this highly stylized model therefore were complemented by a survey of quantitative studies on the national costs of reducing carbon emissions. These studies also emphasize the empirical relevance of cost-effectiveness. Chapter 3 concluded with a comparison of different policy instruments to internalize transboundary environmental externalities.

In Chapter 4, we surveyed the theoretical literature on the incentives for international environmental cooperation and proposed a taxonomy of instruments to support incentive compatibility in international environmental policy. Conceivable strategies to enable sustainable cooperative solutions were grouped into (i) the choice and specific form of the internalization instrument itself; (ii) carrot/stick strategies that make cooperative abatement efforts dependent on the past behavior of other countries (internal stabilization); (iii) transfers and sanctions of various types (external stabilization); (iv) unilateral and accompanying measures by single countries or subcoalitions; and (v) long-term provisions to increase the flexibility of agreements and to improve the framework conditions of international negotiations. The overall finding was that there are in fact various strategies available to provide participation as well as compliance incentives. It was revealed, however, that the requirements for the actors' preferences and capabilities to design and implement complex strategies are usually too demanding to allow for large gains from cooperation. This applies especially to situations where important facts such as the involvement of many countries or the lack of policy instruments on the international level are stylized. It was also found that present (game-)theoretic models of international environmental policy do not sufficiently take into account the importance and the role of institutions as well as specific problems due to informational imperfections.

In Chapter 5, we analysed how the enforcement problem can be overcome by an international environmental agreement including self-financing transfers and resorting to an international institution that works as an intermediary. In this model, side payments are deposited with the intermediary and thus work as a bond. Together with sequential moves of the contracting parties in the implementation of the agreement, these provisions enable credible commitments and solve the time-consistency problem. Self-financing transfers prove to be powerful instruments and to generate substantial gains from environmental cooperation, even if transfers are further restricted to compensations for cost-effectiveness of abatement efforts and if more than two countries are involved. It was also shown that the welfare gains from environmental cooperation may tend to rise with the asymmetry between countries. This result was obtained because transfers and the gains from cost-effectiveness are employed as an instrument to support compliance with the environmental treaty. Since side payments and the gains from trading emissions are generally the greater, the more heterogeneous the countries, the prospects for stable environmental agreements will increase with asymmetry.

In Chapter 6, we addressed the problem of asymmetric information in international environmental agreements which provide for transfers. We compared the financing of net and gross incremental abatement costs in a situation where the calculation of the transfer induces incentives for a strategic misrepresentation of environmental preferences. It was shown that the principle to compensate recipient countries for their *net* incremental abatement costs is generally no longer optimal for the donor countries. This holds even if the donors are able to submit an offer which is optimal for themselves and when the terms of the agreement can be differentiated for each type of recipient (that is, in a separating equilibrium). Also in cases where international transfers have to be based on simple, uniform rules (that is, a pooling equilibrium), conditions can be derived under which both donor and recipient countries favor the application of the gross over the net incremental cost concept. These conditions mirror characteristic features in international environmental policy, namely, countries are very asymmetric and information on the bargaining partners is poor.

In Chapter 7, we proceeded to an analysis of existing international institutions that have been created to support cost-effectiveness in global environmental policy. We described the origins and the mandate of the Montreal Protocol Multilateral Fund, the Global Environment Facility and the concept of joint implementation within the Framework Convention on Climate Change. Operational guidelines and practice of these institutions were evaluated in the light of the preceding analysis.

This study focussed on environmental externalities that have the properties of a pure international public good. Although some of the most pressing environmental problems such as the anthropogenic greenhouse effect or the depletion of the stratospheric ozone layer possess these features, there are obviously many other international environmental problems which have more of an asymmetric, upstream–downstream character. This complicates the analysis, but our results can also be applied to this class of problems. In fact, it is obvious that international transfer schemes play an even more important role in this context and that treaty provisions against enforcement problems and informational shortcomings can be used in the same manner as for purely reciprocal externalities.

Throughout the study a static, partial equilibrium framework has been used. This implies that some crucial features of international environmental problems are neglected. For example, we abstracted from the fact that greenhouse gas emissions constitute a stock pollutant and did not model the dynamic dimension of cost-effectiveness and incentive compatibility.[1] This simplification was necessary to be able to examine the aspects of cost-effectiveness and incentive compatibility in a coherent framework. But nevertheless the main message of our static framework — the important role of side payments and international institutions — can be transferred to a more general, dynamic setting. The basic difference is that with repeated interactions there are even more strategies available for national governments to coordinate their national environmental policies effectively. Also, uncertainty and irreversibility are of greater importance in a dynamic surrounding. Furthermore, we did not take into account distortions in other markets that may have repercussions on optimal international environmental policy and which may allow a *double dividend* to be earned. So far, such general equilib-

---

[1] These aspects have been discussed, however, in the survey on incentive compatibility (see Section 4.3).

rium effects have usually been analysed in the context of purely national environmental policy or unilateral policy measures.[2]

Finally, we assumed national governments to be benevolent towards their own populations, thereby abstracting from political–economic aspects. Although from the latter point of view our analysis is a normative one (as we analyse how governments *should* act if they had the welfare of their people in mind), the analysis is positive in the sense that it accounts for additional restrictions national governments face on the international level and which make global *first-best* solutions generally not attainable. Contributions that analyse environmental decision-making from a political–economic perspective have only recently been made and are very often restricted to non-transboundary externalities. It seems to be a promising direction of future research to overcome this shortcoming. To this end, economic models may also draw inspiration from already existing approaches in the political science literature such as the so-called 'two-level-games'. The latter approach analyses in a game-theoretic framework the interaction of national governments with relevant players on the national level and on the international level simultaneously.

By contrast, the central paradigm of government behavior towards the rest of the world is that of *rational opportunism*. Outside the realm of economic, especially (traditional) game-theoretic research, this notion of rationality is challenged as an appropriate assumption to analyse the incentives for cooperation between sovereign states.[3] From the point of view of *regime theory* (a branch of political science analysing international relations), negotiating an agreement is part of the formation of a regime where countries 'alter their behavior, their relationships, and their expectations of one another over time in accordance with its terms' (Chayes and Chayes 1993, p. 176). This perspective emphasizes the communicative and informative character of the whole process of international negotiations. It modifies the structure of the decision problem, but is treated as exogenous in traditional economic analysis (Young 1989).

The results of the analysis have been derived using highly stylized models. In the light of the various simplifications there clearly are limitations to the scope of the present study. The findings therefore cannot be directly applied to real-world political decision-making and have to be interpreted with some caution. Nevertheless, the approach taken in this study produces clear statements about the usefulness and attractiveness of specific and realistic elements in international environmental policy.

---

[2] Some of these issues have been discussed in Section 4.5.

[3] Recently, this criticism has also been made by economists (see Kirchgässner and Mohr 1996, pp. 214–15).

Some promising directions in future international environmental policy are discussed in the remainder of this chapter.

8.2   Future Directions in International Environmental Policy

An effective protection of international environmental resources is doomed to fail when the aspects of cost-effectiveness and incentive compatibility are ignored, as shown by the discussion in Chapters 3 and 4. International environmental policy-making has to consider these core aspects in an integrated approach. Market-based instruments will perform poorly with respect to cost-effectiveness if their implementation is endangered by opportunistic behavior and lack of enforcement. Similarly, treaty provisions which create incentives for single nations to participate in and comply with environmental treaties may be accompanied by severe cost-inefficiencies, thereby reducing the overall gains from environmental cooperation and the general attractiveness of these agreements. The above problems are especially relevant in the context of global environmental problems where many different countries are involved. Both aspects have undoubtedly been addressed in existing international environmental treaties. The Montreal Protocol incorporates trade sanctions and grace periods intended to ensure the long-term cooperation of the contracting parties. Cost-effectiveness is the primary objective of both the Global Environment Facility and the Montreal Protocol Multilateral Fund. Nevertheless, these arrangements are no more than first steps in very narrow policy fields. The provisions of the Kyoto Protocol, vague with respect to joint implementation and monitoring, are only one example of how much still has to be done.

The importance of compensation schemes, both for cost-effectiveness and incentive compatibility, is another relevant finding for practical policy-making. Transfers are especially important — and often imperative — when the parties involved are strongly asymmetric. They enable trade in emission efforts, and may serve as an instrument to make countries participate in international environmental cooperation, but also to guarantee adherence to signed treaties even without supranational enforcement. The attractiveness of side payments is supported by the fact that they may be granted in other, less explicit forms than cash. Of course, whenever transfers are a feasible option aspects of a 'fair' distribution are especially relevant. The analysis has shown, however, that under certain circumstances it may be of interest to the donors to be 'generous' concerning the amount of side payments if this helps to avoid strategic behavior due to asymmetric information. In the context of joint implementation projects one can therefore make a case to favor the gross over the net incremental cost concept.

A general policy implication of the analysis is that much can be achieved in the protection of transboundary environmental resources when national governments fall back on existing international institutions and use them in an innovative manner. One important role these agencies can play is that of an intermediary between the contracting parties. As long as sufficient independence is guaranteed from national governments, no other power needs to be furnished in addition to that following from the terms of international environmental agreements. Furthermore, the fact that several such agencies with more or less similar tasks already exist may be of advantage, even considering the extra administrative costs. Multiple competing approaches may allow us to find and more quickly develop the approach that makes the best compromise with the specific problems of environmental policy on the international level. The long-term goal, nevertheless, should be to create an institutional framework which allows for decentralized activities of individual actors — under ideal circumstances some kind of global permit market. Existing agencies and the concept of joint implementation thus can serve as a starting-point in the long-term process towards an incentive compatible and market-oriented regulation of these problems. In the context of global warming, though, the first requirement which has to be fulfilled is that a global environmental standard (that is, global emission ceiling) is agreed upon. The discussion on permit trade following the Kyoto Protocol has made it clear that there is nothing to be gained in ecological terms if some (developing) countries are allowed to sell emission permits to other (industrialized) countries, but are themselves not subject to any emission obligation.

From a European perspective, the conviction is perhaps especially strong that substantial progress in the above fields has to be made. Fortunately, the countries belonging to the European Union are in a position to play a path-breaking role in international, and especially global environmental policy. The governments of the EU member states are able to act politically as one single entity and constitute a 'global player', in terms of both the economic and ecological consequences of their policy. The introduction of a European carbon/energy tax may therefore serve as a blueprint for similar projects in other parts of the world and as an alternative to the presently favored permit approach on the global level. Even if the 'carbon leakage' problem turns out to be considerable in the short run, it nevertheless may be worthwhile undertaking this unilateral step: it could be demonstrated how the tax measures are working, and it could be tested which specific institutional arrangements are practicable on the international level. Furthermore, given the widespread sensitivity of policy-makers with regard to 'fair solutions', a strong European commitment may well increase the acceptance of joint efforts in the developing world, thereby reducing the adverse effects of a unilateral policy approach in the long run.

Appendix

A.1 Efficient Bargaining Solutions

The modified Samuelson condition for international public goods in a model with two goods (one composite private good X and one international public good Q) and two countries A and B can be represented according to the following procedure (Shibata 1971):[1]

1. Inversion of the common transformation curve TT' of both countries at TQ'. The slope of the flipped curve TT'' is $-dQ/dX > 0$.

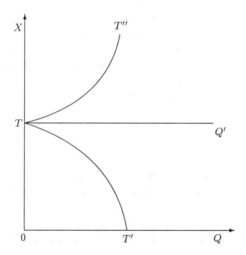

Figure A.1: Inversed transformation curve

2. Vertical addition of the ordinate values of the social indifference curves of country B for each quantity of the international public good Q to the ordinate values of TT''. The slopes of the modified

---

[1]See Arnold (1984, pp. 121–3) for the case of linear production possibility frontiers.

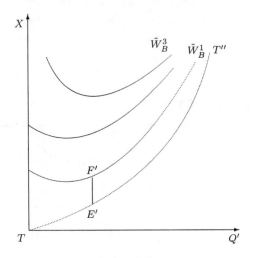

Figure A.2: Modified indifference curves

indifference curves $\tilde{W}_B$ are $(\partial x_B/\partial q_b - dX/dQ)$.

3. Inversion of the modified indifference curves of country B back down again at line TQ'. Addition of the social indifference curves of country A to the origin. Together, we yield graph 2.2.

Because the (modified) indifference curves are tangential for each point on EG in Figure 2.2, $-\partial x_B/\partial q_B + dX/dQ = \partial x_A/\partial q_A$ holds. Since the slopes of the indifference curves in their absolute values correspond to the marginal rates of substitution, the above equation can be written as

$$-\frac{dX}{dQ} = -\frac{dX_A}{dq_A} = -\frac{dX_B}{dq_B} = -\left(\sum_{i=1}^{N} \frac{dx_A^i}{dq_A} + \sum_{j=1}^{M} \frac{dx_B^j}{dq_B}\right).$$

A.2 The 'Permits and Standards' Approach

Assume a uniformly mixed assimilative pollutant e that damages environmental quality A in the form

$$A = a + b \sum_{k=1}^{K} (\bar{e}_k - q_k),$$

where a and b are exogenous parameters that specify the pollution function, $\bar{e}_k$ are emissions of country k in the absence of environmental concerns and q_k are country k's abatements. Abatement costs $C_k(q_k)$ are assumed to be continuous, increasing and strictly convex ($C' > 0$, $C'' > 0$, $C(0) = 0$). Given an exogenous environmental standard $\bar{A}$, the problem of a (world) social planner is to minimize abatement costs

$$\min_{q_k} \sum_{k=1}^{K} C_k(q_k), \text{ s.t.}$$

$$a + b \sum_{k=1}^{K} (\bar{e}_k - q_k) \leq \bar{A},$$

$$q_k \geq 0.$$

The Kuhn–Tucker conditions yield

$$\frac{\partial C_k}{\partial q_k} - \lambda b \geq 0, \quad k = 1, \ldots, K$$

$$q_k \left(\frac{\partial C_k}{\partial q_k} - \lambda b \right) = 0, \quad k = 1, \ldots, K$$

$$a + b \sum_{k=1}^{K} (\bar{e}_k - q_k) \leq \bar{A}$$

$$\lambda \left[a + b \sum_{k=1}^{K} (\bar{e}_k - q_k) - \bar{A} \right] = 0$$

$$\lambda \geq 0; \quad q_k \geq 0, \quad k = 1, \ldots, K.$$

This implies that for interior solutions, marginal abatement costs must be equalized across countries in the optimum. The implementation of the exogenously given standard $\bar{A}$ by tradable permits is achieved by setting the total number of emission permits N such that

$$N = \sum_{k=1}^{K} (\bar{e}_k - q_k) \overset{!}{=} \frac{\bar{A} - a}{b}.$$

When these permits are allocated to the countries and then traded in a perfectly operating market, an equilibrium price p evolves (irrespective of the initial distribution) and the optimization problem for each individual country is

$$\min_{q_k} \left[C_k(q_k) + p(\bar{e}_k - q_k - e_k^o) \right], \quad \text{s.t.} \quad q_k \geq 0, \quad k = 1, \ldots, K$$

where e_k^o is the initial endowment with emission permits of country k. The Kuhn–Tucker conditions yield

$$\frac{\partial C_k}{\partial q_k} - p \geq 0$$

$$q_k \left(\frac{\partial C_k}{\partial q_k} - p \right) = 0$$

$$q_k \geq 0, \quad \forall k \in K.$$

Comparing the conditions for optimality under the individual and the social planner problems shows that they correspond to each other and that cost-effectiveness is reached under a perfectly operating international market for emission permits. The equalization of marginal abatement costs is brought about by the world market price p which is the same for all countries.[2]

---

[2] For the derivation of the cost-minimization theorem with respect to pollution charges, see Baumol and Oates (1988, pp. 165–9).

Bibliography

Ahuja, Dilip (1993) *The Incremental Cost of Climate Change Mitigation Projects*, Working Paper No. 9 (Washington, DC: Global Environment Facility).

Althammer, Wilhelm and Wolfgang Buchholz (1993) 'Internationaler Umweltschutz als Koordinationsproblem'. In *Dezentrale Entscheidungsfindung bei externen Effekten — Innovation, Integration und internationaler Handel*, ed. Adolf Wagner (Tübingen: Francke) chapter 5, pp. 289–315.

Arnold, Volker (1984) 'Umweltschutz als internationales öffentliches Gut: Komparative Kostenvorteile und Verhandlungsgewinne'. *Zeitschrift für Wirtschafts- und Sozialwissenschaften 104*(2), 111–29.

Arnold, Volker (1992) *Theorie der Kollektivgüter* (München: Franz Vahlen).

Aronsson, Thomas, Per-Olov Johansson and Karl-Gustaf Loefgren (1997) *Welfare Measurement, Sustainability and Green National Accounting — A Growth Theoretical Approach* (Cheltenham, UK: Edward Elgar).

Atkinson, Anthony and Joseph E. Stiglitz (1980) *Lectures on Public Economics* (New York: McGraw-Hill).

Bac, Mehmet (1996) 'Incomplete information and incentives to free ride on international environmental resources'. *Journal of Environmental Economics and Management 30*, 301–35.

Barbier, Edward B., John Burgess and David W. Pearce (1991) 'Technological substitution options for controlling greenhouse gas emissions'. In *Global Warming: Economic Policy Responses*, eds R. Dornbusch and J. Poterba (London: MIT Press) pp. 109–60.

Barrett, Scott (1990) 'The problem of global environmental protection'. *Oxford Review of Economic Policy* **6**(1), 68–79.

Barrett, Scott (1992a) *Convention on Climate Change: Economic Aspects of Negotiations* (Paris: OECD).

Barrett, Scott (1992b) 'International environmental agreements as games'. In *Conflicts and Cooperation in Managing Environmental Resources*, ed. Rüdiger Pethig (Berlin et al.: Springer) chapter 1, pp. 11–36.

Barrett, Scott (1994) 'Self-enforcing international environmental agreements'. *Oxford Economic Papers* **46**, 878–94.

Barrett, Scott (1997a) 'Heterogeneous international environmental agreements'. In *International Environmental Negotiations: Strategic Policy Issues*, ed. Carlo Carraro (Cheltenham, UK: Edward Elgar) chapter 2, pp. 9–25.

Barrett, Scott (1997b) 'The strategy of trade sanctions in international environmental agreements'. *Resource and Energy Economics* **19**(4), 345–61.

Baumol, William J. and Wallace E. Oates (1971) 'The use of standards and prices for protection of the environment'. *Swedish Journal of Economics* **73**(1), 42–54.

Baumol, William J. and Wallace E. Oates (1988) *The Theory of Environmental Policy*, 2nd edn (Cambridge, UK: Cambridge University Press).

Benedick, Richard E. (1991) *Ozone Diplomacy: New Directions in Safeguarding the Planet* (Cambridge, MA: Harvard University Press).

Bergesen, Helge O. and Georg Parmann (1997) *Green Globe Yearbook of International Co-operation on Environment and Development* (Oslo, Norway: Fridtjof Nansen Institute).

Black, Jane, Maurice D. Levi and David de Meza (1993) 'Creating a good atmosphere: minimum participation for tackling the "greenhouse effect"'. *Economica* **60**, 281–93.

Bohm, Peter (1993a) 'Incomplete international cooperation to reduce CO_2 emissions: alternative policies'. *Journal of Environmental Economics and Management* **24**(3), 258–71.

Bohm, Peter (1993b) *Should Marginal Carbon Abatement Costs Be Equalized Across Countries?*, Economics Research Paper No. 12 (Stockholm University).

Bohm, Peter (1994a) 'Making carbon emission quota agreements more efficient: Joint implementation versus quota tradability'. In *Economic Instruments for Air Pollution Control*, eds G. Klaassen and Finn R. Forsund (Dordrecht: Kluwer) chapter 9, pp. 187–208.

Bohm, Peter (1994b) *On the Feasibility of Joint Implementation of Carbon Emissions Reductions*, Economics Research Paper No. 2 (Stockholm University).

Böhringer, Christoph and Thomas F. Rutherford (1997) 'Carbon taxes with exemptions in an open economy: a general equilibrium analysis of the German tax initiative'. *Journal of Environmental Economics and Management* **32**(2), 189–203.

Bolin, Bert (1997) 'Key features of the global climate system to be considered in analysis of the climate change issue'. Presentation on the 8th annual conference of the European Association of Environmental and Resource Economists in Tilburg, Netherlands, 26–28 June.

Botteon, Michele and Carlo Carraro (1997) 'Burden-sharing and coalition stability in environmental negotiations with asymmentric countries'. In *International Environmental Negotiations: Strategic Policy Issues*, ed. Carlo Carraro (Cheltenham, UK: Edward Elgar) chapter 3, pp. 26–55.

Braden, John B. and Daniel W. Bromley (1981) 'The economics of cooperation over collective bads'. *Journal of Environmental Economics and Management* **8**, 134–50.

Brekke, Kjell A. (1994) 'Net national product as a welfare indicator'. *Scandinavian Journal of Economics* **96**(2), 241–52.

Brundtland, Gro H. (1987) *Our Common Future*. World Commission on Environment and Development (Oxford: Oxford University Press).

Buchholz, Wolfgang and Kai A. Konrad (1994) 'Global environmental problems and the strategic choice of technology'. *Journal of Economics* **60**(3), 299–321.

Carraro, Carlo and Domenico Siniscalco (1992) 'The international dimension of environmental policy'. *European Economic Review* **36**, 379–87.

Carraro, Carlo and Domenico Siniscalco (1993) 'Strategies for the international protection of the environment'. *Journal of Public Economics* **52**, 309–28.

Carraro, Carlo and Domenico Siniscalco (1995) 'Policy coordination for sustainability: Commitments, transfers, and linked negotiations'. In *The Economics of Sustainable Development*, eds I. Goldwin and A. Winters (Cambridge, UK: Cambridge University Press).

Carraro, Carlo and Domenico Siniscalco (1997) 'R&D cooperation and the stability of international environmental agreements'. In *International Environmental Agreements: Strategic Policy Issues*, ed. Carlo Carraro (Cheltenham, UK: Edward Elgar) chapter 5, pp. 71–96.

Cesar, Herman and Aart de Zeeuw (1996) 'Issue linkage in global environmental problems'. In *Economic Policy for the Environment and Natural Resources: Techniques for the Management and Control of Pollution*, ed. A. Xepapadeas (Cheltenham, UK: Edward Elgar) pp. 158–73.

Chander, Parkash and Henry Tulkens (1995) 'A core-theoretic solution for the design of cooperative agreements on transfrontier pollution'. *International Tax and Public Finance* **2**, 279–93.

Chander, Parkash and Henry Tulkens (1997) 'The core of an economy with multilateral environmental externalities'. *International Journal of Game Theory* **26**, 379–401.

Chayes, Abram and Antonia H. Chayes (1993) 'On compliance'. *International Organization* **47**, 175–205.

Chichilnisky, Graciela and Geoffrey Heal (1994) 'Who should abate carbon emissions? An international view'. *Economics Letters* **44**, 443–9.

Chillemi, Ottorino (1997) 'International environmental agreements and asymmetric information'. In *International Environmental Negotiations: Strategic Policy Issues*, ed. Carlo Carraro (Cheltenham, UK: Edward Elgar) chapter 7, pp. 110–125.

Clarke, Rosemary, Gianna Boero and L. Alan Winters (1996) 'Controlling greenhouse gases: a survey of global macroeconomic studies'. *Bulletin of Economic Research* **48**(4), 269–308.

Cline, William R. (1991) 'Scientific basis for the greenhouse effect'. *Economic Journal* **101**, 904–19.

Cline, William R. (1992a) *The Economics of Global Warming* (Washington, DC: Institute for International Economics).

Cline, William R. (1992b) *Global Warming: The Economic Stakes*, vol. 36 of *Policy Analyses in International Economics* (Washington, DC: Institute for International Economics).

Coase, Ronald H. (1960) 'The problem of social cost'. *Journal of Law and Economics 3*, 1–44.

Connolly, Michael (1970) 'Public goods, externalities, and international relations'. *Journal of Political Economy 78*, 279–90.

Connolly, Michael (1972) 'Trade in public goods: A diagrammatic analysis'. *Quarterly Journal of Economics 86*, 61–78.

Cornes, Richard and Todd Sandler (1986) *The Theory of Externalities, Public Goods, and Club Goods* (Cambridge, UK: Cambridge University Press).

Cropper, Maureen L. and Wallace E. Oates (1992) 'Environmental economics: a survey'. *Journal of Economic Literature 30*, 675–740.

D'Aspremont, Claude A. and Jean J. Gabszewicz (1986) 'On the stability of collusion'. In *New Developments in the Analysis of Market Structure*, eds G.F. Matthewson and J.E. Stiglitz (New York: Macmillan) pp. 243–64.

DeSombre, Elizabeth R. and Joanne Kauffman (1996) 'The Montreal Protocol Multilateral Fund: partial success story'. In *Institutions for Environmental Aid*, eds R.O. Keohane and M.A. Levy (Cambridge, UK: MIT Press) chapter 4, pp. 89–126.

Dockner, Engelbert and Ngo Van Long (1993) 'International pollution control: cooperative vs. non-cooperative strategies'. *Journal of Environmental Economics and Management 25*, 13–29.

Donsimoni, Marie-Paul, Nicholas S. Economides and Heracles M. Polimarchakis (1986) 'Stable cartels'. *International Economic Review 27*, 317–27.

Drèze, Jean and Nicholas Stern (1987) 'The theory of cost–benefit analysis'. In *Handbook of Public Economics Volume II*, eds Alan J. Auerbach and Martin Feldstein, vol. 4 of *Handbooks in Economics* (Amsterdam: Elsevier) chapter 14, pp. 909–89.

Ellis, Gregory M. (1992) 'Incentive compatible environmental regulations'. *Natural Resource Modeling* **6**(3), 225–56.

Elster, Jon (1989) 'Social norms and economic theory'. *Journal of Economic Perspectives* **3**, 99–117.

Endres, Alfred (1993) 'Internationale Vereinbarungen zum Schutz der globalen Umweltressourcen — der Fall proportionaler Emissionsreduktionen'. *Aussenwirtschaft* **48**(1), 51–76.

Endres, Alfred and Michael Finus (1998) 'Playing a better global emission game: does it help to be green?', *Swiss Journal of Economics and Statistics* **134**(1), 21–40.

Enquête-Kommission 'Vorsorge zum Schutz der Erdatmosphäre' des Deutschen Bundestages (1991) *Schutz der Erde. Teilband I* (Bonn: Economica).

Eyckmans, Johan (1997) 'Nash implementation of a proportional solution to international pollution control problems'. *Journal of Environmental Economics and Management* **33**(3), 314–30.

Eyckmans, Johan, Stef Proost and Erik Schokkaert (1993) 'Equity and efficiency in greenhouse negotiations'. *Kyklos* **46**(3), 363–97.

Fairman, David (1996) 'The global environmental facility: haunted by the shadow of the future'. In *Institutions for Environmental Aid*, eds R.O. Keohane and M.A. Levy (Cambridge, MA: MIT Press) chapter 3, pp. 55–88.

Falkinger, Josef, Franz Hackl and Gerald Pruckner (1997) 'A fair mechanism for efficient reduction of global CO_2 emissions'. *Finanzarchiv* **53**(3/4), 308–31.

Fankhauser, Samuel (1995) *Valuing Climate Change* (London: Earthscan).

Fankhauser, Samuel and Snorre Kverndokk (1996) 'The global warming game — simulations of a CO_2 reduction agreement'. *Resource and Energy Economics* **18**, 83–102.

Felder, Stefan and Thomas F. Rutherford (1993) 'Unilateral CO_2 reductions and carbon leakage: The consequences of international trade in oil and basic materials'. *Journal of Environmental Economics and Management* **25**(2), 162–76.

Finus, Michael and Bianca Rundshagen (1998) 'Toward a positive theory of coalition formation and endogenous instrumental choice in global pollution control'. *Public Choice* **96**, 145–86.

Folmer, Henk, Pierre van Mouche and Shannon E. Ragland (1993) 'Interconnected games and international environmental problems'. *Environmental and Resource Economics* **3**(4), 313–35.

Fudenberg, Drew and Eric Maskin (1986) 'The folk theorem in repeated games with discounting or with incomplete information'. *Econometrica* **54**, 533–54.

Genser, Bernd, Andreas Haufler, Frank Hettich and Carsten Schmidt (1999) 'International taxation and pollution control: how should priorities be chosen in the European Union's tax policy agenda?'. In *Institutional Arrangements for Global Economic Integration*, ed. H.-J. Vosgerau (Basingstoke, UK: Macmillan) chapter 10, forthcoming.

Germain, Marc, Philippe Toint and Henry Tulkens (1997) *Financial Tranfers to Ensure Cooperative International Optimality in Stock Pollutant Abatement*, Center for Operations Research and Econometrics Discussion Paper No. 9701 (Leuven, Belgium).

Golombek, Rolf, Catherine Hagem and Michael Hoel (1994) 'The design of a carbon tax in an incomplete international climate agreement'. In *Trade, Innovation, Environment*, ed. Carlo Carraro, vol. 2 of *Fondazione Eni Enrico Mattei Series on Economics, Energy and Environment* (Dordrecht: Kluwer) chapter 3.3, pp. 323–61.

Hagem, Catherine (1996) 'Joint implementation under asymmetric information and strategic behavior'. *Environmental and Resource Economics* **8**(4), 431–47.

Hahn, Robert W. and Robert N. Stavins (1992) 'Economic incentives for environmental protection: integrating theory and practice'. *American Economic Review* **82**(2), 464–8.

Hardin, Garrett (1968) 'The tragedy of the commons'. *Science* **162**, 1243–8.

Heal, Geoffrey (1994) 'Formation of international environmental agreements'. In *Trade, Innovation, Environment*, ed. C. Carraro (Dordrecht: Kluwer) chapter 3.2, pp. 301–22.

Heister, Johannes (1993) *Who Will Win the Ozone Game?*, Kieler Arbeitspapier No. 579 (Institut für Weltwirtschaft an der Universität Kiel).

Heister, Johannes, Ernst Mohr, Wolf Plesmann, Frank Stähler, Tobias
    Stoll and Rüdiger Wolfrum (1995) *Economic and Legal Aspects of
    International Environmental Agreements — The Case of Enforc-
    ing and Stabilising an International CO_2 Agreement*, Kiel Working
    Paper No. 711 (Kiel Institute of World Economics).

Hettich, Frank (2000) *Economic Growth and Environmental Policy: A
    Theoretical Approach*, New Horizons in Environmental Economics
    (Cheltenham, UK: Edward Elgar).

Hoel, Michael (1991) 'Global environmental problems: the effects of uni-
    lateral actions taken by one country'. *Journal of Environmental
    Economics and Management* **20**, 55–70.

Hoel, Michael (1992a) 'Emission taxes in a dynamic international game
    of CO_2 emissions'. In *Conflicts and Cooperation in Managing En-
    vironmental Resources*, ed. Rüdiger Pethig Microeconomic Studies
    (Berlin: Springer).

Hoel, Michael (1992b) 'International environment conventions: the case
    of uniform reductions of emissions'. *Environmental and Resource
    Economics* **2**, 141–59.

Hoel, Michael (1994) 'Efficient climate policy in the presence of free
    riders'. *Journal of Environmental Economics and Management*
    27, 259–74.

Hoel, Michael (1997) 'International coordination of environmental taxes'.
    In *New Directions in the Economic Theory of the Environment*,
    eds Carlo Carraro and Domenico Siniscalco (Cambridge, UK: Cam-
    bridge University Press) chapter 5, pp. 105–46.

Hoel, Michael and Kerstin Schneider (1997) 'Incentives to participate
    in an international environmental agreement'. *Environmental and
    Resource Economics* **9**, 153–70.

Holländer, Heinz (1990) 'A social exchange approach to voluntary coop-
    eration'. *American Economic Review* **80**, 1157–67.

Houghton, John T. et al. (eds) (1996) *Climate Change 1995 — The
    Science of Climate Change*, Contribution of Working Group I to
    the Second Assessment Report of the Intergovernmental Panel on
    Climate Change (Cambridge, UK: Cambridge University Press).

Hourcade, Jean-Charles (1996a) 'Estimating the costs of mitigating
    greenhouse gases'. In *Climate Change 1995 — Economic and Social*

Dimensions of Climate Change, eds James P. Bruce, Hoesung Lee and Erik F. Haites, Contribution of Working Group III to the Second Assessment Report of the Intergovernmental Panel on Climate Change (Cambridge, UK: Cambridge University Press) chapter 8, pp. 263–96.

Hourcade, Jean-Charles (1996b) 'A review of mitigation cost studies'. In *Climate Change 1995 — Economic and Social Dimensions of Climate Change,* eds James P. Bruce, Hoesung Lee and Erik F. Haites, Contribution of Working Group III to the Second Assessment Report of the Intergovernmental Panel on Climate Change (Cambridge, UK: Cambridge University Press) chapter 9, pp. 297–366.

Ihori, Toshihiro (1996) 'International public goods and contribution productivity differentials'. *Journal of Public Economics* **61**, 139–54.

IPCC (1996) *IPCC Second Assessment — Climate Change 1995. Summary for Policy-Makers* (UNEP, WMO).

Jackson, Tim (1995) 'Joint implementation and cost-effectiveness under the Framework Convention on Climate Change'. *Energy Policy* **23**(2), 117–38.

Jorgenson, Dale W. and Peter J. Wilcoxen (1993) 'Reducing U.S. carbon dioxide emissions: an assessment of different instruments'. *Journal of Policy Modeling* **15**(5 and 6), 491–520.

Kennan, John and Robert Wilson (1993) 'Bargaining with private information'. *Journal of Economic Literature* **31**, 45–104.

Kerr, Suzi (1995) *Markets versus International Funds for Implementing International Environmental Agreements: Ozone Depletion and the Montreal Protocol,* Working Paper No. 95–12 (College Park, MD: Department of Agricultural and Resource Economics, University of Maryland).

Kiesling, Herbert J. (1974) 'Public goods and the possibilities for trade'. *Canadian Journal of Economics* **7**, 402–17.

Killinger, Sebastian (1996) 'Indirect internalization of international environmental externalities'. *Finanzarchiv* **53**(3 and 4), 332–68.

Killinger, Sebastian (2000) *International Environmental Externalities and the Double Dividend,* New Horizons in Environmental Economics (Cheltenham, UK: Edward Elgar).

Killinger, Sebastian and Carsten Schmidt (1998) 'Nationale Umwelt-politik und internationale Integration — theoretische Ansätze im Überblick'. *Finanzarchiv* **55**(2), 219–53.

Kindleberger, Charles (1986) 'International public goods without inter-national government'. *American Economic Review* **76**(1), 1–13.

King, Kenneth (1993) *The Incremental Costs of Global Environmental Benefits*, Working Paper No. 5 (Washington, DC: Global Environment Facility).

Kirchgässner, Gebhard and Ernst Mohr (1996) 'Trade restrictions as viable means of enforcing compliance with international environmental law: an economic assessment'. In *Enforcing Environmental Standards: Economic Mechanisms as Viable Means?*, ed. Rüdiger Wolfrum, vol. 125 of *Beiträge zum ausländischen öffentlichen Recht und Völkerrecht* (Berlin: Springer) pp. 199–226.

Koutstaal, Paul (1997) *Economic Policy and Climate Change. Tradable Permits for Reducing Carbon Emissions*, New Horizons in Environmental Economics (Cheltenham, UK: Edward Elgar).

Kox, Henk and Casper van der Tak (1996) 'Non-transboundary pollution and the efficiency of international environmental cooperation'. *Ecological Economics* **19**, 247–59.

Kreps, David M., Paul Milgrom, John Roberts and Robert Wilson (1982) 'Rational cooperation in the finitely repeated prisoner's dilemma'. *Journal of Economic Theory* **27**, 245–52.

Kverndokk, Snorre (1993) 'Global CO_2 agreements: a cost-effective approach'. *Energy Journal* **14**(2), 91–112.

Kverndokk, Snorre (1994) 'Coalitions and side payments in international CO_2 treaties'. In *International Environmental Economics: Theories, Models and Applications to Climate Change, International Trade and Acidification*, ed. Ekko C. van Ierland, vol. 4 of *Developments in Environmental Economics* (Amsterdam: Elsevier) pp. 45–76.

Kwerel, Evan (1977) 'To tell the truth: imperfect information and optimal pollution control'. *Review of Economic Studies* **44**(3), 595–601.

Laffont, Jean-Jacques and Jean Tirole (1996) 'Pollution permits and compliance strategies'. *Journal of Public Economics* **62**, 85–125.

Larson, Bruce A. and James A. Tobey (1994) 'Uncertain climate change and the international policy response'. *Ecological Economics 11*, 77–84.

Lipnowski, Irwin and Shlomo Maital (1983) 'Voluntary provision of a pure public good as the game of "chicken"'. *Journal of Public Economics 20*, 381–6.

Mäler, Karl-Göran (1989) 'The acid rain game'. In *Valuation Methods and Policy Making in Environmental Economics*, eds Henk Folmer and Ekko C. van Ierland, vol. 36 of *Studies in Environmental Science* (Amsterdam: Elsevier) chapter 12, pp. 231–52.

Mäler, Karl-Göran (1990) 'International environmental problems'. *Oxford Review of Economic Policy 6*(1), 80–108.

Mäler, Karl-Göran (1991) 'Incentives in international environmental problems'. In *Environmental Scarcity: The International Dimension*, ed. Horst Siebert (Tübingen: Mohr) pp. 75–93.

Manne, Alan and Richard Richels (1993) 'The EC proposal for combining carbon and energy taxes: the implications for future CO_2 emissions'. *Energy Policy 21*(1), 5–12.

Markusen, James R. (1975a) 'Cooperative control of international pollution and common property resources'. *Quarterly Journal of Economics 89*, 618–32.

Markusen, James R. (1975b) 'International externalities and optimal tax structures'. *Journal of International Economics 5*, 15–29.

McMillan, John (1979) 'The free-rider problem: a survey'. *Economic Record 6*, 95–107.

Merrifield, John (1988) 'The impact of selected abatement strategies on transnational pollution, the terms of trade, and factor rewards: a general equilibrium approach'. *Journal of Environmental Economics and Management 15*, 259–84.

Michaelis, Peter (1997) *Effiziente Klimapolitik im Mehrschadstoffall*, vol. 280 of *Kieler Studien* (Tübingen: Mohr).

Mintzer, Irving M. (1993) *Implementing the Framework Convention on Climate Change – Incremental Costs and the Role of the GEF*, Working Paper No. 4 (Washington, DC: Global Environment Facility).

Misiolek, Walter S. and Harold W. Elder (1989) 'Exclusionary manipulation of markets for pollution rights'. *Journal of Environmental Economics and Management 16*, 156–66.

Mohr, Ernst (1991) 'Global warming: economic policy in the face of positive and negative spillovers'. In *Environmental Scarcity: The International Dimension*, ed. Horst Siebert (Tübingen: Mohr) pp. 187–212.

Mohr, Ernst (1995) 'International environmental permit trade and debt: the consequences of country sovereignty and cross-default policies'. *Review of International Economics 3*(1), 1–19.

Mohr, Ernst (1996) 'Sustainable development and international distribution: theory and application to rainforests'. *Review of International Economics 4*(2), 152–71.

Mohr, Ernst and Jonathan Thomas (1998) 'Pooling sovereign risks: the case of environmental treaties and international debt'. *Journal of Development Economics 55*(1), 153–69.

Munasinghe, Mohan et al. (1996) 'Applicability of techniques of cost–benefit analysis to climate change'. In *Climate Change 1995 — Economic and Social Dimensions of Climate Change*, eds James P. Bruce, Hoesung Lee and Erik F. Haites, Contribution of Working Group III to the Second Assessment Report of the Intergovernmental Panel on Climate Change (Cambridge, UK: Cambridge University Press) chapter 5, pp. 145–77.

Murdoch, James and Todd Sandler (1997) 'The voluntary provision of a pure public good: the case of reduced CFC emissions and the Montreal Protocol'. *Journal of Public Economics 63*, 331–49.

Myerson, Roger B. (1979) 'Incentive compatibility and the bargaining problem'. *Econometrica 47*, 61–73.

Myerson, Roger B. and Mark A. Satterthwaite (1983) 'Efficient mechanisms for bilateral trading'. *Journal of Economic Theory 29*, 265–81.

Nordhaus, William D. (1979) *The Efficient Use of Energy Resources* (New Haven, CT: Yale University Press).

Nordhaus, William D. (1991a) 'The cost of slowing climate change: a survey'. *Energy Journal 12*(1), 37–66.

Nordhaus, William D. (1991b) 'A sketch of the greenhouse effect'. *American Economic Review* **81**, *Papers and Proceedings*, 146–50.

Nordhaus, William D. (1991c) 'To slow or not to slow: the economics of the greenhouse effect'. *Economic Journal* **101**, 920–37.

Oberthür, Sebastian (1997) 'Montreal Protocol: 10 years after'. *Environmental Policy and Law* **27**(6), 432–40.

OECD (1991) *Responding to Climate Change — Selected Economic Issues* (Paris: OECD).

OECD (1992) *Climate Change — Designing a Tradeable Permit System* OECD Documents (Paris: OECD).

Olson, Mancur (1965) *The Logic of Collective Action. Public Goods and the Theory of Groups* (Cambridge, MA: Harvard University Press).

Olson, Mancur and Richard Zeckhauser (1966) 'An economic theory of alliances'. *Review of Economics and Statistics* **48**, 266–79.

Olson, Mancur and Richard Zeckhauser (1967) 'Collective goods, comparative advantage, and alliance efficiency'. In *Issues in Defense Economics*, ed. R.N. Mc Kean (New York, London) pp. 25–48.

Palmer, Karen, Wallace E. Oates and Paul R. Portney (1995) 'Tightening environmental standards: the benefit–cost or the no-cost paradigm?'. *Journal of Economic Perspectives* **9**, 119–32.

Parson, Edward A. and Owen Greene (1995) 'The complex chemistry of the international ozone agreements'. *Environment* **37**(2), 16–43.

Pearce, David (1990) 'Economics and the global environmental challenge'. *Journal of International Studies* **19**(3), 365–87.

Pearce, David (1991) 'The role of carbon taxes in adjusting to global warming'. *Economic Journal* **101**, 938–48.

Pearce, David (1995) 'Joint implementation: a general overview'. In *The Feasibility of Joint Implementation*, ed. C.J. Jepma, vol. 3 of *Environment and Policy* (Dordrecht: Kluwer) chapter 1, pp. 15–31.

Petrakis, Emmanuel and Anastasios Xepapadeas (1996) 'Environmental consciousness and moral hazard in international agreements to protect the environment'. *Journal of Public Economics* **60**(1), 95–110.

Ploeg, Frederick van der and Aart de Zeeuw (1991) 'A differential game of international pollution control'. *Systems and Control Letters* **17**, 409–14.

Ploeg, Frederick van der and Aart de Zeeuw (1992) 'International aspects of pollution control'. *Environmental and Resource Economics* **2**, 117–39.

Ploeg, Frederick van der and Jenny E. Lighthart (1994) 'Sustainable growth and renewable resources in the global economy'. In *Trade, Innovation, Environment*, ed. C. Carraro (Dordrecht: Kluwer) chapter 2.5, pp. 259–80.

Porter, Michael E. and Claas van der Linde (1995) 'Toward a new conception of the environment–competitiveness relationship'. *Journal of Economic Perspectives* **9**(4), 97–118.

Radner, Roy (1980) 'Collusive behavior in noncooperative epsilon-equilibria of oligopolies with long but finite lives'. *Journal of Economic Theory* **22**, 136–54.

Richter, Wolfram and Wolfgang Wiegard (1993) 'Zwanzig Jahre "Neue Finanzwissenschaft" — Teil I: Überblick und Theorie des Marktversagens'. *Zeitschrift für Wirtschafts- und Sozialwissenschaften* **113**, 169–224.

Sachverständigenrat zur Begutachtung der gesamtwirtschaftlichen Entwicklung (1998) *Jahresgutachten 1998/99: Vor weitreichenden Entscheidungen.* Drucksache 14/73 des Deutschen Bundestages (Bonn).

Samuelson, Paul A. (1954) 'The pure theory of public expenditure'. *Review of Economic Studies* **36**, 387–9.

Sandler, Todd (1996) 'A game theoretic analysis of carbon emissions'. In *The Political Economy of Environmental Protection — Analysis and Evidence*, ed. Roger D. Congleton (Ann Arbor, MI: University of Michigan Press) chapter 11, pp. 251–72.

Sandler, Todd (1997) *Global Challenges: An Approach to Environmental, Political, and Economic Problems* (Cambridge, UK: Cambridge University Press).

Schmidt, Carsten (2000) 'Incentives for international environmental cooperation: theoretical models and economic instruments'. In *International Environmental Economics: A Survey of the Issues*, eds

Günther Schulze and Heinrich Ursprung (Oxford: Oxford University Press) chapter 6, forthcoming.

Schulze, Günther and Heinrich Ursprung (2000) 'Environmental policy in an integrated world economy: the political–economic view'. In *International Environmental Economics: A Survey of the Issues*, eds Günther Schulze and Heinrich Ursprung (Oxford: Oxford University Press) chapter 4, forthcoming.

Shibata, Hirofumi (1971) 'A bargaining model of the pure theory of public expenditure'. *Journal of Political Economy* **79**, 1–29.

Stähler, Frank (1992) *Pareto Improvements by In-kind Transfers*, Kieler Arbeitspapier No. 541 (Institut für Weltwirtschaft an der Universität Kiel).

Stähler, Frank (1993) *On The Economics of International Environmental Agreements*, Kieler Arbeitspapier No. 600 (Institut für Weltwirtschaft an der Universität Kiel).

Steiner, Urs (1997a) *Inefficient National Environmental Regulation as a Signal of High Abatement Costs*, Working Paper 97-2 (Aarhus: Department of Economics, Aarhus School of Business, Denmark).

Steiner, Urs (1997b) *Signalling in International Environmental Agreements: Using Pre-Agreement Emission Level as a Signalling Device*, Working Paper 97-9 (Aarhus: Department of Economics, Aarhus School of Business, Denmark).

Sugden, Robert (1984) 'Reciprocity: the supply of public goods through voluntary contributions'. *Economic Journal* **94**, 772–87.

Terasaki, Katsushi (1992) 'Optimum supply of international public goods'. *Keio Economic Studies* **29**(1), 45–62.

Tietenberg, Tom H. (1985) *Emission Trading: An Exercise in Reforming Pollution Policy* (Washington, DC: Resources for the Future).

Tietenberg, Tom H. (1990) 'Economic instruments for environmental regulation'. *Oxford Review of Economic Policy* **6**(1), 17–33.

Tietenberg, Tom H. (1994) 'Implementation issues for globally tradeable carbon entitlements'. In *International Environmental Economics: Theories and Applications to Climate Change, International Trade and Acidification*, ed. Ekko C. van Ierland (Amsterdam: Elsevier) pp. 119–49.

UNCTAD (1992) *Combating Global Warming — Study on a Global System of Tradeable Carbon Emission Entitlements* (Geneva: United Nations Conference on Trade and Development).

United Nations (1996) *Statistical Yearbook — Forty-first Issue* (New York: United Nations).

Verbruggen, Harmen and Huib M.A. Jansen (1995) 'International coordination of environmental policies'. In *Principles of Environmental and Resource Economics*, eds Henk Folmer, H. Landis Gabel and Hans Opschoor (Aldershot, UK: Edward Elgar) chapter 10, pp. 228–52.

Victor, David G. (1991) 'Limits of market-based strategies for slowing global warming: the case of tradeable permits'. *Policy Sciences* **24**, 199–222.

Watson, Robert, Marufu Zinyowera and Richard Moss, eds (1996) *Climate Change 1995 — Impacts, Adaptations and Mitigation of Climate Change: Scientific–Technical Analyses*, Contribution of Working Group II to the Second Assessment Report of the Intergovernmental Panel on Climate Change (Cambridge, UK: Cambridge University Press).

Weitzman, Martin L. (1974) 'Prices vs. quantities'. *Review of Economic Studies* **41**, 477–91.

Welsch, Heinz (1992) 'Equity and efficiency in international CO_2 agreements'. In *Energy Markets and Environmental Issues: A European Perspective*, eds Einar Hope and Steinar Strøm, Proceedings of a German–Norwegian Energy Conference, Bergen, 5–7 June 1991 (Oslo: Scandinavian University Press) chapter 12, pp. 211–25.

Wicksell, Knut (1896) *Finanztheoretische Untersuchungen — nebst Darstellung und Kritik des Steuersystems Schwedens* (Jena: G. Fischer).

Williamson, Oliver E. (1983) 'Credible commitments: using hostages to support exchange'. *American Economic Review* **73**, 519–40.

World Bank (1990) *Funding for the Global Environment: The Global Environment Facility*, Discussion Paper (Washington, DC: World Bank).

Xepapadeas, Anastasios and Amalia Yiannaka (1997) 'Measuring benefits and damages from carbon dioxide emissions and international agreements to slow down greenhouse warming'. In *International Environmental Negotiations: Strategic Policy Issues*, ed. Carlo Carraro (Cheltenham, UK: Edward Elgar) chapter 9, pp. 150–71.

Young, Oran R. (1989) 'The politics of international regime formation: managing natural resources and the environment'. *International Organization 43*, 349–75.

Zhang, ZhongXiang and Henk Folmer (1995) 'The choice of policy instruments for the control of carbon dioxide emissions'. *Intereconomics 30*(3), 133–42.

Index